Sensoria

Sensoria

*Thinkers for the
Twenty-First Century*

McKenzie Wark

VERSO
London • New York

First published by Verso 2020
© McKenzie Wark 2020

1 3 5 7 9 10 8 6 4 2

Verso
UK: 6 Meard Street, London W1F 0EG
US: 20 Jay Street, Suite 1010, Brooklyn, NY 11201
versobooks.com

Verso is the imprint of New Left Books

ISBN-13: 978-1-78873-506-3
ISBN-13: 978-1-78873-505-6 (HBK)
ISBN-13: 978-1-78873-508-7 (UK EBK)
ISBN-13: 978-1-78873-507-0 (US EBK)

British Library Cataloguing in Publication Data
A catalogue record for this book is available from the British Library

Library of Congress Cataloging-in-Publication Data
A catalog record for this book is available from the Library of Congress

Typeset in Sabon by MJ & N Gavan, Truro, Cornwall
Printed and bound by CPI Group (UK) Ltd, Croydon CR0 4YY

In memory of Niall Lucy

Contents

Introduction

Toward the Common Task

What is the point of scholarship? In any other time, this might have seemed a churlish question to ask. But in the United States and increasingly elsewhere too, the question now calls up three equally prompt and self-evident kinds of answers.

One response is that it has no point at all. This is now an opinion with a lot of powerful backing. Another is that it has no point other than to socialize the high-risk work of invention, so that private interests can do the lower risk work of "innovation" and profit from it. The third answer protests these other two but not in particularly satisfying terms. Scholarship is hard to defend as a means to enlightenment or liberation; these seem rather abstract and now self-undermining goals.[1] Ironically, scholarship about the limits to enlightenment and liberation casts doubt on the scholarship as much as the other two lines of questioning.

There is a fourth answer, but it does not get much traction any more: scholarship is an end in itself, a free and self-directed inquiry that takes its own time.[2] It describes, at best, what might happen in elite institutions propped up by the venerable seed money of slave owners, robber barons, or an imperial state, but not what the rest of us get to do. It is too remote a utopia from the actually existing university that runs on debt and precarious labor.[3]

The mission of scholarship appears so hollowed out today that some advocate a more fugitive means of study, one that treats the university as a resource (and not much more) in which to create the under commons, with its own pedagogy and forms of collaboration.[4] That has a lot to recommend it, were it not that there seem to be problems at such a scale that such a practice cannot grasp. There may soon not be an institution for the under commons to be under.

Instead let me start by saying something simple: that scholarship is about the common task of knowing the world.[5] Each of those little words contains multitudes. *Common* refers to what is shared but also the ordinary, even the vulgar. *Task* demarcates a kind of labor, but it is also a kind of play. The action behind the verb *knowing* connects the shared and ordinary, the laboring but playful activities already telegraphed in this little phrase.

The most difficult but also capacious word here is, of course, *world*. Perhaps it is best approached indirectly, through the parable of the blind scholars and their elephant: Each touches, senses, and knows a part of the elephant and declares the elephant to be like what they touch: tusklike, trunklike, or taillike. Each hears the other saying something incompatible with the thing that they themselves touch.

The first limit to the parable is that maybe there's no whole elephant to be seen, either.[6] A scholar who could see the elephant would not know any better than the blind ones, because while the account by the scholar who sees might include the grey color of its skin, they may know nothing of its texture or smell. Nobody gets to know the totality.

The second limit to this parable is that it may not even be possible to combine all of these partial accounts of the elephant into a true and whole picture of the elephant as a totality, as a world. The parts don't quite add up to a whole. Each way of knowing shapes in part the thing it comes to know, producing parts that are parts of different wholes. Knowing is never quite going to come together again, and there may be nothing at all helpful any more in the fiction that it might.

This was always the paradox about the project of knowing the world. The knowing depended on myths that posit a whole, unknown world at the start and another, different whole world, the unity of the world of knowledge, at the end. The knowing is in between two things that are some kind of non-knowledge, an imagined start and a projected future. Nobody much believes in this anymore. Knowledge has lost its religion, that which bound it together, through time and across the disciplines.[7] It is futile to try and hide this from anyone, least of all ourselves. The university, like the church before it, is now a habit without gods.

Knowledge doesn't add up. Nothing guarantees that its parts are parts of a whole. There is no shortage of attempts to fill this void with claims to privileged knowledge of the world as a totality. All will be well, each discipline tells us, if we accept their world as sovereign, as the true totality, as the whole elephant. Some of these claims to world-knowing are so powerful that they are also world-making. The economists and the engineers, for example, claim there are worlds that lend themselves to calculation or solution, respectively. The world is only resources to be allocated or problems to be solved.

Less powerful ways of knowing point out the limitations of such worlds but are blind to the limitations of their own sphere. The scholar of literature or philosopher or anthropologist or historian can be fulsome in their critique of others but have little to say about their own extravagant counterclaims to sovereignty. They are also prone to a sort of pathetic will-to-power, in which they claim an imaginary sovereignty over the world as it ought to be in the face of more powerful ways of knowing the world that can affect how it is.

So rather than claim to see the elephant whole, or claim to perceive with one's inner eye what an ideal elephant should be, let's just acknowledge that all forms of knowing come to know only a part of the world. Every way of producing knowledge is enabling, and its particular techniques make parts of the world knowable. And yet every way of producing knowledge is also blind to what it does not perceive outside of its own form of knowing.[8]

3

This state of things is particularly troubling, given that there's a widespread sense that the world, whatever it is, and whatever it may be, is in a lot of trouble. That is the elephant in the room. The most common name for this at the moment is the Anthropocene. In an earlier book, *Molecular Red,* I started to ask about what might constitute theory for the Anthropocene.[9] I now add that I think it is timely to ask what a practice of knowledge for the Anthropocene could be, particularly if we take the COVID-19 pandemic to be not just a global crisis of applied knowledge in its own right, but a preview of what demands the Anthropocene will continue to place on knowledge production.

Each way of knowing the world touches a part of the elephant. Rather than give in to claims to know the whole elephant in advance, let's work out collaboratively, as a common task, some practices of putting parts of the elephant as we sense and know them next to one another. Not so much to produce a seamless picture of the whole, but to understand the differences between all of the partial sensings. The common task is to produce a knowledge of the world made up of the differences between ways of knowing it.

In this book, I want to look at three different ways of knowing the world, to find points of contact between them and also points of difference. Those three ways of knowing are centered respectively on aesthetics, ethnography, and design. One way to think about this might be that it starts with surfaces, with the aesthetic form of cultural and media artifacts through which the world appears. Then it moves on to ways of knowing how different kinds of humans connect to those surfaces, broadly conceived as enthnographic. And finally we turn to the technical, to the design of informatics machines that humans will interact with and within.

I chose to start with aesthetics because, being from media studies, I think our access to the world is always mediated. It helps to pay attention to the forms in which the world is sensed, to how your awareness of your part of the elephant is mediated. If the sensory apparatus taken as a whole is the sensorium, then perhaps we could think in a more plural way about different *sensoria*, here conceived as a plurality of cultural, technical, and social forms of apparatus through which the world is known. The common task might then be (in part at least) the work of putting sensoria in play, with and against one another, while limiting the claim of each to be sovereign over the others.

The various sensoria might thus be the different worlds we think we know, but where the appearance of a world is an artifact not only of the design of the way of sensing some part of the world but of habits that have accumulated about the world to which that part might belong. All ways of knowing are mixes of the empirical and the rational, of perceptions and conceptions. Rather than attempt to cure misperception through reason, or unreason through sensation, perhaps it's a matter of mapping the borders of different bundles of reason and perception as they congeal together in particular ways of knowing.

The common task of knowing the world reverses the relation between the disciplinary and the interdisciplinary. To the disciplinarian, the interdisciplinary is always something of an afterthought. It does not challenge but rather reaffirms the sovereignty of the disciplines. It proclaims that because there are disciplines, sovereign over the objects of knowledge at their center, then the interdisciplinary can only exist at the margins to affirm the disciplines as centers. But what if we reverse this procedure? It is only the edges of ways of knowing that are interesting.

That different ways of knowing cannot really be reconciled is not a bug but a feature of the common task. The problematic and unsettled concepts at the margin might be the most interesting and useful things that any way of knowing can offer another. Thus the world might be known provisionally, speculatively, tentatively, without any one way of knowing having to be sovereign over the others.

Another parable might be useful here. What is the surface area of the elephant? According to the internet, it could be up to eighty-eight meters squared.[10] But if we looked more closely, with a finer resolution, it could be even more than eighty-eight meters squared. At the finer resolution, the folds in its skin reveal yet more folds. What if we increase the resolution still more? There are yet more folds, more surface. On and on we could go.

One could say that each successive view at a higher resolution is more accurate. But is it more true? Is it more useful? Is it *more knowledge?* In some contexts, surely; but in others, surely not. Where qualitative forms of knowledge are concerned, the whole structure of knowledge production seems to be organized around more detail. The "but it is more complicated than that" position is treated as a winning argument. The less addressed problem in knowledge production is how to pull back from the scale where the details expand to fill one's sensoria to a less detailed but still useful or interesting picture, one in which other things besides our own special interest might come into view.

The common task of knowing the world is not an end in itself. Nor can it come to an end and produce a conclusive knowledge. It is always only temporary and provisional. The common task is a detour on the way to something more important.[11] That something might now be the other common task of enduring in the world provisionally, incompletely, named the Anthropocene. The Anthropocene names a world transformed by collective human labor under the power of the commodity form. That world appears increasingly hostile to the endurance not just of our species-being but of many others as well.

It is tempting to cast this as a crisis.[12] As a narrative device, crisis focuses attention, but it can short-circuit the common task of producing a knowledge of this world of the Anthropocene. There's a rush to rename it, and in renaming it, call it something that makes it the special property of a particular way of knowing the world, to the exclusion of all others. It becomes an alibi for exacerbating the problem of knowing the world, at a time when not knowing is itself a key part of the problem.

This is when the elephant in the room called the Anthropocene is even acknowledged. A lot of knowledge production still gaily jets around as if this was somebody else's department. But as my friend and New School colleague Dominic Pettman says: "Elephants are too polite to mention the human in the room." Or rather, the world's indifference to us, its negative presence as that which, in its generality, does not really appear in any particular technical and cultural sensorium, becomes the thing that can only appear, if at all, out of a common task. This is a common task that I think is best conducted on the basis of a rough equality of all ways of knowing. Not everything is knowledge, but there might not be any universal way of knowing what is knowledge and what isn't.

Sensoria contains brief assessments, focusing on key concepts, of twenty-odd general intellects, some of whom are well-known.[13] I have tried to look beyond my New York–centric view of the world and beyond the confines of the academy. Not surprisingly, I have failed in the task of producing a completely diversified overview; I have just the parts of the elephant I can touch from where I stand.

In my reading, all of these general intellects manage to generate out of their particular ways of working some concepts that can be connected or contrasted with others derived from other kinds of knowledge work. That to me is what a general intellect is: someone who generates concepts out of particular knowledge work in particular departments of the intellectual division of labor. Not all are academics; some are artists or writers. Art and literature seem to me to have analogous problems to scholarship in the common task of knowing the world.

This book is meant to be useful. At the low resolution view, where you take in a fair swath of elephant but with not much detail, what I think is most useful are concepts. I'm looking for ways to compress and condense by focusing on concepts. If a good fact is mostly true about something in particular, a good concept is slightly true about a lot of things. Both fall short of the common task of knowing the world. That can only be begun by lacing concepts together from different labors. It is toward that objective that this book is aimed.

I

Aesthetics

Sianne Ngai: Zany, Cute, Interesting

I commonly encounter two problems when I try to teach aesthetics. One is that today's students don't seem to relate to categories of aesthetic experience and judgment such as the *sublime* and the *beautiful*. Another is that in today's cosmopolitan classroom, these seem like rather western categories. An approach that might help here is Sianne Ngai's *Our Aesthetic Categories: Zany, Cute, Interesting.*[1] The *our* in the title is a delicious provocation.

The book presents two problems of its own: first, it is written from within the upper echelons of literary-critical and theoretical work, as conducted in our top universities, a world to which I do not belong. Can it be made interesting for those of us in more ordinary day jobs? Second: is it possible to extract from it some concepts that can help with the making of a counterhegemonic culture in our times?

Rather than the sublime and the beautiful, Ngai offers three categories, which one can already see at work on the surface of social media, distributed more or less as "zany blogs, cute tweets and interesting wikis."[2] Even just as common words, *zany*, *cute*, and *interesting* seem intuitively right as keys to what many people want to look at, laugh with, sigh over, and share with others. If you want to make a meme, in the general sense of a unit of media that will be shared by others, those three all work.[3] The question is, why?

To cut to the punchline: "The best explanation for why the zany, the interesting, and the cute are our most pervasive and significant categories is that they are about the increasingly intertwined ways in which late capitalist subjects labor, communicate and consume."[4] They are the material through which we can have perceptions and share judgments that seem most closely related to what we do, say, and use in the twenty-first century.

Ngai frames this as a tension between the relative novelty of these aesthetic categories and something that appears as more of a constant—capitalism. The pressure I want to put on this is to ask whether they are indicative not of "late" capitalism, but "early"' something else.[5] But first, let's flesh out the three categories.

The zany: it's a *performative* aesthetic that is hot and sweaty, anxious and excessive. It is physical and sometimes libidinal. It is about activities where play becomes a job or work gets too playful. It involves imitation and mimicry, as if trying to copy what someone else does but doing it clumsily. It may be done as a joke but taken seriously or done seriously and taken as a joke: think Lucille Ball or Hugo Ball. Injury is possible: think Charlie Chaplin on the assembly line. It borders on camp, or what Jack Halberstam calls the *queer art of failure*, as in Sandra Bernhard or Kikki and Herb.[6] But the zany is more likely to convert triumph into failure than failure into triumph. Think the coyote's endless labor of trying to catch the roadrunner.[7]

The zany performance can be too rigid or too elastic. Either way, there's instability between doing a job and performing a role, or between cultural and occupational performance, or between play and labor. The zany can be desperate or stressed, but it is not Dionysian frenzy; it is more precarious and forced, like bad porn. Obliged to play, the zany can be sexy but not joyous.

The stock character of the *zanni* was originally an itinerant servant, a peasant forced by drought or war into the city. The *zagna* was the female counterpart. The zanni and zagna are supposed to repair the amorous relationships of others. Comedy ensued. The zanni came to refer to a second mime imitating another very broadly, an anarchic improviser. He was a "substitute for another guy." He mutated into the *Cable Guy* and as such is linked to post-Fordist labor and is caught in-between modes of production, in this case between industrial work and service work.

The zanni shows up again as Kramer on *Seinfeld*: like Jerry, only more so. All the show's characters perform versions of what Paolo Virno calls *virtuoso labor* (what for Angela McRobbie and others is *affective labor*).[8] Ngai also thinks of this as *feminized labor*, a term Paul Preciado would push back on, in the assumptions it makes about what is feminine.[9]

Feminized labor is certainly at play in movies like Richard Pryor's *The Toy*, in which he dresses as a waitress to get a job. Ngai thinks there are ambiguities for women about skills formerly associated with their special role in social reproduction now being used in the workplace. If there's a genre that performs this kind of performativity, reality TV shows like *Top Chef*, *Project Runway*, or *Drag Race* are examples of it. They are all about aesthetic judgments on forms of virtuoso or affective labor.

The cute: The word derives from the word *acute*. The word itself is a cute version of an edgier word. The zany is to be held at a distance; the cute is intimate, domestic. We have powers over cute things, and yet they still seem to make demands of us. The zany is about production; the cute is about consumption. The zany is about the worker; the cute is about the product. The zany is hot and may involve sharp implements; the cute is warm and fuzzy. If the zany is about performing subjects, the cute is about subject–object relations, including transitional objects, like the plushie the child can love or (if the kid is anything like my daughter) just abandon in the strangest places.

Cuteness lacks beauty's novelty, singularity, and untouchability—and power. The cute can be handled and fondled. It is proximate to kitsch, to easy consumption, to the simulating of affect.[10] The cute commodity often seems to be asking: Are you my mother? The cute thing can be a fetish, masking its own making, but it can also be utopian, a model of a world of use value without exchange value.

Marx imagines commodity fetishes a bit like child actors, squealing and appealing for their buyers.[11] Cuteness is perhaps a kind of fetish redoubled. It tries to work on the fantasy of the fetish itself. It pines for the utopia of the qualitative, which seeks refuge under capitalism in the fetish. Cuteness is a fantasy of the commodity addressing its protector. One feels like one is carrying out its wishes. Its exaggerated passivity can provoke sadism or care. It can also hint at a pastoral fantasy of use value that could be rescued and kept safe, as in the *Toy Story* movies. The cute provokes a desire for intimacy to cut out exchange. Its powerlessness can itself be powerfully erotic.

Ngai: "the ultimate index of an object's cuteness may be its edibility."[12] It is sweet but edged with disgust. Keston Sutherland points out that the metaphor Marx uses in *Capital* for abstract labor is *Gallerte*, which in English might translate as aspic, brawn, or gelatine—all achieved by boiling down animal parts.[13] The transformation of concrete labors into abstract labor *renders* the laborer into something akin to the notorious pink goo or pink slime that industrial, processed meat now contains. Ngai: "If undifferentiated labor in this text gets figured as a quivering, gelatinous food implicitly made up of ground-up human workers, the inverse of or antidote to this image of being dissolved into food might be the image of a face emerging from inside a cookie."[14]

One can connect this reversibility of the cute to Walter Benjamin's observation that the gaze of the cute creature can be considered our own gaze, looking on at the process of commodification itself, with which we compulsively identify, and in the face of which it is tempting to appear small and vulnerable and plead for special care.[15] The cute renders production as if it were a domestic activity, but one charged with eroticism and violence. Ngai wonders if it's any accident that Japanese culture exploded with its own version of the cute, the *kawaii*, in the era of rapid postwar industrialization. Perhaps it was a way of learning to love defeat on a national scale, but one redoubled in the private sphere as learning to love exploitation. The term *kawaii* sounds fairly close to *kowai*—the scary. Cute eroticism can be sweet, but biting—fanged phenomena.

While one thinks most readily of stuffed animals, the cute might also be in play in such refined works as Gertrude Stein's *Tender Buttons*.[16] In spite of its proximity to kitsch, the cute can be an avant-garde tactic. Here it is "less a fantasy of art's capacity for revenge on a society that renders it harmless, than a more modest way of imagining art's ability to transform itself into something slightly less easy to consume."[17] Ngai here offers a really interesting reading of one of Francis Ponge's miniature poems, in which an orange is deformed in the act of consumption, in some small mute act of resistance.[18]

In a lovely twist, Ngai writes: "It is as if the authority figure's 'Hey, you!' in Louis Althusser's scene of interpellation fell short of arriving at the second person pronoun, doubling back on itself to become an act of hailing one's own incomplete hail."[19] I would have a slightly more sinister take on this: a world in which every surface becomes a weaponized adorable, not hailing but cooing: "Hey ... Hey ... Hey."[20]

There was something adorable about Theodor Adorno. And something cute even about his masterpiece *Minima Moralia*, his self-helpless book for and from damaged life, with its coy refusal of dialectical resolution. In it are a lot of kitsch items, like the useless gift articles produced by a specialized industry for people who no longer know how to give.[21] This junk is still closely tied to art, as kitsch lurks in art. So perhaps one can reverse the gesture and find the aesthetic in the cute, as a kind of fetish that protects against fetishism.

The interesting: If the zany is about subjects, and the cute is about subject–object strangeness, then the interesting is about things. Or maybe *information* about things or even the *circulation* of forms of information. It is not a performative or commodity aesthetic, but a discursive one. If the zany is hot, and the cute is warm, then the interesting is cool, ironic, detached, even clinical. It's a small surprise of information, of some variation from a norm. It can have a documentary impulse. It is interested in comparison, in anomalies and systems; it alternates between reason and surprise.

For Isabelle Stengers, what is interesting in science is a proposition that associates the largest number of actors.[22] The interesting also assembles the social, but what is sociologically interesting also has an aesthetic aspect. It measures the tension between understanding and wonder. Theories are not interesting when obvious, improbable, or unprovable. Ngai:

> From the hard sciences to sociology to literary studies, the interesting thus seems to be a way of creating relays between affect-based judgement and concept-based explanation in a manner that binds heterogeneous agencies together and enables movement across disciplinary domains.[23]

The interesting is an aesthetic without content, for the modern ironic self, like the detectives Nick and Nora in Hammett's *The Thin Man*.[24]

It's an aesthetic category one might connect to the *flâneur* and the *dérive*. Ngai links it to the rise in the circulation of printed matter, to which I might, in the spirit of T. J. Clark, add circulation through the modern city.[25] From Baudelaire to Debord, the *dérive* emerges as an anthropological version of the interesting, a method on the boundary between the regularity of the city and its possibility for anticipatory utopian moods.

The interesting lacks universality. "The interesting is thus a style of serial, comparative individualization." And yet the

interesting enables movement between aesthetic and nonaes-
thetic judgment, between pleasure and cognition: "the feeling
that underpins it seems to lie somewhere between an object-
oriented desire and an object-indifferent affect." Experience
is just what one agrees to notice, when interest flickers from
passive to active awareness. It is prior to affect: a generic,
minimal judgment. As curiosity, it could be the libido of theory,
both a driver and danger to reason. It's a feeling of not yet
knowing, an absence of a concept, "a kind of zero-degree aesthetic judgement."[26]

The interesting anticipates but is continuous. It is not
arresting, not a pause in time, like the sublime or beautiful.
It happens in a flowing duration but makes and marks a difference. It can thus only be historical. It might—finally—be
a secular aesthetic. The interesting can be irritating, with its
repetitive flick between the familiar and the unfamiliar, identity
and difference, continuity and break. But its variance from the
norm can be small, its affect minimal, its risk manageable. As
Raymond Williams notes, *risk* is the link between aesthetic and
economic senses of "interest."[27]

For Susan Sontag, photography makes everything interesting.
Barthes tried to arrest the serial repetition of the photographic
studium with his more singular *punctum*. Here one might want
to connect the interesting to Vilem Flüsser's famous essay on
photography as a machine that incorporates everything as an
image.[28] In modern literature, the interesting is Beckett, Perec,
or Stein's *The Making of Americans*, and more recently, Tom
McCarthy's *Remainder*, which one could read as a novel
about the novel as the temporal repetition that produces the
interesting.[29]

In a surprising move, Ngai links the interesting in the novel,
particularly the realist novel and its modern variants, to conceptual art. They are all interested in investigating generic
appearances, the serial, the algorithm, the schema, paper-
work and official procedures. Conceptual art is a forensic art.

Conceptual art shares a paradox in detective fiction identified by Franco Moretti: it must tell ever new stories but must reproduce the same schema.[30]

The interesting addresses a world of speeded-up information by asking for a slowed-down attention. Sometimes, the information about the art becomes the art, as in On Kawara postcards. If modern art was once a special kind of commodity, then a special kind of service, now it is a special kind of derivative financial instrument.[31] Ngai: "Interesting conceptual art was both an instance of and an art about this absorption of modes of circulation into modes of production."[32] But I think we blew through that moment toward a full subsumption of both into control of the value chain through the information vector.

And so:

Diachronic and informational, forensic and dialogic: the aesthetic of the interesting has the capacity to produce new knowledge. From Adorno on the products of the culture industry to Cavell on Hollywood screwball comedies, [to Ngai on the interesting], all contemporary criticism is thus, in some sense, an implicit provision of evidence for why the object that the critic has chosen to talk about is interesting.[33]

In this way a critic might still influence public judgment, crossing the border between general and specialized, making subcultures cohere, watching the detectives.

The zany is a subject, the interesting an object, and the cute a hybrid. All are in-between play and labor, and they signal an era in which work becomes play and play becomes work. All three are both ways of feeling and ways of relating, and they mark an era in which both work and play are also tied into a constant effort to make or maintain sociality. These seem common experiences for those parts of the overdeveloped world where more and more people seem to do service work, "creative" work, work with information.

The particular affective responses involved are hardly grand ones. The cute evokes feelings through its vulnerable and diminutive form. The zany is itself a feeling of flailing help-lessness. (Ngai does not include erotic frenzy but one might as well, particularly if hyperbolic and joyless.) The interesting is a moving target, tracking along with the difference between norms and anomalies. These might all be trivial or bathetic feelings—but they are not detached, disinterested, or leisurely contemplation of the beautiful. Nor are they the overwhelming force of the unmasterable sublime, which one nevertheless puts back in its box with the gesture of respect or recognition of delight. They nest between those two extremes. We are dealing with weak forms and subtle powers that make the histrionics of the sublime in Lyotard or Land look a bit dated.[34]

In a novel formulation, Ngai suggests that art really has become autonomous. Moreover, the other great ambition for art, its merger with everyday life, has also come true at the same time. Both utopias came to pass, but not quite in the form anyone envisaged. They happen through rather than against the commodity form. Art survived through weakness, through a faint facility for standing-in for nonalienated labor, as a vague and friendly ghost rather than the specter haunting Europe. The aesthetic is still with us, but in banal form, lacking religious solemnity. You can cuddle up to it at night or glance it in a museum. "Hey…", it says. It can be awesome but never inspire awe. It has no higher power to appeal to and not much up its sleeve.

That aspect of art that really did fuse with the everyday becomes almost indistinguishable from neurotic symptoms: Interest cycles through irritating obsessions and boredom; cute-ness reeks of manipulation that provokes phobias and disgust; zaniness performs hysteria or mania. Everyday art is the kipple of once-great genre tropes: cuteness is the pastoral in a .jpeg; the zany is a comedic return and reconciliation in a .gif; the interesting is realism in a Facebook quiz.

The ubiquity of these more secular aesthetic categories may be related to "the increasing routing of art and aesthetic experience through the exchange of information."[35] The aesthetic now attaches to performance, commodity, and information. This connects a series of historical phenomena:

> the convergence of art and information; the loss of tension between art and the commodity form; the rise of an increasingly intimate public sphere and of an increasingly exchange-based private one; the proliferation and intensification of activity in both public/private domains that cannot easily be dichotomized into play or work.[36]

While more secular than the sublime, all three also put pressure on the category of *beauty*: cuteness violates the distance to the object, zaniness troubles the concept of spontaneous play, while the gaze of the interesting is clinical but remains unmoved.[37] The aesthetic experience is just not to be found where classical western aesthetics thought it was. Ngai: "Can distance, play and disinterested pleasure—essential images of freedom rather than compulsion or determination—still be considered reliable 'symptoms' of the aesthetic, if late capitalist culture's most pervasive aesthetic categories pose such a challenge to each as such?"[38]

Schlegel and Fredric Jameson now appear as the synthetic observers of transitional moments. Ngai:

> If, in response to the loss of the sacred under conditions of secular, industrial modernity, the eighteenth and nineteenth centuries plunged headlong into the resacralization of the aesthetic, the contemporary moment seems defined by a desacralization of the aesthetic turn, but a desacralization caused precisely by the aesthetic's hyperbolic expansion.[39]

Contrary to Jameson, Hiroki Azuma got the postmodern moment right when he noticed a shift from a grand narrative to a vast database—of cute elements or *moe-points*—as what was already emerging in Japan in the nineties.[40]

Aesthetic theories may themselves have their aesthetic modes, the beautiful being no doubt the most common. Jameson's aesthetics may have tried to pull off the sublime: You were meant to feel as if you stared into the abyss of the totality itself. If we think of Adorno's *Minima Moralia* as cute, then what do interesting or zany aesthetic theories look like? In these terms, Ngai's own book seems to work in the interesting mode. Perhaps the new only appears against the background of a constant—in this case, eternal capitalism. It can have novel features, but somehow its essence remains the same. It can be late but all tomorrow's parties still go on and on and are all the same.

What would not just a zany aesthetic, but a *zany aesthetic theory*, look like? In retrospect, I think I tried it in *A Hacker Manifesto* and *Gamer Theory*.[41] The titles themselves name kinds of performing-subjects, who, like the zanni in his time, do emerging kinds of labor. *Gamer Theory* itself was performative, appearing online as a networked book. It worked within Oulipian constraints and was certainly not cool but a lot of hot, hard work.[42] It wasn't as compellingly zany as Eddo Stern's *Tekken Torture*, a modified fighting game that gave real electric shocks when players were hit by their opponents, but it felt that way.

Unlike the interesting, the zany really works *against* its constraints. There's an acceptance of a given form and temporal constant in the interesting that the zany pushes exhaustively and exhaustingly past. Maybe with a touch more of that mania we can then unmoor the aesthetic experience of the interesting, the zany, and the cute from the assumption of an eternal capitalism. Maybe this isn't late capitalism, but early something else.

What might be novel is the ownership and control over the entire value chain through command of the information vector itself. Here I'd like to connect Ngai to the pioneering work of

Randy Martin, whose interest was in forms of performative aesthetics that might include her category of the zany but are perhaps a bit broader. The zany is anxious about doing it right. The escape hatch the performative art (and sport) that interested Martin found is close to the queer art of failure, in that it recognizes a new volatility in its conditions of operation. It lets go of the guiderail.

The secularization of the aesthetic seems homologous with the subsumption of the value chain under control of information. The power of what I call the *vectoralist class* is an aesthetic power, a power over appearances, over the stocks, flows, and (more importantly) the vector via which information is managed and material production is ordered. The aesthetic—in the sense of the apprehension of information—integrated the everyday into commodification but also changed what the commodity form is. It is not just that information became a commodity but that the commodity could now take the form of information itself.

Tiziana Terranova suggests that counterhegemonic struggles are now about tactics in a turbulent flow of information. In this connection, Ngai's identification of three operative aesthetics is useful and can be instrumentalized as styles of engagement. These are aesthetics about the subsumption of creative effort of what I called the *hacker class*, into the commodification of information and the informationalization of the commodity. Clearly this era of the zany, the cute, and the interesting may also pass. The Anthropocene may require a revolution in modes of perception, affect, and cognition.

But all this too may be automated. I sometimes joke with my "millennial" students and "post-millennial" kids that our last job will be to figure out how to be cute so our new artificial intelligence (AI) overlords will keep us mere humans as pets. Or perhaps they will find the weird data we throw off interesting—although we will still have to be careful not to become persons of interest. Maybe our AI overlords will evolve a posthuman language in which to LOL at our zany mammalian antics. But Ngai's book is no joke and may well be the basis for a manual for appearing to each other, that we might feel and know and think each other, and endure.

Kodwo Eshun: Black Accelerationism

Sensory language leaves us with no habit for lying,
We are hostile aliens, immune from dying. —The Spaceape

There are two bright stars of London culture whose premature deaths I still feel. One is Stephen Gordon (1970–2014), aka The Spaceape. The other is Mark Fisher (1968–2017). Both made works that to me are haunted by the nameless dread of the Anthropocene. But they were also forward slanting culture agents, whose work was constantly abrading the dead skin of the times. Mark Fisher:

Capitalism has abandoned the future because it can't deliver it. Nevertheless, the contemporary left's tendencies towards Canutism, its rhetoric of resistance and obstruction, collude with capital's anti/meta-narrative that it is the only story left standing. Time to leave behind the logics of failed revolts, and to think ahead again.[43]

As Fisher and Gordon were both well aware, an orientation toward an imminent, immanent future is a hard thing to achieve in a culture shaped in the present out of the past, as a selective tradition. Marx: "The tradition of all dead generations weighs like a nightmare on the brains of the living."[44] Inherited ways of writing make the present over as if it were more of the same. Perhaps music might be more attuned to the present than the past. Music too is made in the present out of past materials, but in its field of resonance one might detect unknown pleasures and feel unfathomed spaces. As Kodwo Eshun writes in *More Brilliant Than the Sun*: "Everything the media warns you against has already been made into tracks that drive the dance floor."[45]

A word for this might be *accelerationism*.[46] If it had a key idea, it is that it is either impossible or undesirable to resist or negate the development of the commodity economy coupled with technology. Rather, it has to be pushed harder and faster; it has to change more rather than less. It is an idea, a feeling, an orientation that might make most sense among those for whom the past was not that great anyway. And so, not surprisingly, the best text on accelerationism was also about Blackness—Kodwo Eshun's *More Brilliant Than the Sun*.

It's helpful to make a preliminary distinction here between what Aria Dean calls *Blacceleration* or *Black Accelerationism* and *Afrofuturism*, although the former may be a subset of the latter.[47] Black Accelerationism is a willful pushing forward that includes an attempt to clear away certain habits of thought and feeling in order to be open to a future that is attempting to realize itself in the present.

Afrofuturism is a more general category in which one finds attempts to picture or narrate or conceive of Black existence on other worlds or in future times, which may or may not have an accelerationist will to push on. If Black Accelerationism is a particular temporal and spatial concept, Afrofuturism is a genre that includes both temporal and spatial concepts within the general cultural space of science fiction. That in turn might be a subset of modernism, with its characteristically nontransitive approach to time.[48]

The term *Afrofuturism* was coined by Mark Dery, drawing on suggestions in the work of Greg Tate.[49] It's become a lively site of cultural production but also scholarly research, providing a frame for thinking about the science fiction writing of African American authors such as Samuel Delany and Octavia Butler or more recently N. K. Jemisin. It has also become a popular trope in contemporary cultural production. The Marvel superhero movie *Black Panther* (2018) is a veritable anthology of its visual figures. Afrofuturism also shows up in music videos by Beyoncé, FKA Twigs, and Janelle Monáe.[50]

Monáe's video *Many Moons* contains one of the key figures of the genre. It shows androids performing at an auction for wealthy clients, including white, vampiric plutocrats and a Black military-dictator type. The androids are all Black and are indeed all Monáe herself. The android becomes the reversal, and yet also the equivalent, of the slave. The slave was a human treated as a nonperson and forced to work like a machine; the android is an inhuman treated as a nonperson but forced to work like a human.

These figures have a deep past. But first, I want to explore one of their futures or a related future. After writing *More Brilliant Than the Sun*, Eshun co-founded the Otolith Group with Anjalika Sagar. The first three films they made together, *Otolith* parts I, II, and III, offer a different "future" and a cultural space in which to think of Black Accelerationism.[51]

Otolith is in the genre of documentary fiction or essay film, descended from the work of Chris Marker and Harun Farocki. The conceit involves a future character who is a descendent of present-day Otolith co-founder Anjalika Sagar, who lives in orbit around our planet and who is working through the archives of her own family.

Otolith links the microgravity environment to planetary crisis, where orbital or *agravic* space is a *heterotopia* inviting heightened awareness of disorientation.[52] "Gravity locates the human species."[53] This is a speculative future in which the species bifurcates, those in microgravity function with a modified otolith, that part of the inner ear that senses the tilting of the body. In the terms of the revived structural analysis of myth offered by Eduardo Viveiros de Castro, this is a myth about the end of both the human and the world.

Sagar's imaginary future descendant looks back, through her own ancestors, to the grand social projects of the twentieth century: Indian and Soviet state socialism, the international socialist women's movement, and (as in Anna Tsing) the Non-Aligned Movement. One of Sagar's ancestors had actually met Valentina Tereshkova, the first woman in space.[54]

The last part of *Otolith* meditates on an unmade film by the great Satjayit Ray, *The Alien*.[55] Its central conceit, of an alien lost on earth who is discovered by children, strangely enough turned up later in the Hollywood film *ET*. Otolith speculates on whether Hindu polytheism foreclosed the space in which an Indian science fiction might have flourished. The popular Indian comic books that retell the stories of the Gods are indeed something like science fiction and call for a rethinking of the genre.

Otolith also gestures toward American science fiction writer Roger Zelazny's *Lord of Light* (1967), which imagines a quite different future than that of *Otolith* but that similarly tries to decenter imaginative possibility.[56] In this book, the only survivors of a vanished earth are Hindu. Their high-tech society is also highly stratified. Its rulers have God-like powers and the technology to "reincarnate." The central character, described in the book as an "accelerationist," challenges this class-bound order.

During the Cold War, while much of American literature was basically suburban white boys talking about their dicks, science fiction did a lot of the real cultural work.[57] Zelazny's book is not a bad example of how far American science fiction could get in imagining a non-western world that was neither to be demonized nor idealized and whose agents of change were internal to it. Samuel Delany and Octavia Butler went even further in using worldbuilding as a literary device for asking about how concepts like race and gender, or even the human, come to be in the first place.[58] In science fiction, unlike in literary fiction, worldbuilding has to at least be plausible.

Afrofuturism is a landscape of cultural invention that we can put in the context of a plural universe of imagined future times and other spaces, which draw on the raw material of many kinds of historical experience and cultural raw material. And just as Afrofuturism functions as a subset of science fiction modernity, there might also be many kinds of accelerationism. The posthuman ends up being more than one thing if one can get one's head around currently existing humans as being more than one thing.[59] The orbital posthuman of *Otolith* might in many ways repeat a figure from that little-known accelerationist classic, JD Bernal's *The World, The Flesh and the Spirit*.[60] But it does so inflected by particular cultural histories.

Which brings me to *More Brilliant Than the Sun*. It is a text whose strategies include putting pressure on language through neologisms and portmanteau constructs, in order to let the future into the present.[61] Eshun sets himself against modes of writing about Black music that are designed to resist hearing anything new. "The future is a much better guide to the present than the past." Thus, "the rhythmachine is locked in a retarded innocence." You are not supposed to analyze the groove, or find a language for it. Music writing becomes a futureshock absorber: "You reserve your nausea for the timeless classic." Eshun's interest is rather in "Unidentified Audio Objects."[62]

We no longer have roots, we have aerials. Eshun is resistant to that writing that wants the authentic and seeks for it in music, that wants to locate it in organic community, whether in the Mississippi Delta for the blues or the burning Bronx for hip-hop.[63] He is resistant to the validating figure of "the street" as the mythical social or public place where the real is born.

From the Net to arcade simulations games, civil society is all just one giant research-and-development wing of the military. The military industrial complex has advanced decades ahead of civil society, becoming a lethal *military entertainment complex*, reprograming predatory virtual futures. Far from being a generative source for popculture, as Trad media still quaintly insists, the street is now the playground in which low-end developments of military technology are unleashed, to mutate themselves.[64]

As Black Lives Matter has so consistently confirmed.[65]

For Eshun, disco is "audibly where the 21st century begins,"[66] even if most genealogies of pop delete its intimations of the sonic diaspora of Afrofuturism. Like Paul Gilroy, Eshun thinks of Black culture as diasporic rather than national, but unlike Gilroy, he is not interested in a critical negation of the limits of humanism in the name of a more expansive one.[67] His Black culture "alienates itself from the human; it arrives from the future."[68] It refuses the human as a central category. If the human is not a given, then neither can there be a Black essence. There's no "keeping it real" in this book. The writer's job is to be a *sensor* rather than a *censor*.

The field of study here is not so much music itself as the ambiences music co-generates with spaces, sound systems, and bodies. It's not an aesthetics of music so much as what the late Randy Martin would have recognized as a kinaesthetics. One could even see it as a branch of psychogeography, but not of walking—rather, of dancing.[69]

The dance does not reveal some aspect of the human, but rather has the capacity to make the human something else. Eshun follows Lyotard in extending Nietzsche's insistence that the human does not want the truth. Here, the human craves the inauthentic and the artificial.[70] This is the basis of a sonic accelerationism: the objective is to encourage machine-made music's "despotic drive" to subsume both its own past and the presence of the human body.[71]

Black Accelerationism, operating mostly but not exclusively through music, aims "to design, manufacture, fabricate, synthesize, cut, paste and edit a so-called artificial discontinuum for the futurerhythmachine."[72] As Hiroki Azuma maintains, machines don't alienate people.[73] They can make you feel more intensely. They enable a hyperembodiment rather than disembodiment.

Let's work backward through the sonic material Eshun feels his way through. What's not to like about late nineties Detroit techno?[74] Here we might start with what for Eshun was one of the end points. Drexciya is an unidentifiable sonic object that comes with its own Afrofuturist myth. The Drexciyans navigate the depths of the Black Atlantic. They are a webbed mutant marine subspecies descended from pregnant slaves who were thrown overboard during the Middle Passage, as if they had escaped all of slavery's scenes of subjection.[75]

Drexciya use electronic sound and beats to replay the alien abduction of slavery as sonic fiction, or as what Sun Ra called an *alterdestiny*.[76] As Lisa Nakamura shows, certain popular Afrofuturist material like the *Matrix* movies make the Black or the African the more authentically human and rooted.[77] What appeals to Eshun is the opposite claim: that Blackness can accelerate faster away from the human. It's an embrace rather than a refutation of the slave-machine figure, pressing it into service in pressing on.

There was a time when avant-garde music was beatless. Drum and bass went in the opposite direction: "drumsticks become knitting needles hitting electrified bedsprings at 180 bpm." The *sensual topology* offered by 4hero or A Guy Called Gerald use drum machines not to mimic the human drummer but replace it, to create abstract sonic environments that call the body into machinic patterns of movement. "Abstract doesn't mean rarified or detached but the opposite: the body stuttering on the edge of a future sound, teetering on the brink of new speech."[78]

Rhythm becomes the lead instrument, as on A Guy Called Gerald's *Black Secret Technology*:

> dappling the ears with micro-discrepancies ... When polyrhythm phase-shifts into hyper-rhythm, it becomes unaccountable, compounded, confounding. It scrambles the sensorium, adapts the human into a "distributed being" strung out across the

webbed spider-nets and computational jungles of the digital diaspora.[79]

One could say more about how quite particular musical technologies program in advance a kind of phase-space of possible sonic landscapes. The human sound-maker is then not the author but rather the output of the machine itself. For Eshun this is a way to positively value the figure of Blackness as close to the machinelike and remote from the fully "human." Perhaps an insistence on Blackness as fully human rather overvalues the human. And if whiteness is supposedly most close to the human, then there's every reason to think less of the human as a category in the first place. This rhetorical move is central to Black Accelerationism. The coupling of Blackness with the machinic is what is to be valued and accelerated, as an overcoming of both whiteness and the human.

If there's a sonic precursor and stimulator for that line of thought, its acid house music as a playing out of the unintended possibilities of the Roland TB-303 bass synthesizer. It was meant as a bass accompaniment for musicians to practice to, but sonic artists such as Phuture made it a lead instrument, exploring its potential not to imitate bass but to make otherworldly sounds. Eshun: "Nothing you know about the history of music is any help whatsoever."[80]

Eshun mostly works his way around hip-hop, being rather disinterested in its claims to street authenticity, not to mention its masculine bravado.[81] He makes an exception for the late eighties work of the Ultramagnetic MCs. Here the song is in ruins, language is reduced to phonemes. The rapper becomes an abstract sound generator, dropping science. Eshun quotes Paul Virilio from *Pure War* to the effect that "science and technology develop the unknown."[82] Science is associated not with what is demonstrated or proven but the opposite, which might be the condition of possibility of science in the more conventional sense.

As is common among those who read a lot of Deleuze during the last century, Eshun favors an escape from the rational and the conscious, a slipping past the borders into the domain of affections and perceptions. In the language of Gerald Raunig, it's an attempt to slip past the individual into a space of *dividual* parts, in this case, of skins rippling with sonic sensation.[83] It's not consciousness raising so much as consciousness *razing*.

Here, sound that works on the skin, on the animated body rather than the concentrating ear, might take the form of feedback, fuzz, static. In the eighties these were coming to be instruments in themselves rather than accidental or unwanted byproducts of instruments that made notes. One can hear (and feel) this in the Jungle Brothers or Public Enemy—the sound of a new earth, a Black planet.

It is not the inhuman or the nonhuman or the overhuman that is to be dreaded. What one might try to hear around is rather the human as a special effect. "The unified self is an amputated self."[84] The sonic can produce what the textual always struggles to generate—a parallel processing of alternate states or points of view. This is not so much a double consciousness as the mitosis of the I.[85] This is a sonic psychogeography that already heard the turbulent information sphere that Tiziana Terranova's writing later conceptualizes. But it's more visceral than conceptual, or rather, both at once: "concepts are fondled and licked, sucked and played with."[86] Sonic landscapes are intimate but not exactly commodities, and certainly not, in Ngai's terms, cute.

Of the recognized hip-hop pioneers, the most lyrically and conceptually adventurous was the late Rammellzee, who worked in graffiti, sculpture, and visual art as well as producing some remarkable writings, all bound together with a gothic futurist style he called *Ikonokast Panzerism*.[87] His work appeared always with a layer of armor to protect it from a hostile world. He already saw the hip-hop world of the streets and the police as a subset of a larger militarization of all aspects of life. His particular struggle was against the military perceptual complex, and his poetic figure for this was the attempt to "assassinate the infinity sign."[88]

Rammellzee ingested and elaborated on futures opened up by the discovery of the possibility latent in the direct-drive turntable of the breakbeat. *Adventures on the Wheels of Steel* by Grandmaster Flash could stand-in as an emblem of that moment. Breakbeat opens up the possibility of the studio as a research center for isolating and replicating beats. The dj becomes a *groove-robber* rather than an ancestor worshipper. "Hip-hop is therefore not a genre so much as an omni-genre, a conceptual approach towards sonic organization rather than a particular sound in itself."[89]

The turntable becomes a tone generator, the cut a command, discarding the song, automating the groove. It's a meta-technique for making new instruments out of old ones. John Cage had already been there, arriving at the turntable not through encounters with gay disco so much as through a formalist avant-garde tradition. As Eshun wryly notes: "Pop always retroactively rescues unpop from the prison of its admirers."[90]

Couple the turntable with the Emulator sampler and you have a sonic production universe through which you can treat the whole of recorded sound as what Ngai thinks of as the interesting or Azuma thinks of as a database rather than as a grand narrative. Or rather, that technosonic universe can produce you. In Eshun's perspective, the tech itself authors ways of being. The Emulator sampler discovers the sampled break and uses Marley Marl as its medium.

New sounds are accidents discovered by machines. "Your record collection becomes an immense time machine that builds itself through you."[91] The machine compels the human toward its parameters. The producer is rather like the gamer, as I understood the figure in *Gamer Theory*: an explorer of the interiority of the digital rather than romantic revolt beyond it.[92] Digital sound reveals the body to itself, as a kind of sensational mathematics for kinaesthetes.

If there is a "Delta blues origin story" here for digital Black music, it is an ironic one. It is the German band Kraftwerk.[93] But rather than delegitimizing Black digital music, Eshun has an affirmative spin on this. Black producers heard themselves in this echt-European machine music. They heard an internal landscape toward which to disappear. Sonic engineers such as Underground Resistance volunteer for internal exile, for stealth and obfuscation. Even for passing as the machine, as when Juan Atkins releases works under the name Model 500.

"Detroit techno is aerial, it transmits along routes through space, is not grounded by the roots of any tree ... Techno disappears itself from the street, the ghetto and the hood ... The music arrives from another planet." A production entity like Cybotron "technofies the biosphere."[94] Or escapes from it, building instead a city of time.

> Escapism is organized until it seizes the means of perception and multiplies the modes of sensory reality... Sonic Fiction strands you in the present with no way of getting back to the 70s ... Sonic Fiction is the manual for your own offworld breakout, re-entry program, for entering Earth's orbit and touching down on the landing strip of your senses ... To technofy is to become aware of the co-evolution of machine and human, the secret life of machines, the computerization of the world, the programming of history, the informatics of reality.[95]

The dj intensifies estrangement, creating alien sound design. Music making is deskilled, allowing for more hearing, less manual labor. The sound processes listeners into its content. Detroit techno comes with a plethora of heteronyms, in parallel rather than serial. And it counterprograms against the sensuality of Funkadelic.[96] "Techno triggers a delibidinal economics of strict pulses, gated signals—with techno you dance your way *into* constriction." It favors the affectless voice over the glossolalia of soul. Techno is funk for androids escaping from the street and from labor. "Techno secedes from the logic of empowerment which underpins the entire African American mediascape."[97]

As in the work of Donna Haraway, the machinic and Blackness are both liminal conditions in relation to the human; they are treated not as ironic political myths but as programs to implement with all deliberate speed.[98]

> There is a heightened awareness in HipHop, fostered through comics and sci-fi, of the manufactured, designed and posthuman existence of African-Americans. African aliens are snatched by African slave-traders, delivered to be sliced, diced and genetically designed by whiteface fanatics and cannibal Christians into American slaves, 3/5 of their standardized norm, their *Westworld* ROM.[99]

In somewhat Deleuzian terms, Eshun traces a line of flight from Blackness through the machine to becoming imperceptible.[100] "Machine Music therefore arrives as unblack, unpopular and uncultural, an Unidentified Audio Object with no ground, no roots and no culture."[101] But far from erasing Blackness, this disappearance is only possible through Blackness or its analogs.

The digital soundscape is a break in both method and style from the analog that it subsumed and which in turn processed earlier forms of media technology after its own affordances. Key moments here might be George Clinton's Funkadelic and Lee Perry's Black Ark. These versions of analog signal processing took pop presence and processed it into an echo or loop. Space invades the texture of the song. Distortion becomes its own instrument. "Listening becomes a field trip through a found environment."[102]

Funkadelic was an alien encounter imagined through metaphor of the radio, connecting human-aliens to station

WEFUNK, "home of the extraterrestrial brothers." Its repetitive urging was to give in to the inhuman, to join the Afronauts funking up the galaxy. It was built out of tapeloops, doo-loops, mixadelics, and advertising slogans for nonexistent products. Underneath the off-pop hooks, Funkadelic altered the sensory hierarchy of the pop song. "The ass, the brain and the spine all change places ... The ass stops being the behind, and moves up front to become the booty." This was not the bodyshape proposed by pop. "Moog becomes a slithering cephalopod tugging at your hips."[103]

Funkadelic accelerated and popularized sonic concepts that in part came from jazz, or more specifically what Eshun calls the *jazz fission* of the 1970s. This encompasses the cybernetic, space age jazz of George Russell, "a wraithscape of delocalized chimes ... Russell's magnetic mixology accelerates a discontinuum in which the future arrives from the past." Also in this bag are the 1970s albums of Miles Davis and Herbie Hancock, where effects pedals become instruments in their own right. Here's Eshun evoking the sound of Herbie Hancocks's *Hornets*: "Moving through the echoplex, construction is cloned from a singular sensation into an environment that dunks you headfirst in a horde of heat-seeking killer bees."[104]

Effects defect from causes, detach from instruments. It's the expansion of an era when industrial communication split sounds from sources, as R. Murray Shafer has already suggested.[105] It was hard to hear at first. Take, for instance, Alice Coltrane's controversial remixing of John Coltrane's *Living Space*. It in turn might be made possible by Sun Ra's work from the mid-1950s onward, with his alternate Black cosmology.[106] For Sun Ra, to be Black is not to be figuratively the Israelite, fleeing bondage, but to actually be descended from the Egyptians, to belong to a despotic power—which rules elsewhere in the galaxy. Soul music affirms Blackness as the legacy of the suffering human. In contrast, Ra is an alien god from the future. This is not alienation but affirmation of the alien.

Sun Ra lends himself to an Afrofuturist reading, which would highlight his claim to be from Jupiter, to be the author of an alterdestiny. And in Eshun there's a more specifically Black accelerationist reading, or perhaps hearing, or maybe sensing. It's not an alternative to this world, but a pressing on of a tendency, where through the exclusion from the human that is Blackness an escape hatch appears in an embrace of one other thing that is also excluded: the machinic. Sun Ra's Arkestra was for some of its existence a bit of a male monastic cult.

Accelerationism is often presented as a desire for a superseding of a merely human model of cognition, but it is still rather tied to a valuing of cognition that has particular cultural roots. Perhaps cognition is not up to speed.[107] Eshun:

> There's a sense in which the nervous system is being reshaped by beats for a new kind of state, for a new kind of sensory condition. Different parts of your body are actually in different states of evolution. Your head may well be lagging quite a long way behind the rest of your body.[108]

Otolith II posed three questions: "Capital, as far as we know, was never alive. How did it reproduce itself? How did it replicate? Did it use human skin?"[109] The operative word here is *skin*, implicated as it is in what Gilroy calls the *crisis of raciology*. Perhaps one could ask if capitalism has already superseded itself and done so first by passing through the pores of the skin of those it designates others. But one might wonder whether, if this is not capitalism, it might not be something worse. Eshun already has an aerial attuned to that possibility, filtered through the sensibility of (for example) Detroit techno, with its canny intimations of the subsuming of the street into a militarized surveillance order, from which one had best discreetly retire.

One could keep searching back through the database of Afrofuturism, beyond Eshun's late twentieth century forays, as Louis Chude-Sokei does in *The Sound of Culture.*[110] As it turns out, what is perhaps the founding text of Futurism is a perversely Afrofuturist one: Marinetti's *Mafarka: The Futurist,* first published in 1909. It's an exotic tale of a Muslim prince's victory over an African army, and his desire to beget a son, part bird, part machine, who can rise up to conquer the sun.[111]

Or one might mention Samuel Butler's anti-accelerationist *Erewhon,* the ur-text on the human as the reproductive organ for the machine. Its imaginary landscape bares the traces of Butler's experience in New Zealand, in the wake of colonial wars against the Maori. Or, as Angela Davis notes, even though tied against their will to the plantation, even though they may never have seen one and only heard the sound in the distance, the Black spirituals early on started to imagine the getting on board the freedom train.[112] The technics of the railway was already an imaginary vector out of the slave condition, a sweet chariot of iron and smoke.

It may turn out that the whole question of acceleration is tied to the question of race. Haraway usefully thinks the spatial equivalence of the non-white, the nonman, the nonhuman in relation to a certain humanist language. But thought temporally, humanism has a similar problem. Spatially, it is troubled by what is above it (the angelic) or below it (the animal).[113] Temporally, it is troubled by what is prior to it (the primitive) or what supersedes it, including a great deal of race panic about being over-taken by the formerly primitive colonial or enslaved other. Particularly of that other, in its unthinking, machinelike labor, starts to look like the new machines coming to replace the human. In this regard, the rhetorical strategy of Black Accelerationism is to positively revalue what had been previously negative and racist figures. As such, and as in Viveiros de Castro, it's a permutation on the old mythic forms made productive in a new way.

Lisa Nakamura: Digitizing Race

Lisa Nakamura is a pioneer of the study of what used to be tagged as "race in cyberspace."[114] Now that the internet is everywhere, and race and racisms proliferate on it like fungus on damp newspaper, her work deserves renewed critical attention. Her book *Digitizing Race: Visual Cultures of the Internet* is over a decade old, but it turns out that looking perceptively at ephemeral media need not render the resulting study ephemeral at all.

Digitizing Race draws together three things. The first is the postracial project of a certain (neo)liberal politics that Bill Clinton took mainstream in the early nineties. Its central conceit was that all the state need do is provide 'opportunities' for everyone to become functional subjects of postindustrial labor and consumption. The particular challenges of racism were ignored.

The second is a historical transformation in the internet that began in the mid-nineties, which went from being military and scientific (with some creative subcultures on the side) to a vast commercial complex.[115] This led to the waning of the early nineties internet subcultures, some of whom thought of it as a utopian or at least alternative media for identity play, virtual community, and gift economies. In *A Hacker Manifesto*, I was mostly interested in the last of these. Nakamura is more interested in what became of identity and community.

One theme that started to fade in internet culture (or *cyberculture* in the language of the time) had to do with passing online as something other than one's meatspace self. This led to a certain gnostic belief in the separation of online from meatspace being, as if the differences and injustices of the latter could just be left behind. But the early cyberculture adepts tended to be a somewhat fortunate few, with proximity to research universities. As the internet's user-base expanded, the newcomers (or noobs) had other ideas.

The third tendency Nakamura layers onto the so-called neoliberal turn and the commercialized and more-popular internet is the academic tendency known as visual studies or visual culture studies.[116] This in part grew out of, and in reaction against, an art historical tradition that could absorb installation art but did not know how to think digital media objects or practices. Visual culture studies drew on anthropology and other disciplines to create the "hybrid form to end all hybrid forms."[117] It also had something in common with cultural studies, in its attention to low, ephemeral, and vulgar forms, treated not just as social phenomena but as aesthetic ones as well.

Not all the tendencies within visual culture studies sat well together. There could be tension between paying attention to digital media objects and paying attention to vulgar popular forms. Trying to do both at once was an exercise in self-created academic marginality. The study of new media thus tended to privilege things that look like art; the study of the low, the minor, or the vulgar tended to favor social over aesthetic methods and preoccupations. Not the least virtue of Nakamura's work is that she went out on a limb and studied questions of race and gender *and* in new and ephemeral digital forms *and* as aesthetic practices.

One way to subsume these three questions into some sort of totality might be to think about what Lisa Parks called *visual capital*.[118] How is visual capital, an ensemble of images that appear to have value, created and circulated? How does social differentiation cleave along lines of access to powerful modes of representation? Having framed those questions, one might then look at how the internet came to function as a site for the creation and distribution of hegemonic and counterhegemonic images of racialized bodies.

Here one might draw on Paul Gilroy's work on the historical formation and contestation of racial categories, or the way Donna Haraway and Chela Sandoval look to cyborg bodies as produced by biotechnical networks, but within which they might exercise an ironic power of slippery self-definition.[119] Either way, one might pay special attention to forms of image-making by nonelite or even banal cultures as well as to more high-profile mass media forms, cool subcultures, or avant-garde art forms.

There are several strands to this story, however, one of which might be the evolution of technical media form. From Nick Mirzoeff, Nakamura takes the idea of visual technology as an enhancement of vision, from easel painting to digital avatars.[120] In the context of that historical background, one might ask what is old and what is new about what one discovers in current media forms. This might be a blend of historical, ethnographic, and formal-aesthetic methods.

A good place to start such a study is with interfaces, and a good way to tie together the study of cinema, television, and the internet is to study how the interfaces of the internet appear in cinema and television. Take, for instance, the video for Jennifer Lopez's pop song, "If You Had My Love" (1999). The conceit of the video is that Lopez is an avatar controlled by users who can view her in different rooms, doing different dances in different outfits. The first viewer is a young man who appears to be looking for something to jerk-off to; other imaginary viewers include teenage girls and a rather lugubrious interracial threesome, nodding off together on a sofa.[121] We become voyeurs on their voyeurism. But the interface itself is perhaps the star, and J-Lo herself becomes an effect. With the interface, the imaginary user can make J-Lo perform as different kinds of dancer, slotting her into different racial and cultural niches. The interface offers "multiple points of entry to the star."[122] She—it—can be chopped and streamed. It's remarkable that this video made for MTV sits so nicely now on Youtube.com, whose interactive modes it premediates.

Another example: There was (and still is) a lot of commentary on *The Matrix* (1999), but not much of it lingers over the slightly embarrassing second and third movies in the franchise.[123] They are "bad films with their hearts in the right place."[124] Like the J-Lo video, they deal among other things with what Eugene Thacker in *Biomedia* called *immediacy*, or the expectation of real-time feedback and control through an interface.[125] As Nakamura drolly notes, "This is an eloquent formulation of entitlement." Where the *Matrix* films get interestingly weird is in their treatment of racial difference among interface users under "information capitalism."[126]

The Matrix pits Blackness as embodiment against whiteness as the digital. What goes on in the background to the main story is a species of Afrofuturism, celebrating the erotics of the Black bodies as that which is most remote from the whiteness of technics. It's the opposite of Black Accelerationism, in which a close proximity of the Black body to the machine is in advance of whiteness and to be desired. In *The Matrix* version, the Black body holds back from the technical and retains attributes of soul, individuality, corporeality, and this is its value. Nakamura: "Afrofuturist mojo and black identity are generally depicted as singular, 'natural' … 'unassimilable' and 'authentic.'" But with the bad guy Agent Smith, "Whiteness thus spreads in a manner that exemplifies a much-favored paradigm of e-business in the nineties: viral marketing."[127] The white Agents propagate through digitally penetrating other white male bodies.

At least race appears in the films, which offer some sort of counterimaginary to cyber-utopianism. But as Coco Fusco notes, photography and cinema don't just record race—they produce it.[128] An algorithmic technics may in the main exacerbate the production of racialized difference.[129] Lev Manovich notes that it's in the interface that the photographic image is produced now, and so for Nakamura, it is the interface that bears scrutiny as the place where race is made. In *The Matrix*, race is made to appear for a notionally white viewer.

The presence of blackness in the visual field guards whites from the irresistible seduction of the perfectly transparent interface ... Transparent interfaces are represented as intuitive, universal, pre- or postverbal, white, translucent, and neutral—part of a visual design aesthetic embodied by the Apple iPod.[130]

Apple's iconic early ads for the iPod featured blacked-out silhouettes of dancing bodies, their white earbud cords flapping as they move, against bold single-color backgrounds. For Nakamura, they conjure universal consumers who can make product choices, individuated neoliberal subjects in a colorblind world. Like the "users" of J-Lo in her video, they can shuffle between places, styles, cultures, ethnicities—even if some of the bodies dancing in the ads are meant to be read as not just black-out but also Black. Blackness, at the time at least, was still the marker for the authentic in what white audiences desired from Black music. In this world, "Whiteness is replication, blackness is singularity, but never for the black subject, always for the white subject."[131]

Nakamura:

This visual culture, which contrasts black and white interface styles so strongly, insists that it is race that is real. In this way the process of new media as a cultural formation that produces race is obscured; instead race functions here as a way to visualize new media image production ... In this representational economy, images of blacks serve as talismans to ward off the consuming power of the interface, whose transparent depths, like Narcissus' pool, threaten to fatally immerse its users.[132]

If Blackness usually stands for authentic embodiment in this visual culture, then being Asian stands for proximity to the tech.[133] The Asian shows up only marginally in *The Matrix*. Its star, the biracial Keanu Reeves, was like J-Lo racially malleable for audiences. In his case he could be read as white by whites and Asian by Asians if they so desired. A more ironic and telling example is the 2002 film *Minority Report*. Tom Cruise— was there a whiter star in his era?—has to get his eyes replaced, as retinal scanning is everywhere in this film's paranoid future. Only the eyes he gets belonged to a Japanese person, and the Cruise character finds himself addressed as a particularly avid consumer everywhere he goes. Hiroki Azuma and Asada Akira had once advanced a kind of ironic Asian Accelerationism, which positively valued a supposed closeness of the Asian with the commodity and technology, but in *Minority Report* it's an extreme for the white subject to avoid.[134]

Race at the interface partakes now in what Paul Gilroy notes is a crisis of raciology, brought on by the popularization of genetic testing.[135] The old visual regimes of race struggle to adapt to the spreading awareness of the difference between genotype and phenotype. The film *GATTACA* (1997) is here a prescient one in imagining how a new kind of racism of the genotype might arise. It imagines a world rife with interfaces designed to detect the genotypical truth of appearances.

Nakamura ties these studies of the interface in cinema and television to studies of actual interfaces, particularly lowly, unglamorous, everyday ones. For instance, she looks at the avatars made for AOL Instant Messenger (AIM), which started in 1997 as an application running in Microsoft Windows. Of interest to her are the self-made cartoonlike avatars users chose to represent themselves to their "buddies." "The forma- tion of digital taste cultures that are low resolution, often full of bathroom humor, and influenced by youth-oriented and transnational visual styles like anime ought to be traced as it develops in its native mode: the internet."[136]

At the time there was little research on such low forms, par- ticularly those popular with women. Low-res forms populated with cut and paste images from the Care Bears, Disney, and Hello Kitty are not the ideal subjects of interactivity imagined in cool cyberculture theory. But there are questions here of who has access to what visual capital, of "who sells and is bought, who surfs and is surfed."[137] AIM avatars were often based on simple cut and paste graphics, but users modified the standard body images with signs that marked out their version of cultural or racial difference. This was a moment of explosion of ethnic identity content on the web—to which there was a racist backlash yet to come.[138]

AIM users could download avatars from websites that offered them under various categories—of which race was never one, as this is a supposedly postracial world. The avatars were little gifs, made of body parts cut from a standard template with variations of different hair, clothing, slogans, and so on. These could be assembled into mini-movies, remediating stuff from anime, comics, games; as a mix of photos and cartoons, flags, avatars.

One could read Nakamura's interest in the visual self-presencing of women and girls as a subset of Henry Jenkins's interest in fan-based media, but she lacks his occasionally overenthusiastic embrace of such activity as democratic and benign.[139] Her subaltern taste-cultures are a little more embattled and compromised. The kind of femininity performed here —laced with cuteness—is far from resistant and sometimes not even negotiated. These versions of what Hito Steyerl would later call the *poor image* are hard to redeem aesthetically.[140] Cultural studies had tried to ask meta-questions about what the objects of study are, but even so, we ended up with limited lists of proper new media objects, of which the AIM avatar was not one.

The same could be said of the website alllooksame.com. The site starts with a series of photographs of faces and asks the user to identify which is Japanese, Chinese, or Korean. (Like most users, I could not tell, which is the point.) The category of the Asian American is something of a post–Civil Rights construct. It promised resistance to racism in panethnic identity but paradoxically treated race as real. While alllooksame.com is an odd site, for Nakamura it does at least unite Asian viewers in questioning visual rhetoric about race.

Asian American online practice complicates the digital divide, being on both sides. The Asian American appears in popular racial consciousness as a "model minority," supposedly uninterested in politics and eager to get ahead in information capitalism or whatever this is. Yet she or he also appears as the refugee, the undocumented, the subsistence wage service worker. For Nakamura, this means that the study of the digital divide has to look beyond the race of users to other questions of difference and also to questions of agency online rather than mere user numbers.

In some racialized codings, the "Asian" is high-tech and assimilates to (supposedly) western consumerist modes. In others, the encounter between postcolonial literary theory and new media forms produces quite other conjunctures. To collapse a rich and complex debate along just one of its fault lines: imperial languages such as English can be treated either as something detachable from its supposed national origin or as something to refuse altogether.

The former path values hybridity and the claiming of agency within the language of the colonizer. The latter wants to resist this and sticks up for the unity and coherence of a language and a people. And, just to complicate matters further, this second path is also a European idea—the unity and coherence of a people and its language being itself an idea that emerged out of European romanticism.

Much the same fault line can be found in debates about what to do in the postcolonial situation with the internet, which can also be perceived as western and colonizing—although it might make more sense now to think of it as colonizing not on behalf of the old nation-states as on behalf of an emerging postnational geopolitics of what Benjamin Bratton calls *the stack*. Nakamura draws attention to some of the interesting examples of work on non-western media, including

Eric Michaels's brilliant work on video production among western desert Aboriginal people in Australia and the work of the RAQS Media Collective and Sarai in India, which reached out to non-English speaking and even nonliterate populations through interface design and community access.[141]

Since her book was published, work really flourished in the study of non-western uptakes of media, not to mention work on encouraging local adaptions and hybrids of available forms.[142] If one shifts one's attention from the internet to cellular telephony, one even has to question the assumption that the west somehow leads and other places follow. It may well be the case that most of the world leap-frogged over the cyberspace of the internet to the cell space of telephony. Yuk Hui even asks if there are non-western cosmotechnics.[143]

The perfect counterpoint to the old cyberculture idea of online disembodiment is Nakamura's study of online pregnancy forums—the whole point of which is to create a virtual community for women in some stage of the reproductive process. Here Nakamura pays close attention to ways of representing pregnant bodies. The site she examines allowed users to create their own signatures, which were often collages of idealized images of themselves, their partners, their babies, and (in a most affecting moment) their miscarriages. Sometimes sonograms were included in the collages of the signatures, but they separate the fetus from the mother, and so other elements were generally added to bring her back into the picture.

It's hard to imagine a more kitsch kind of cuteness. But then we might wonder why masculine forms of geek or otaku culture can be presented as cool when something like this is generally not. By the early 2000s the internet was about 50/50 men and women, and users were more likely to be working class or suburban. After the here-comes-everybody moment, the internet started to look more like regular everyday culture. These pregnant avatars ("dollies") were more cybertwee than cyberfeminist (not that these need be exclusive categories, of course).[144] But by the early 2000s, "the commercialization of the internet has led many internet utopians to despair of its potential as a site to challenge institutional authority."[145]

But perhaps it's a question of reading outside one's academic *habitus*. Nakamura: "'Vernacular' assemblages created by subaltern users, in this case pregnant women create impossible bodies that critique normative ones without an overt artistic or political intent."[146] The subaltern in this case can speak but chooses to do so through images that don't quite perform as visual cultural studies would want them to.[147] Nakamura wants to resist reading online pregnancy forums in strictly social-science terms and to look at the aesthetic dimensions. It's not unlike what Dick Hebdige did in retrieving London youth subcultures from criminological studies of "deviance."[148]

The blind spot of visual cultural studies, at least until recently, was vernacular self-presentation. But it's hard to deny the pathos of images these women craft of their stillborn or miscarried children. The one thing that perhaps received the most belated attention in studies of emerging media is how they interact with the tragic side of life—with illness, death, and disease. Those of us who have been both on the internet and studying it for thirty years or so now will have had many encounters with loss and grief. We will have had friends we hardly ever saw in real life who have passed or who grieve for those who have passed. In real life there are conventions for what signs and gestures one should make. In online communication they are emerging also.

Nakamura was right to draw attention to this in *Digitizing Race*, and she did so with a tact and a grace one can only hope to emulate:

> The achievement of authenticity in these cases of bodies in pain and mourning transcends the ordinary logic of the analog versus the digital photograph because these bodily images invoke the "semi-magical act" of remembering types of suffering that are

45

inarticulate, private, hidden within domestic or militarized spaces that exclude the public gaze.[149]

Not only is the body with all its marks and scars present in Nakamura's treatment, it is present as something in addition to its whole being.

> We live more, not less, in relation to our body parts, the dispossession or employment of ourselves constrained by a complicated pattern of self-alienation ... Rather than freeing ourselves from the body, as cyberpunk narratives of idealized disembodiment foresaw, informational technologies have turned the body into property.[150]

Here her work connects with that of Maurizio Lazzarato and Gerald Raunig on machinic enslavement and the dividual respectively, in its awareness of the subsumption of components of the human into the inhuman.[151]

But for all that, perhaps the enduring gift of this work is (to modify Adorno's words) to not let the power of another or our own powerlessness stupefy us.[152] There might still be forms of agency, tactics of presentation, gestures of solidarity—and in unexpected places. Given the tendency of the internet culture in the decade after *Digitizing Race*, perhaps it is an obligation now to return the gift of serious and considered attention to our friends and comrades—and not least in the scholarly world. The tragic side of life is never far away. The least we can do is listen to the pain of others and speak in measured tones of one another's small achievements of wit, grace, and insight.

Hito Steyerl: Art Is Beauty That Does Not Try to Kill Us

Thinking of getting into the art world? According to Hito Steyerl, here's what you may find:

Public support swapped for Instagram metrics. Art fully floated on some kind of Arsedaq. More fairs, longer yachts for more violent assholes, oil paintings of booty blondes, abstract stock-chart calligraphy. Yummy organic superfoods. Accelerationist designer breeding ... Conceptual plastic surgery ... Bespoke ivory gun handles. Murals on border walls.[153]

"Good luck with this," she concludes, "You will be my mortal enemy."[154]

The art world does not seem like a promising place from which to write and think critically about the world as it is, let alone its possibilities for being otherwise. It seems to have floated free from any other world. And yet in *Duty Free Art*, Steyerl finds a way to make its autonomy interesting. Its separation affords her the possibility of observing, if not the totality of the world, then at least a few more sides of it than many others see. What she sees is planetary civil war, sharpening class conflict, and the enclosure of the informational commons into proprietary theme parks.

From her art world vantage point, history appears to have a tempo no longer accessible to humans, running backward, from a vacant future to a festering past. "What was public is privatized by violence, while formerly private hatreds become the new public spirit." A spirit drunk on twitterbots, fake news, internet hacks, and "artificial stupidity"[155]—mostly in the service of actual or aspirational authoritarian rule.

It was the lapsed Marxist Werner Sombart who probably coined the term *creative destruction*, although it is also associated with Joseph Schumpeter.[156] Today's ruling class embraces it without the ambivalence and irony the term once had, under the more anodyne labels *disruption* and *innovation*, which in actuality means the decimation of jobs, mass surveillance, and algorithmic confusion. The practice of design is celebrated, but weapons design is not mentioned in polite company.

Art appears floating above all that. Its autonomy rests in part on its weird economy of value. It is about singular things rather than mass commodities. It is also an economy of *presence*, which is in turn an odd subset of what Yves Citton thinks of as an *ecology of attention*.[157] Sometimes the encounter with the artist is of more value than the work, because the artist is rarer. Artists are cheaper to transport than art, because they don't require the specialized handling and insurance. This means that the artist has to be permanently available to be present and usually without getting paid. This attention to the artist is bad for the artist's own powers of attention. The artist gives off an aura of unalienated labor and unmediated presence but is actually living in a fragmented, disjoined *junktime*.[158]

Various proposals for an art strike, by Lee Lozano, Stewart Home, and others, have never quite worked out, because the artist does not exactly perform labor in the first place.[159] But maybe there is a kind of attention strike that goes on all the time. Your body is there, present and correct, but you are distracted, checking Instagram. Your attention is on strike, and that distraction is then captured as value through one or another networked, computational device.

If your body is present but your attention is not, then perhaps that's a sort of proxy for presence. A proxy is there in place of something else; it at least counts for something and registers as a valid stand-in. Steyerl wants to ask who or more likely what is getting to make the distinctions between valid and invalid stand-ins. When is one's existence recognized as giving off a signal and when is it just noise? That might be the fault line today between existing and not-existing, in a polity, a culture, an economy, even in the definition of what might be allowed to live.

Perhaps because the art world is rather slow on the uptake with all things technical, it's a useful vantage point from which to think it's much bigger and more powerful rivals in the information and image trade. Take for example what is happening in computational photography.[160] The lenses on cellphone cameras are not that great, so the production of the image rests in part with computation, which is more and more inclined to make images out of what the computer thinks you want to see. It decides on your behalf what in the visual field is signal and what is noise.

What happens in an individual camera happens on a bigger scale in the policing of images of sex and violence online. When is an image signal, and when is it noise? It only appears as if algorithms are deciding all this for us now. There is a lot of what Astra Taylor calls *fauxtomation*, where such work is outsourced to a globally subcontracted workforce.[161] But developers are on the case, designing "probabilistic porn detection."[162] It works by feeding millions of images into a computer so it can find the patterns, so the computer can determine whether that's a ginger cat next to a teapot, or some obscure sex position, such as Yawning, Octopus, Fraser MacKenzie, Watching the Game, Stopperage, Chambers Fuck, and Persuading the Debtor. You can look those up for yourself to see if they're real or if Steyerl made them up, but then all the services with which your computer communicates about its actions will know you wanted to know.

What's at stake when algorithms clear noise from information? Steyerl updates Jacques Rancière's distinction between the *crowd* or *public* and the *mob* or *multitude*.[163] The former can make demands, which they should do through their representatives, or proxies. The latter is noise, to be met with the riot police. Our representatives are in some cases still people, and sometimes they are elected. But we also have images that function as our proxies, if we are lucky enough not to be excluded as noise. It may not be a one-way street, however. "As humans feed affect, thought, and sociality into algorithms, algorithms feed back into what used to be called subjectivity."[164]

The image is an effect of an algorithm, which may be a proxy for something, but it may have generated that for which it is a proxy through *scripted operations*. These operations model in code what it is they are supposed to double, whether it is a population or the subject of an individual photograph. What computation produces as signal out of noise is generated by a probabilistic template of what ought to be there: "Likeness becomes subject to likelihood."[165]

The business of producing image and information proxies is of course immensely gameable.[166] There's all kinds of proxy cold war going on, not all of it the fault of "The Russians." Indeed, "The Russians" are now a proxy stand-in for the whole crazy game of information warfare, fought as often as not with noise. There's all sorts of actors, acting through stand-ins, duplicates, dupes, sock puppets. It is what the situationists called *détournement* on an epic scale, producing what elsewhere I called the *spectacle of disintegration*.[167]

Global civil war contains shooting wars too, also fought through proxies. These are the military equivalent of shell companies. "The border between private security, private military company, freelance insurgents, armed stand-in, state-hackers and people who just got in the way has become blurry." It's not so much a deviation from a norm as *the new normal*.[168] "To state that online proxy politics is reorganizing geopolitics would be similar to stating that burgers tend to reorganize cows."[169]

Steyerl: "Not seeing anything intelligible is the new normal. Information is passed on as a set of signals that cannot be picked up by human senses."[170] The critical approach is less about interpreting hidden power structures underneath an orderly culture as it is a practice of questioning the routine habits of *apophenia*, the selecting of patterns in random data. Your camera's computer detects what it thinks you want to see in the noisy data captured by its lens. (Kittens!) Your social media service detects what it thinks is acceptable content amid the dick pics. A deadlier version is National Security Agency's Skynet, trained to find "terrorists" in cellphone data from Pakistan. But were the thousands killed by missile and drone actually terrorists?[171] Hard to say, as there's no empirical test or benchmark for Skynet's procedures.

Perhaps it's a matter of finding different patterns, based on different protocols. Steyerl wants to show the connection between the design of death and the design of life. Her emblem is what Harun Farocki called the suicide camera, or what I once called *missilecam*, the nose-cone camera sending signals of its progress as it approaches its target.[172] Steyerl: "the camera was not destroyed in this operation. Instead, it burst into billions of small cameras, tiny lenses embedded into cellphones."[173] Now we are overrun with the fallout of zombie cameras that failed to die.

The camera may once have framed the world as if it were there to be made into a picture for a person. But now humans are just part of a landscape that machines picture for other machines. "If the models for reality increasingly consist of sets of data unintelligible to human vision, the reality created after them might be partly unintelligible for humans too."[174]

Who can forget the internet weirdness of Google's *DeepDream* images, which reveal the presets of machinic vision and yet which managed to visualize the unconscious of circulation, with added cuteness? As Sianne Ngai reminds us, the *cute* can also have its scary side, as when DeepDream decides that what emerges out of a plate of spaghetti and meatballs is a series of disembodied puppy-heads. It had a habit of recognizing patterns that aren't there. "It demonstrates a version of corporate animism in which commodities are not only fetishes but morph into franchised chimeras."[175]

Humans are an inconvenience for machines. It's a commonplace to think of work as turning humans into robots, but the humans always seem to remain repulsively mammalian. One way that computation has resolved the human into the world of the machine is through games. Alan Turing's famous Turing Test was a way of deciding if something is human.[176] If we think the way something communicates with us is human, then it is. He based it on a parlor game, involving the guessing of someone's gender just from notes passed under the door.

John von Neumann tried to formalize the whole problem of decision and decidability with game theory. If we can simplify the stakes and certain tricky concepts such as *rationality*, *utility*, and *information*, then decision can be a science. Following Philip Mirowski, Steyerl argues that the difficulty of human decision-making was resolved in economic theory by taking humans out of the equation.[177] If the rationality of humans is a problem for economic theory, replace humans with computation, with rational nonhumans, and let them loose on the world. "It is striking how much reality has been created as a consequence of different iterations of game theory."[178]

Steyerl: "The point is that games are not a consequence of computers making the world unreal. On the contrary, games make computers become real. Games are generative fictions."[179] Steyerl borrows my term for this: we live in *gamespace*.[180] "So, regardless of whether humans ever were 'rational' in the way game theory assumed, a lot of people have now been trained to understand rationality in this way and to imitate its effects."[181] Gamespace becomes more real, because more rationalizable, than the world it was supposed to model. And we are now all inside it, along with everything else.

For a while, we were all obliged to pass online reverse-Turing tests to prove to machines that we were something like a human. *Captcha*, which made you write out letters you saw in a fuzzy picture, tested whether you could impersonate a human to a machine, not whether a machine can impersonate a human to a human. This is no longer necessary now that Google has a scripted operation that models what a human is.

Computational models can decide not only whether you are human enough to be online but what you will want to do when you get there and what you will like. These models have an aesthetic dimension, in that they model your taste as a kind of ideal form and serve you with things that are like what it presumes you are like. In everyday aesthetics as in economics, models rule. Whether it's a fashion model or a financial algorithm, the universe of forms is a sort of Platonist ideal that becomes the world, becomes gamespace.

Only the art world appears to have a solution to this. Attempts have been made to manage art algorithmically, such as ArtRank, which advises investors on which art to buy based on its proprietary metrics. But more usually, the autonomy of the art world banishes the ideal, the model, the beautiful form, from the world and quarantines it in museums. Where once the avant-gardes wanted to unleash the beauty of art on life, we may now count it as good fortune that at least one species of ideal, elegant, beautiful form is kept separate from the world—that of art.

Looking back out at the world from the quarantine of the museum, the task for humans is now to understand how machines picture the world. "Maybe the art history of the twentieth century can be understood as an anticipatory tutorial to help humans decode images made by machines for machines … Mondrian is perhaps an unconscious exercise for humans trying to learn how to see like a machine."[182]

Museums are not what they used to be, however. In Benedict Anderson (or before that, in Harold Innis), the space of a nation-state could be regulated by the space-binding media of printed newspapers and also by the time-binding media of the museum.[183] But the national museum is now flanked by other phenomena. Consider Freeport art storage, where art remains permanently in transit—and duty free. One facility is reputed to hold thousands of Picassos. It's an art world example of what Keller Easterling calls *extrastatecraft*—a kind of secret museum, a "luxury no man's land."[184]

Or consider the documents to be found in *WikiLeaks* that may show that the architect Rem Koolhaas was in negotiations to design a museum for the Syrian government. His office will not confirm their authenticity. Many dictators now favor contemporary art museums, biennales, and art fairs as a way to look fashion-forward in the dictator world. The national museum may have once provided some sort of temporal anchor for the modern state, but the contemporary art museum can't perform that purpose. Following Peter Osborne, Steyerl sees contemporary art as a proxy for a kind of transindividual *junktime*.[185] They are a proxy for the nonexistent global commons. It's like the commons, but out of harms' way—autonomous.

"Seen like this, duty free art is essentially what traditional autonomous art might have been, had it not been elitist and oblivious to its own conditions of production."[186] Here Steyerl builds on Peter Bürger's famous critique of the failure of the avant-gardes and suggests a little of what might be culled from the wreckage.[187] But we have to keep in mind art's conditions of possibility now: dictator's contemporary art foundation, arms dealer's tax shelter, hedge funder's trophy, art student's debt bondage, aggregate spam, leaked data, unpaid precarious labor, all accumulating as value in the freeport.

Steyerl frankly takes advantage of a position in the art world, whose simulated autonomy is doubled edged. The art world is a point from which to observe the destruction of many features that were once characteristic of a certain modern, capitalist world and the installing of some other mode of production and control, still based on exploitation and oppression, but of an algorithmic and derivative rather than disciplinary and industrial kind. Both the autonomy of the art world and the disruption of the historical world may yet, in subtle, minor ways, be dialectically reversible. Their negation of the world might be negated in little ways.

On the side of art, Steyerl wants to stay close to what Gregory Sholette called the dark matter of the art world, such as all the invisible affective labor performed by gallery assistants, curatorial assistants, interns, art students, and the like.[188] She even defends the International Art English that has sprouted out of the billion art world press releases now pouring into our inboxes. Steyerl has a thing for low genres, and the art world press release, written by the assistant or the intern, is surely one of the lowest.

Steyerl's knack for rethinking very low genres reminds me of the work of Lisa Nakamura, particularly when Steyerl looks at romance scams, that subset of internet scam where the scammer gets the mark to fall in love with them and then takes their money. Steyerl reads them through Thomas Elsaesser's work on melodrama, a form all about impossibility, delay, submission, and repressed or forbidden feelings.[189]

The romance scam comes with customized products from a hyperprivatized culture industry, targeting those excluded from metro dating markets as too old, too fat, or too much a parent. Race and empire play a role, as the scammers are often from outside the metropolitan world. As does language, as translation software might be used to produce an odd semblance of English or some other metropolitan language. To Steyerl, these are "languages from a world to come."[190] After all, there's usually a trace of hope in any epistolary form.

Such moments are rare. The internet is no longer a space of possibility. It became, we are told, the best of all possible worlds. The internet, like cinema, like all the preceding technical gods, is dead. The internet is now surveillance, free labor, copyright control, troll-enforced conformism. As for cinema: "Cinema today is above all a stimulus package to buying new televisions, home projector systems, and retina display iPads."[191]

Where the cinema became the core of a specialized culture industry, the internet rewires all of production and circulation, subjecting the making of things to the control of information protocols. Steyerl: "What kind of corporate/state entities are based on data storage, image unscrambling, high-frequency trading, and Daesh Forex gaming? Who are the contemporary equivalents of farmer-kings and slave-holders?"[192] I call them the *vectoralist class*. Where the capitalist class owned the means of production, the vectoralist class owns the vector of information. That is the ruling class of our time. What I think Steyerl's perceptive vision offers us (to update Fredric Jameson) is not the cultural logic of late capitalism but the algorithmic logic of early something else.[193]

Reality is now made of and by images and models designed for computers and sometimes even by them.

> Improbable objects, celebrity cat gifs, and a jumble of unseen anonymous images proliferate and waft through human bodies via WiFi. One could perhaps think of the results as a new and vital form of folk art, that is if one is prepared to completely overhaul one's definition of folk as well as of art.[194]

And to understand both the folk and the art, it might help, as Lev Manovich has also counseled, to understand the proprietary software within which the folk thinks it designs the art, but which might actually shape both to its own designs.

Before it's too late. Steyerl does not hesitate to use the F-word: fascism. Perhaps what we're looking at now are "derivative fascisms."[195] Fascism is a gap in representation itself. What some call the "neoliberal" moment appeared to be one in which forms of political representation declined in favor of forms of market participation. But then these too receded, leaving economic exclusion, debt overhang, and riots in their wake.

Some inherited forms of cultural and aesthetic politics might not work in this context. As followers of Antonio Gramsci, cultural studies advocated seizing the means of cultural representation.[196] This was part of a long march through the institutions meant to secure political representation and state power. But now an inflation of cultural representation correlates more with political disenfranchisement. Everyone can have their cultural proxy, even if, as Yves Citton reminds us, it is a long way down the Google search results. But political representation, political proxies, seem not to function. Fascism happens when political representation collapses; it's a short circuit, reality by fiat. It appears to do away with mediations, proxies. Fascism blocks reality, it is a "blind spot filled with delusion and death."[197]

Maybe it's time to try different aesthetic tactics.

The Soviet avant-garde tried to counter a socialist realist aesthetic of ideal models with *productivism*, an art that hewed close to labor, the machine, and their product.[198] Perhaps what Mark Fisher calls today's *capitalist realism* might be met with what Steyerl calls an aesthetic practice of *circulationism*, which finds ways to circulate not only images but value.[199] Maybe it could short-circuit existing networks. Maybe short circuits are the problem, and it could instead reinstate what Bernard Stiegler calls the *long loops* of culture, art, and education.[200]

The figure of circulation might be linked here to a certain reversibility of terms. *Duty free art* may be the art that circulates through international art fairs or freeports. It might even be a kind of decentralized currency, an analog bitcoin, encrypted in International Art English. But it might also be an art that shucks off the old duties to history, faith, and nation and exploits its own liminality as a radical project.

Speculation may refer to a world in which derivative markets overshadow markets in actual things, trading not just in actual time but every possible forking timeline. "It represents mood swings around derivatives of derivatives."[201] Speculation might also be a philosophical tool, for risky thought with a looser relation to its object, which may find new objects hitherto undetected. In the spirit of Randy Martin, Steyerl senses a world of volatile relations between referents and signs, persons and proxies.

Steyerl: "What is the opposite [of] design, a type of creation that assists pluriform, horizontal forms of life, and that can be comprehended as part of a shared humanity?"[202] Against a gamespace that is everywhere and leaves no option but to try to game it from the inside, desirable games might be restricted in time and space, able to be reset, scores erased. They would have rules that are not proprietary secrets and can be modified by the users.

Steyerl is no accelerationist: "Acceleration is yesterday's delusion."[203] But she might still be interested in an aesthetic of detecting the forms of information that contour the totality of this world as it is experienced from the inside and also what it can contribute to making it otherwise. This might take the form of particular hacks or of the equally challenging task of imagining the totality otherwise.

The Situationist artist Constant Nieuwenhuys is a touchstone for Steyerl here.[204] His central question was how to design an infrastructure where humans could play freely, on top of a gamespace of machine logistics that ordered the world of things. This was Constant's *New Babylon* (1956–74), in which his New Babylonians could be world nomads, rather like an international art biennale imagined as a free global party.[205]

Maybe it was not a realistic plan. In Steyerl's aesthetics, it's the gap between *New Babylon* and the world that is the value of the utopian. The point is not to make the world over into sameness with the model, the ideal, the algorithm, but to think and act in the difference. This is not quite how I read it, but perhaps our approaches can be squared. I treat *New Babylon* as radically practical. I read Constant as doing what Charles Fourier did, which is to pursue the practical so relentlessly that our actual totality appears by contrast to be fake, made up, impossible. Because it is. It won't last, and we all know it.

For me the limit to stressing the autonomy of the art work is that it becomes an object of contemplation, of a particular mode of attention. But it's not a matter of imposing the work on the world and falsifying it. It is rather a matter of pursuing the practical question, the question of the good life, so thoroughly as to show how the commodity form has falsified the world, made it unable either to be beautiful for us or beautiful without us.

Yves Citton: Ecologies of Attention

I once tried to watch Andy Warhol's *Empire* (1964) for as long as I could. I lasted maybe twenty minutes. The whole eight-hour film is a single shot of the Empire State Building. It got boring, but then a bird flew by and it was like being struck by lightning.

One could think of the subject of all Warhol's art as the act of paying attention. It is worth having Warhol in mind while reading Yves Citton's *The Ecology of Attention*. Warhol is not mentioned in it, but he does cover both ends of the attention problem. On the one hand, Warhol made work that is very demanding of attention; on the other, he got his own image to circulate as an instant attention attractor. He understood the value of attention.

He was not the first, of course. Citton begins with Gabriel Tarde, who starts a line of thinking about an economy of visibility whose currency is fame.[206] It became an economy in a double sense, in that fame can be measured, and the attention it garners can be scarce. An increasing wealth of information means a scarcity of something else. Economists treat attention as a commodity, to be hoarded or strategically acquired. Citton wants to put some critical pressure on that view, by paying attention to what it leaves out. Perhaps the design of the attention-gathering apparatus is suboptimal.

Attention is not a new concern. The ancient art of rhetoric was about taking and holding it.[207] Among the moderns, attention to innovation in style has long been a way of renewing attention. One might connect this to the way Sianne Ngai thinks about the aesthetics of the *zany*, *interesting*, and *cute*, each of which draws attention to, and also away from, aspects of modern life, to production, circulation, and the commodity, respectively. Warhol pioneered forms of all three as ways of attracting attention.

Citton offers an attention ecology rather than an attention

economy. The latter tends to start with individualized attention as if it always existed, whereas an attention ecology takes an interest also in how attention regimes produce individuals in the first place.[208] This ecology can be rather noisy, more like the turbulent information soup studied by Tiziana Terranova than the simple sender → receiver of the classic communication diagrams.[209]

One cannot make causal statements about the media any more than one can about the weather. Neither works like a gun or a hypodermic. Media, like weather, may have material, agential, and formal causes, but not final causes. They don't tend toward a goal. And it may help to think more about formal causes a little more than agents or materials. This was McLuhan's innovation, to think of media as not being about objects or subjects, but forms that shape both.[210] The form of a given media shapes how things can appear to us and what kinds of subjects we can be in regarding them.

This is not too far from what Karen Barad calls an *agential realism*, where the agents are produced retrospectively by an apparatus that assigns them their distinctive identities.[211] Hence, one can think of media as a matter of attending together, where the attention is shaped in particular ways, carving out things to perceive and know and individuating us into our selves through the act of attention. The feelings I have of a self are cut from the flow of transindividual *affect* that may be the main thing media are actually for and about.[212]

A view which sees an ecology—rather than a more restricted economy—of attention might wonder if it is working quite as it should. Even assuming we are all the rational actors of economic folklore, one can wonder if we can really attend to what might matter and decide accordingly. Such an optimistic view depends on us having access to useful information to attend to in the first place. "The rationality of our behavior is constantly jeopardized by the deficiency of the information we have about the environment. In other words: we never have the means to pay enough attention."[213] Our behaviors are irrational because our actions are constrained by the surreal spectacle to which we are supposed to constantly attend.

An economy attending only to a metrics of attention has no way of measuring or even really knowing what is needed to reproduce the conditions of attentiveness themselves. Bernard Stiegler has a usefully counterintuitive argument about this: the problem is not that we are narcissistic, but that we are not narcissistic enough.[214] The dominant attention economy is too impoverished to enable us to individuate ourselves from it. We don't go through Freud's stage of *primary narcissism*, from which one might return and get some perspective on the world. Instead, we remain within an undifferentiated and pre-individual state, a group narcissism, in which state we get a bit crazy, trying to both belong and be separate without a primary separation to secure either. For Stiegler, mass shootings are symptoms of this failed media ecology. Citton's diagnosis is a little different but not incompatible.

Citton channels Paul Valéry: attention is the struggle against entropy. It's the effort to direct oneself to what matters and in the process both preserve and adapt the forms of the world. Like Paolo Virno, Citton is interested in clichés, proverbs, habits of speech—what he calls *schemas*.[215] These are the collective reserve of accumulated experience that we test and hopefully can modify when they come in contact with new perceptions of the world. I would connect this to what Bogdanov called *tektology*, which one could see as the organization of collective attention through a self-aware practice of filtering and modifying the schemas or worldviews that our collective labors have inherited from our predecessors.[216]

Like Bogdanov, Citton is interested in something that is at once a politics and an aesthetics of attention. There are four different regimes of attention, of acquired schemas or habits, perhaps even genres. One could call the four regimes *alertness, loyalty, projection,* and *immersion*.[217] Alertness attends to warnings and threats, to what has to be excluded. Loyalty is the opposite pole; it is about trust, mutuality, solidarity, community, what "binds" us through the long term. Projection is looking outward from the familiar, looking for what is mine or ours. Immersion is allowing the strange or the new to come in.

Immersion fascinates, projection bedazzles, loyalty hypnotizes, alertness excites. One might have need of all four, but the current attention economy privileges some over others. Certain kinds of games, for example, highlight alertness. So does Fox News. A certain kind of art and a certain kind of pedagogy, on the other hand, might try to counterprogram with loyalty and immersion, with an acceptance of others and a joint project of new sensation, negotiated through what Ngai calls the interesting, in which the artist eases us toward the new sensation by securing our trust with formats that hold and repeat the strange or overlooked elements of the work. Warhol's *Empire* might be an example here: repeating the one thing, but gently on the eye.

But what's more common, when it's not the alert, is projection. Attention economies like us to feel at home, as if the world is no more than our living room with brighter colors. It's a way of working with the constraint: that our attention is limited but information is abundant. We're encouraged to see a handful of what in media industry parlance are called "properties" as an extension of home, a landscape onto which to project, populated by a handful of stars and characters.

In Guy Debord or Vilém Flusser there's the beginnings of a critique of the political economy of stardom.[218] As Debord said, stars model the acceptable range of desires to which one might look. As Flusser saw, the attention paid such objects increases their value. Here I might put more stress on how attention both adds value but may also exhaust it. Jean Baudrillard thought seduction ran a fine line between exposure and concealment.[219] Dominic Pettman thinks we may be overexposed and have reached *peak libido*, falling into diminishing returns on visibility.[220]

Citton: "from the moment we start living off visibility, everything that lifts us out of obscurity is worth having."[221] Attracting attention even starts to appear as an ethical goal. One is supposed to "raise awareness" of worthy goals and to oneself in the process. As Baudrillard already saw in the seventies, the logic of visibility has its evil side.[222] Acts of terrorism and shooting sprees exploit this same visibility. They are the hideous other side to Debord's motto of the spectacle: "that which is good, appears; that which appears, is good."[223]

Citton usefully connects the logic of media as value to finance. The culture industries now work less like manufacturers and more like banks. Their market capitalization is a derivative of the attention value of a portfolio of the "properties" they claim to own or claim to be able to keep extracting from the information commons and privatizing. The culture industry is the finance industry whose financial instruments monetize the unconscious. I think we could extend this by connecting Citton to the work of Randy Martin. Perhaps it is not just that media becomes finance, but finance becomes media.

Financialization might then be just one piece of a transformation of the commodity economy under the control of information. Matteo Pasquinelli draws our attention to prevalence of ternary structures, inserting themselves between information providers and receivers, *parasites* channeling off a surplus of the flow generated by attention,[224] which then shape attention in the interests of generating their surplus. This might give rise to whole new categories of political and cultural struggles about the geopolitics of what is visible and not visible, or about what Nick Mirzoeff calls the *right to look*.[225]

Besides our day jobs, if we have them, we have a whole other job these days, doing free labor for Google, Facebook, and others. The culture industries at least let us relax while they did the job of entertaining us. What I call the *vulture industries* of social media outsource that to us as well. The vulture industries might form a component, alongside finance and some other curiously information controlling businesses, of a distinctive kind of ruling class. Citton uses my term for it: the *vectoralist class*. This ruling class concentrates power by controlling stocks, flows, and protocols of information and keeping an information surplus for itself.

In Citton's reading, the vectoralist class is more than a power over information. It is a power over attention and visibility—even knowability—as well. Its rise is premised on the digital as the latest wave of what Stiegler calls *grammatization*.[226] For Stiegler the invention of writing, the seriality of the production line and digital tech are all part of the same, long, historical phenomenon of grammatization. It reduces the sensory continuum to digital bits, imposing a grammar on their order. It standardizes the world, now including everything from software (Manovich) to urban design (Easterling).

Grammatization leads to information abundance, channeled in vectors of control, but then subject also to ternary forms that interpose themselves between ceaseless information and limited attention spans. One example is Google, whose PageRank algorithm is modeled on academic citation ranking procedures.[227] Another is Facebook, modeled initially on the look-books of elite American universities. They might between them crudely cover the two ternary procedures most common: ranking and rating. The former uses an algorithm to choose what humans want; the latter uses humans to choose what algorithms want. In both cases the attention of the humans is for sale to advertisers.

What results is a fairly novel kind of cultural inequality. Citton:

> What counts ... is not whether something gets included (or not): it is being at the height of visibility, right at the top of

the first page of search results. The new proletarians are not so much the "excluded" as the "relegated." The organization of our collective digital attention by Google structures our field of visibility on the basis of a PRINCIPLE OF PRIORITIZATION: the power of the vectoralist class consists in the organization of priorities, rather than the inclusion or exclusion from the field of visibility.[228]

Citton quotes Paul Valéry: "attention is vector and potential."[229] Attention is a pressure, an effort, a Spinozan *conatus*—a tendency toward endurance and enhancement. Attention comes from *ad-tendere*, to tend toward. Citton emphasizes an irreducible, qualitative aspect of attention. What the industries of the vectoral class do is turn the vector into the scalar. But in this media regime, the arrow always has to be measured. An attention ecology is reduced to an attention economy.

Citton:

> The vectoralist class is not exploitative because of its "power to move anything and everything" but because of its requirement that "value be realized" in countable terms. Such is THE TRUE CHALLENGE OF THE DIGITAL CULTURES now emerging: how can you take advantage of the vectoral power of the digital without allowing yourself to be inprisoned in the scalar cage of digitalization? Only the art of interference, the elusive art of hackers, can rise to such a challenge—which is at the heart of the attention ecology in the age of its electrification.[230]

I take a slightly different view: the problem is not so much that the vector becomes the scalar, for that attention has to be measured. The problem might be more *what* is attended to, and *what* is measured. Perhaps we could pay attention to what this commodity economy can't include as something measured, but which is not some ineffable qualitative and vital force. It is rather some quite measurable things whose measure does not compute because it does not take the form of exchange value. That might be one aspect of ecology, for example. Earth science can measure climate change, but this economy can't really pay attention to it.[231]

So what's to be done? Citton thinks we can start paying attention to attention itself as something that can be learned, cultivated, practiced, designed, in ways that produce forms of both collective and individuated becoming. To do so involves stepping down a scale, from attention ecologies to forms of joint attention and finally to individuated attention. It is helpful to fixate on neither the big picture nor the individual, but to look at what could mediate in-between.

Joint attention could be like Sartre's *being-for-another*: I know myself through imagining that others attend to me when I attend to something.[232] I picture my observations as themselves observed. There might be quite a few varieties of this joint attention, particularly when people are in groups. There can be co-attention to the same event, at a concert, or reciprocal attention on the dance floor. (This is an aspect Eshun doesn't really cover.) We don't all have to feel the same, but our feelings in joint attention are a continuum, and we usually do our best to harmonize with it. That shared feeling might be the hardest part to capture in a media form. As many have noted, conversations in real life can tamp down potential spirals of anger; emojis don't really do the trick.

Teaching situations are full of moments of joint attention going right or going wrong. Teaching can often be a matter of improvising ways of steering attention. Citton follows Cathy Davidson in thinking that if there's a problem with attention in the classroom, it may not be as simple as blaming the kids or their phones.[233] To isolate one material or agential cause is to miss how it's a matter of a formal cause, an ecology in which school, teacher, students, and phone are all components. If kids are bored with school, maybe school could engage them differently and in more interesting things. Davidson calls this the new three Rs: rigor, relevance, and relationships. Which might be a way of saying that some key things to teach are things about attention itself as a difficult art.

It was sometimes imagined that making learning more "interactive" would make it work better. Citton thinks there are reasons to retain the masterly as well as the interactive approaches to teaching. It's a matter of whether a teaching style is working to focus attention and at the same time convey the art of attention itself. Maybe even the notorious massive open online courses might work for certain kinds of learning, if structured around something other than the education tech for the sake of it, saving money, or capitalizing on the prestige of a brand-name university. As Citton suggests, Rancière's famous *ignorant schoolmaster* might not have known the French he was teaching, but he knew how to sculpt attention to it.[234]

Ecology here seems to me a kind of impossible goal—like justice in Derrida or communicative action in Habermas or the world republic in Karatani—which might either be a regulative ideal or a sort of atemporal presence.[235] Ecology, like God, does not exist and is probably impossible. Yet it remains in the background. But there might be more than one ecology. Our visions of it extend out from our actual labors and practices. It looks different depending on what you attend to.

Citton mentions two ecologies: the radical and the managerial. The radical ecology of attention comes out of things like the Occupy Wall Street or Black Lives Matter movements. It wants to rebuild the whole practice of what can be seen, heard, known, shared, from the ground up. The managerial ecology of attention comes out of things from institutional forms that try to hold the line against the complete subsumption of attention into the regime of exchange value. It operates on a slightly bigger scale and is perhaps less bracing in its ambitions. Citton wants us to attend to both rather than choose between them. After all, part of steering away from attention in the modes of alertness and projection is to background the habit to digitize, to binarize, to make it all about us or about them.

The space for a politics and an art of attention thus covers a range of sites, from the radical to the managerial, and might be about all four forms of attention, but perhaps with a different emphasis. Attention is a form of care for the defense of the group, but it is also for maintaining its qualities and stabilizing its habits while being open to the new. To pay more attention to the reproduction of abilities is to include things feminism insists are undervalued as they are classified as women's work. Here we could connect the theme of attention to that of emotional labor. As Hito Steyerl observes of the art world: why does it always fall to women to attend to how everyone feels about the show or the project? To pay more attention to openness to the new is to pay attention to what artists do when they pay attention and to the things they are trying to show us might be interesting. Warhol is an example of that.

Where political groups are concerned, attention may be key to avoiding the opposite problems of endless splits and rigid groupthink. If one attends to the transindividual feelings of a group, one may be able to tune it, without insisting that everyone think or feel the same way. As Anna Tsing has shown, political actions can be successful even with very divergent worldviews involved. This might be a matter of the transindividual *imaginal politics* that Chiara Botticci extracts from the psychoanalysis of Castoriadis.[236]

Citton runs together two other techniques of attention that should be separate: the psychoanalytic and the surrealist. Both are interested in bracketing off the rational content of communication. But I think the psychoanalytic ends up suspecting that there is an underlying form. It is a hermeneutics of suspicion. It attends to what is not said, not shown. What I would call the surrealist is a bit different. It takes place not under the sign of Hermes, always suspecting there is something lacking, as that of Iris, goddess of the iridescent, multicolored, overflowing excess.[237]

Both might have their uses as ways of practicing an art of

attention. Or even of inattention. Perhaps (as Walter Benjamin suggested) there can be an *emancipatory distraction*, a freedom from what one is supposed to see and where one is supposed to go.[238] The urban arts of the *flâneur* (and *flâneuse*) or of the *dérive* or urban drift come into play here.[239] There are ways of perceiving the city contrary to the habits that work and leisure impose upon us, from which to dream of another city for another life.

Citton ends rather than starts with individual attention, because he is interested in asking not how it can be instrumentalized by an attention economy but how it is produced in the first place by an attention ecology. He cites Williams James: "my experience is what I agree to attend to."[240] But where did this "William James" come from and with whom does it think it is agreeing? Philosophies of individual attention have gone through phases, from Locke and the sensualists who saw psychic attention as passive to romantics for whom it is more active, to the moderns who saw it more as physiological and those contemporaries for whom it's about neuroscience.

Here one could connect this to the history of attention in science, as science studies has examined it. Science used to be a thing a gentleman did, in which he was a modest witness to an observable phenomenon. As the division of labor in science developed and mere lab technicians read the dials and recorded the results, it was less about a special quality of a gentleman's perceptions and more about things that could be attended to in standardized ways.[241]

But as Donna Haraway and others have noted, attention in science has roots in certain models of male comportment. The gentleman-scientist was modest in his claims about the world, the gentlewoman was modest in her bodily behavior.[242] One could add here a little about what the well-bred lady was supposed to attend to: religion and family. It's ironic that while the good novel became a replacement for the Good Book in more recent models of the attentive world for women of a certain class, it was once the bad object. Here one has to enter a skeptical note about the claim that it's the loss of novel reading that has destroyed attention. Techniques of attention require a more subtle history.[243]

Here Citton is with Katherine Hayles in emphasizing the range of modes of attention that book culture afforded.[244] One can concentrate on the novel, or one can skim dictionaries or encyclopedias or use the index to find related passages in different books. Close reading is not the only attentional skill that has value. The fetish for it as a singular attentive skill might be more about an impoverishment of the arts of attention that goes way back. Like Félix Guattari, Citton is not nostalgic, but neither is he an enthusiast for technical solutions to the problem of attention whose main function is to enrich their makers.[245]

What we need then are arts of attention in the plural and that counterprogram in and against those controlled by the vectoralist class. Citton has a taste for more high art forms, but free jazz is not for everybody. One also needs samplers, selections, and compilations for attentional forms that are less specialized. An example: Jill Solloway's TV version of the novel *I Love Dick*, which samples attentive forms of the female gaze from video art.[246] It may be no bad thing that popular media includes samples of them. Good popular artists are djs of other people's attentive inventions.

Returning to the four modes of attention, Citton comes up with a useful shorthand, which to conserve attention I'll present like this: Projection + loyalty = classical art. Alertness + projection = culture industry. Immersion + alertness = modern art. Loyalty + immersion = arts of interpretation. He suggests we concentrate our efforts in the fourth quarter. One might pursue with some interest how it maps onto Alex Galloway's conception of the art of the intraface.[247]

There might actually be ways of intervening in all four quadrants. Citton mentions two already: the radical and the managerial. Both aim at a certain kind of visibility. A third might be the art of discretion as seen in the later work of Guy Debord and Alice Becker-Ho.[248] It's about ways of being and being concealed at the same time and legible to those in the know as more than one seems but otherwise incognito. A fourth might be a kind of imaginative and counterintuitive meme-making, something like Baudrillard's *fatal strategy*.[249] It is an inverse and complement to discretion, a form of seduction.[250] Not a measured concealing but a measured revealing, a revealing precisely of what is hidden, a calling of attention to the place where there's nothing to which to attend.

If one is to make good art, good politics, or good media, it might help to start with the current attention economy and a knowledge of its limits. One can make good work in it, but what it will consider good work is what it can measure. One might want to think of the good as another kind of value or at least another kind of measure.

If one wants a takeaway, a too long; didn't read: Attend to the in-between spaces. Avoid the binaries. Observe the connections. And act on them.

Randy Martin: After Capitalism, the Derivative

"After me, the deluge," declared King Louis XV, at what was almost but not quite the high-water mark of Absolutism. These days one might say, after capitalism, the derivative. The late work of Randy Martin takes up the startling premise that the commodity form has mutated into something else. *Knowledge LTD: Towards a Social Logic of the Derivative*, the last book he wrote before his untimely death, tries to tease out several implications of this idea, while recapitulating his entire lifetime of study of the aesthetic, the ethnographic, and the technic.[251]

We forget that Marx's *Capital* starts with the appearance of what is *new* in the world of its time: the abundance of commodities. So why always keep starting with commodities now that they are old, rather than starting with a form of exchange whose abundance is relatively new, with derivatives? Martin: "derivatives are a transmission of some value from a source to something else, an attribute of that original expression that can be combined with like characteristics, a variable factor that can move in harmony or dissonance with others."[252]

A commodity appears as a unitary thing, a discrete object, calling forth an individual subject as its intimate partner on the market. Behind that appearance lies a whole hidden world of production, where particular labors are themselves commodified and combined, where products are made and a surplus labor extracted. As Amy Wendling shows, in Marx, it is something of a thermodynamic model, where production is a meshing of labor and machines, each with its own kind of energy.[253]

A key to thinking this process is its abstraction.[254] Particular, concrete labors become abstract labor; particular commodities extruded from their factories all embody some quantity of that labor, the ultimate determinant of their exchange value. But what if abstraction had not stood still since Marx's time, when the commodity form was generalized? What if it didn't stop at abstracting from the body of the worker, the object produced, and the individual subject as consumer?

On top of the abstraction of the particular labors, materials and machines that are realized in the classic commodity form, there might now be another, which is by some measures a bigger thing in the world. This other abstraction is the *derivative*, a form of information through which each of the component flows in commodification can be subdivided, valued, combined, and sold again and again as financial instruments. On top of the quantitative abstraction of the energetics of production is a quantitative abstraction of the information about all of the possible future states of that system, each of which can be separately priced and sold.[255]

Martin: "If derivatives do now what commodities did in Marx's account, they too, result from, bear, and release particular social relations and forms."[256] This might not be the capitalism of your great-grandparent's era, and while one could try to explain it with metaphors and concepts drawn from that past, these might obscure what is qualitatively peculiar about its form today. What might be different is not just the appearances but the underlying connection between particular things and the totality of abstract relations that generate them as appearances. Commodities could be thought of as particular parts of an abstract whole; derivatives are further subdivisions of those parts that can be further abstracted into many possible totalities.

Marxist theory is at something of an impasse at the moment. The cultural turn of Stuart Hall and others raised some pertinent issues, not least about race and gender and the postcolonial world, but it got bogged down in the details, in appearances.[257] Unfortunately, the dominant response is to simply return to the ways of thinking about the underlying abstract totality of the era prior to that turn. Rare are attempts, like Martin's, at a dialectical overcoming of the impasse, in which the appearances of the late twentieth century are subsumed in a more historical and contemporary understanding of the totality that might produce them. Martin took the cultural turn, then turned again, finding distinctive and novel homologies at three levels: aesthetics, politics, and economics.

It might help that the cultural appearances to which Martin pays attention is not the usual fiction, cinema, music, or other aesthetic products that were central to debates about so-called postmodern culture. His early work was mostly about dance, which does not quite so neatly fit into the theories of the postmodern as pastiche (Jameson), simulation (Baudrillard), game (Lyotard), panic (Kroker), or database (Azuma).[258]

The postmodern moment for Martin was when a general derivative logic extended across economic, political, and cultural principles of movement. It emerged out of the struggles of the seventies. As in Hardt and Negri, Martin puts the emphasis on subaltern agency, but it is not labor that drives the qualitative change toward the derivative.[259] It is what Martin calls *decolonization*, which happens on a much wider front.[260] Indeed, part of its novelty is the abundance of points of challenge. Decolonization unmakes the seeming naturalness of domination and escapes from nation, empire, self, masses, all of which posed as forms of autonomy but were actually forms of authority.

The derivative is a byproduct of various decolonizations, which are not just a negation of power, but also an affirmation of self-assembly.[261] Martin:

> the derivative flows from decolonization and takes the undoing of what was whole, the unbounding of what was enclosed, the bundling of what was scattered ... as its conditions of possibility ... From the decolonization of culture, seeds are spread everywhere and sources released and captured, sampled and posted, through expansive webs of self-dissemination.[262]

Like Paolo Virno, Martin is interested in dance as emblematic of a kind of self-organizing virtuoso labor.[263] For Martin, the dancer's body "has been valued and supported in a kind of impossible economic anorexia ... Dancers are prized for their creativity, flexibility, absence of material needs."[264] Virno thinks of this as post-fordist *virtuosity* but Martin thinks of it as kind of *social kinesthetic*. This is more like Raymond Williams' *structure of feeling*, in which a certain historical formation is lived and breathed.[265] Like structure of feeling, a social kinesthetic might be a disposition that exists prior to its articulation, as a sensibility or habit. Dancers are the perfect labor force, a model of work without strife—or strikes.[266]

Dance is a site for thinking about how the body in movement makes value. In a factory, bodies move, products extrude, but then those commodities are alienated from their maker, enter circulation, and end up inside circulation in forms of credit and debt. Dance is different. Bodies move in space, credit and debt are tendered between dancers and audiences for a particular duration. Circulation is inside production.

Dance is also a derivative, a series of minor variations derived from something common. Small changes lead to large gains. Dance makes the kinesthetic legible, and the derivative of this understanding can then be substituted into other domains of practice. This is essentially what Martin did. For him, dance is derivative of the social kinesthetic in the same way that finance is derivative of the commodity form.

Postmodern dance was a new iteration of the social kinesthetic, a rupture from the universalizing tendencies of the classical and the modern.[267] The classical is an order that comes from without that has to be embodied. Its origins are in feudal Absolutism, as codified dance was initially derived from Louis XIV's movements. Sovereignty is transferred from the king to the artist-genius-celebrity, operating in art as autonomous realm. The classical kinesthetic privileges a vertical movement: the king imitates God, the dancer the king, the subject the dancer.

If one had to give one instance of the modern, then Martha Graham (whose studio was at The New School for a while) is an excellent choice. In the modern, the choreographer becomes the sovereign artist-genius. It's a kinesthetic that includes the vertical but also an inward-curling, arcing, or whiplike spiral. Genius is disclosed through self-mastery of the body's inherent capacity. Movement is for movement's sake within an autonomous space of art.

The postmodern turns against the exalted body of the creator, revealing the labor of the body. Judson Church, a few blocks south of the New School, is the fulcrum here.[268] That was where Merce Cunningham's experiments were elaborated upon by Trisha Brown, Meredith Monk, Fred Herko, Yvonne Rainer, and others. Dance is always derived from other movement, but postmodern dance at least acknowledges this and is less interested in claiming sovereignty or autonomy. Judson dance was an arbitrage of movement forms in different situations including the sit-in and the demo. It's a kind of dance that can attribute valuation but doesn't govern and that includes space and objects within its practices. It brings bodies together according to physique and physics rather than commanded by external authorities, terrestrial or celestial.

The classical gesture brings all power to a center to be imitated. The modern is about the interior depth of centered sovereign creator. The postmodern countertendency is centrifugal, spinning out, not in. It is a persistent decolonization within the modern, "replacing God with gravity."[269] Movement is developed out of the body itself—using methods influence by Zürich Dada fellow traveler Rudolf Laban.[270] Martin:

> Rather than descending from the line of God through the body
> of the sovereign or from deep within the creator's body, post-
> modern technique emphasizes the spaces in between the bodies
> of dancers or the spatial and kinesthetic relations that obtain
> between dancers and their environment.[271]

Martin sees parallels between Judson dance and more vernacular movement practices such as hip-hop's Rock Steady Crew and Z-Boy skaters.[272] These were horizontal habits that expressed a global abundance of movement, iterative and derivative. These were of a piece with the musical cultures of the time, based on samples and breaks: "The break, from this perspective, could be considered a space of arbitrage, a place where a manufactured difference between two sources becomes a generative realization of some value."[273] One could connect this to Eshun on techno or Azuma on database culture.[274]

These derivative forms emerged among populations "at risk," meaning mostly at risk of proletarianization, or worse, caught up by the *predatory state*.[275] Upward or forward mobility is blocked, so their kinesthetic elaborates sideways moves. They are the inverse phenomena to the contemporaneous financialization and concentration of wealth. One could put more stress on the forms of recuperation developed in this era of the disintegrating spectacle, but kinesethetics of the 1970s did its best to outrun them, through "moshing, mashing and mixing."[276] It was an era of emerging sovereignties living pleasure within danger. One could think of this as a response to the era of *precarity* as Angela McRobbie and others call it, although it's a more compromised word than it sounds, linked to both debt and prayer.[277] Martin prefers to think in terms of *volatility*.

The quandaries of the category of *public* form the middle section of the book and draw not on Martin's experience as a dance scholar within cultural studies but as a researcher in cultural policy studies.[278] Here Martin's study is focused on American public institutions, but other parts of the overdeveloped world may increasingly come to resemble it.

The "public" is many rather than one thing and is distributed across the economic, political, and cultural. It appears as a stand-in for "the good." But the public became a derivative of the private. "The public associated with the commons, consensus, and cooperation has been eclipsed by private self-interest, fragmentation and competition."[279] A derivative undoes the integrity of the part and whole and reassembles attributes into forms of indebtedness, contingency, exchange value. This is what happened to public goods, those that are not private and not made for profit.

The public is managed by a third sector beyond state and market—philanthropic and nonprofit organizations.[280] They care for the commons but put donors in the position of judging social allocations. Private foundations become a distinct institutional sector, taking over state functions in an era of tax cuts. They transfer public resources into private hands and as such are of a piece with employer health care plans, the home mortgage interest rate deduction, tax-exempt retirement accounts, and other forms of selective privatized welfare.

Philanthropy has become something less than a gift.

> When giving becomes a form of investment, the notion of public good shifts from something that the market cannot provide to a claim on what is good for the public ... The public as a derivative of private values does not simply render all goods onto the market. Instead, it infuses civic engagement with expectations of appreciable gain ... Hence, far from a simple conversion to the market, as suggested by concepts such as privatization, deregulation, and neoliberalism, the philanthropic complex ... is at once regulatory, constitutive of publics, and compatible with a proselytizing conservatism as much as moralizing liberalism.[281]

Philanthropy aligns the "rich" and "poor" by generalizing private property, the ur-form of which is the microloan. Access to credit is now touted as a "human right."[282] The human is conceived exclusively as market actor. Microloans have high rates of return with high interest and low default. They exploit unpaid family labor and have low overheads. The aggregation of these loans through a digital information vector makes poverty bankable by exploiting social solidarity and trust procedures. Poor women are good debtors, often held in place by patriarchal kin. Through them a derivative of the local becomes part of a global financial infrastructure.

In place of democratic accountability is a concept of fiduciary oversight of the social, as if the social were made of nothing but individual debtors. "Framing public goods in terms of investment that maximize returns alleviates them from the burden of being available to all, especially when opportunity trumps equality as a key underlying value."[283] For nonprofits, the capacity to raise and expend funds is its own sign of success. "The sensibility of the venture philanthropist is to inhabit the present with their wealth and to incarnate less a universal will as an investor-based excellence."[284]

Philanthropy and its public meet through the derivative

forms of big stars and big data. Polling is the public pacified, the general will reduced to consumer choice. But where polling was once interested in aggregating difference into a national popular whole, now it is more about political and cultural market niches and interest groups, or "derivative publics,"[285] each of which has its own celebrity experts, its Nate Silvers.[286] Martin:

> Legitimacy and authority shift into the realm of uncertainty. No-one knows what the public thinks, what performances are worth, what politics opinions enact, yet all are compelled to search for value and to act on the differences they perceive … Poised between noise and information, between non-knowledge and knowledge, derivatives emerge from the space between the measurable and the immeasurable—not simply making a quanta actionable but charging the medium in which they move with certain qualities.[287]

This argument connects Martin to the work on cognitive capitalism of Yann Moulier Boutang.[288]

The other derivative of the public is the celebrity, the charismatic outsider, whose role is to re-enchant the disenchanted masses. Stars are expressions of what is valued, a qualitative abstraction from touchy publics.[289] "The center holds less not because it is impossible to quantify but because it remains in motion, at the heart of volatility, throbbing, shifting away from the prospect that it can anchor the effluvial masses."[290] The stability of the public is undone by its own operations.

The public is now a good made in the nonprofit sector. The many are known by measuring the few at the volatile center or through the celebrity avatar of the shifting edge. "The derivative logic undoes the partition of public and private. A flood of the political ensues."[291] This is an interesting insight: far from being a postpolitical age, it's the opposite. There is an abundance of politics. What Chantal Mouffe would call *antagonism* overflows its institutional bounds.[292]

The expert elite who manage the technical aspect of its derivative form produces backlash. Political antagonism is recoded as cultural difference, producing the *culture wars*—antagonism reduced to culture and blamed for its own inability to assimilate to a rational norm. The culture wars are for Martin an anxiety provoked by partial decolonization. It's a fear, shared by conservatives and liberals alike, that "democratization would be the enemy of democracy."[293]

The instruments devised to manage risk produce it in politics too. There is a surplus of ungovernable uncertainty.

> Politics overflows its banks; regulatory capacities are disintermediated; political value is assembled from shared attributes that come from far and near; affiliation is rendered volatile; the face value of the political exceeds the underlying means of representation and formal channels of participation; sentiments are judged in anticipation of their completion as consequences.[294]

Martin calls this *excess criticality*:

> That politics does not reside in a single sphere, filled by some volute of a popular mass whose energies can be assimilated and co-opted, shifts dramatically the very conception of mobilization as an aggregate of individual decisions taken. Rather, excess criticality occupies the kind of epistemic and ontic state of the dark pools, shadow banks, and arbitrage conditions by which new currencies of political value are generated.[295]

Excess criticality has two "sensibilities of surplus."[296] The first still seeks an expansion of rights, to health, education, housing, jobs, but also to freedoms and protections, an expanding democratization. The second is a total critique that is immanent to that democratization and pushes it against its limit. Expert-based politics failed to keep up with excess criticality and resulted in a generalized distrust of "elites." With the demise of professionally managed political pluralism, there are demand for limits to criticality to preserve a democratic procedure, even as it has ceased to function.

This volatility of aesthetics and politics is homologous with that of economics. The economy is supposed to be that which is excluded from the political but includes a national population. The crisis is about what is included and excluded. It took a massive political intervention to save the economy from itself in 2008, by a visible regulatory hand that was itself beyond regulation. The intervention was less to fix the thing than to change public perception. The bailout transferred public money to the private sphere, and it was apparently self-evident that this was in everyone's interest.

The economy is supposed to be a device for converting knowing into being, but one has to believe in it in order for it to deliver wealth. The economy met its end in 2008 because it became unknowable even to itself. But no better way of knowing could be found, and the knowledge crisis remains. "Contrary to the fable of triumphant neoliberalism ... more regulation, not less, is required."[297] Deregulation rewrites statues rather than abolishing them.

Contrary to the professions of faith of its worshippers, the economy actually needs active management. It is a supposedly self-regulating distributor of prices that combines knowledge from individuals who each know their own preferences. The market is supposedly the sum of all knowledge individual monads provide, which they cannot master because what they have is incomplete. Knowledge is not given to anyone as totality; only market can be that, once it has shoved all knowledge through the cookie-cutter mold of price.

Financial markets are knowledge aggregation in its purest form, an economy of almost pure information, although as Mirowski points out, economists are never too clear about what information actually is.[298] In the economy of finance, derivatives are based on models of risk that can be priced. In portfolio theory, risk is spread through diversification. Short-term fluctuations in prices can be hedged; long-term is a bit tricky and more volatile. It is hard to manage futures that are not like the past using models drawn from that past. Risk can be knowable; *uncertainty* is unknowable. Derivatives are a way to hedge risk and extract a return from an unknowable future by hedging its various possibilities. Derivatives can even extract a surplus from uncertainty itself.

Expertise can no longer prevent volatility. There's a link between a financialization of nonknowledge and the state attacks on expertise that accelerated under Reagan and Thatcher. They attacked the credibility of their own governing class. Knowledge no longer has an autonomous value. It has to show a return. The mass of knowledge on which finance rested became its impediment. There's a loss of trust in the particular expertise that managed particular risks, in education, health, or security, for example. Finance became the manager of generalized risk in the form of nonknowledge, the acme of what I call the vectoralist class.

The managerial class turned out to have no internal class cohesion, and it was easy enough to separate "star" managers and attach them to finance. Martin:

> The occupational girth of the professional managerial class continues to expand, driven by managerialism, intellectual property, industrialization of culture, and the like … But its basis of association and its internal logic of association are to be decomposed and reformed from autonomous control of expert domains to highly specialized and technical knowledge that is subject to managerial requisites rather than self-rule.[299]

What is surplus or excess in relation to knowledge? For Martin, it's the unknown. Risk management in professional fields, from health to security to energy to finance, generate value from the unknown. Knowledge is now so abundant that it cannot all be used, and its excess can generate disaster. Knowledge is a kind of credit, but the unknown is a kind of debt. This industrialization of knowledge is like the earlier transformation of farmers into workers. There's a loss of a particular connection to the means of production. Enclosure now extends far into the professions.

Since expert knowledge can't fix "economy," nonknowledge has its day. Nonknowledge comes in a few flavors. The unknown known is, or was, discoverable by expertise. The known unknown is imaginable but impossible to verify. The unknown unknown is a generative absence of knowledge confronting risk and uncertainty. The burden of enduring all of these shifts onto individuals. "Non-knowledge rules in the world risk society."[300] Nonknowledge generates *derivative logics*. These prosper now that nonknowledge is a force of production.[301]

"Financialization ... entails a shift in policy emphasis from providing security to managing risk."[302] The swelling of that risk leads to more and more hedging. There's a kind of "regulatory disintermediation."[303] Lots of rule-making is now outside of the state. (In much the same way, the regulation in the design world is now about standards, as Keller Easterling observes.) The economy was once a model for the conservation of energy based on utility as determined by partial but rational actors.

> Whereas what has been described as the economy imagines that price is the moment of resolution of difference, the derivative operates through the conditions of generalized uncertainty as a bearer of this ongoing contestation over value in which the relation between knowledge and nonknowledge is governed.[304]

Not only is the totality of derivatives bigger than the commodity economy, it is prior to it. Prices are formed in options and futures markets before they are set in cash markets: "The core operation of derivatives is to bind the future to the present through a range of contractual opportunities and to make all manner of capital across disparate spheres of place, sector, and characteristic commensurate with one another." Derivatives are a kind of "meta-capital." Admittedly, "stuff still gets made and sold, even if through thickets of debt and credit."[305] And yet I wonder if at its apex this is still "capitalism" or something worse.[306]

Martin:

> if commodities appeared as a unit of wealth that could abstract parts into a whole, derivatives are a still more complex process by which parts are no longer unitary but are continuously disassembled and reassembled as various attributes are bundled and their notional value exceeds the whole economy to which they may once have been summed.[307]

Capitalism designed processes of mass assembly that made standardized products. Derivatives run that process in reverse, slicing into the bulk of those products and reassembling them by risk attribute. They are worth more as derivatives than as commodities. "Subjecting the world to the logic of derivatives means acting as if no transaction is final and there is always a globally realizable potential for improved performance."[308]

Martin:

> By abstracting capital from its own body ... derivatives do to capital what capital itself has been doing to concrete forms of money and productive conditions such as labor, raw materials, and the physical plant. Hence, while derivatives serve as a globally exchangeable money form, they also break down the distinction between money and capital. At the same time, they make available to capital accumulation what would be considered new materialities of ideas and perceptions, weather and war, bits of code stripped from tele-technology or DNA, the microscopic and cosmic.[309]

The derivative organizes the forces of production of the information vector.

Derivatives increase opacity and amplify volatility and risk. They then treat the volatility they produce as a horizon for their own opportunity.

> They turn the contestability of fundamental value into a trade-able commodity ... The derivative serves as a kind of shuttle between the particular risk factors it bundles together and the general glare of optimum market performance as an imaginary horizon to which the measure is subject.[310]

This is not just a matter of a world of "fictitious capital" or "mere circulation." Financial logics enter directly into the workplace. The housing, education, health, and automotive industries integrate finance directly with production. Even daily life becomes financialized.[311] Anyone with either money or debt works a second shift managing these assets and liabilities. "Derivatives perform a dispossession of self and ownership."[312]

That there is a political or aesthetic outside to the economic is a fantasy structure the derivative abolishes. Derivatives now constitute the totality. The derivative is not an economic object that politics can regulate. It is itself regulatory. It is nonknowledge itself, commodified. Derivatives don't price things; they price uncertainty.

> Finance works through flows. It moves production inside of circulation. It is a kind of compulsory movement that mandates going forward. Even in times of crisis, we must keep going at all costs. The price paid for this compulsion is that finance claims to see everything but has no knowledge of how it moves, or has no language for its own movement.[313]

Derivatives appear as detachable but actually reveal a mutual indebtedness. Debt "servicing" becomes everyone's problem. Derivatives make future outcomes actionable in the present, appearing as a way to regulate and control futures. "Finance is based on those with observable information profiting from the bulk of those lacking it who create an environment of noise."[314] Uncertainty itself is rendered productive.

> Rather than something firmly tethered that then got away, what would it mean to understand the emergence of this dissonant

social relation that cuts across the global and the intimate, spheres of production and circulation, future and present, knowledge and non-knowledge?[315]

For Martin, nonknowledge is an open field of nonabsorbed surplus, which means that a politics or aesthetics specific to this era, rather than nostalgic for another, could apply itself to socializing this surplus, starting from the form in which it now appears.[316]

What I would want to add to Martin is an attention to the forces of production that made the derivative possible, what I call the *vector* or what Benjamin Bratton calls *the stack*. Then one could examine the derivative at work in other fields, such as the sciences. One might also then sharpen the class analysis at work and see finance as a component of a class that extracts value from surplus information—what I call the *vectoralist class*. One might then also pay closer attention to the various subordinate classes this layered mode of production exploits, what I call the *farmer*, the *worker*, and the *hacker classes*. Beyond that are those excluded from a political economy in which they could even assume a class location. Here one might trace how things like the social kinesthetic of hip-hop resurfaces in the movement for Black lives.[317]

The derivative is the form of appearance of a qualitatively different abstraction at work in the world, what I call a *third nature*, built on top of, and extracting a surplus from, the second nature that social labor built at the command of capital.[318] But as Virno reminds us, the term *second nature* in Marx always carried a tone of ideological falseness.[319] Likewise, as John Bellamy Foster and others remind us, the totality of our times is no less real and yet no less false and is only accelerating the metabolic rift between the totality of social relations and their dependency on a "first" nature that now appears as a spread of risks to be optioned, swapped, and hedged.[320]

II

Ethnographics

Jackie Wang: Prisoners of the Algorithm

Ethnography begins at home. Since I've lived, as a "resident alien," in the United States for some twenty years, I want to start here, with some insights into an America that a white person like me hardly sees. Then I'll move on to look at writers who generate quite different concepts out of quite different geopolitical circumstances.

There are many ways of not being at home at home. In Jackie Wang's *Carceral Capitalism,* the unhomely enters through her brother being in prison. "There is a political knot at the center of my life, a point of great density, around which orbit my questions about the world and how it is structured."[1] Wang writes of the various court dates, repeatedly deferred, for his appeal hearing:

> What is prison? Immobility, yes, but also the manipulation of time as a form of psychic torture … It warps the temporalities of everyone in the orbit of the disappeared person … Our lives were punctuated by this anxiety-inducing cycle of anticipation and deferral.[2]

Incarceration can make time volatile as well as repetitive.

A series of things snap into focus about everyday life. Her brother is in prison in Florida while she is in graduate school at Harvard. These seem like completely different worlds. How is the division between those worlds decided, justified, policed? How might the exclusion of her brother, and of millions like him, his social death, or perhaps rather his civic death, be an intrinsic part of the world in which she (and most of the rest of us) get to live? How might those worlds, despite their differences, be increasingly governed by similar logics, of surveillance, data collection, predictive algorithms, and debt?

To even think this takes some effort, as it means that certain people have to be acknowledged to be people. Wang never tells us why her brother is in prison, because it should not matter. He is a person to her. He could be a person to us, if we accepted his personhood without qualification, without needing him to be innocent first. This is the pressure Wang wants to put on our thinking: to get over limiting our care and attention to those we deem, in some arbitrary way, to be innocent. Which is not to insist that we are all guilty, as that is part of the same logic. Rather to acknowledge that we are all implicated.

This brings us directly to the internal tension within the Movement for Black Lives. The most mobilizing cases have been instances of Black children who have been out in some social space that the white imaginary can grasp, like a playground or a parking lot, and who have been murdered by the police for no apparent reason at all. Pictures of these children in school graduate gowns circulate. Defenders of police murderers, and of white supremacy in general, are quick to insinuate that these children were doing something wrong, or behaved in a threatening manner, or are rumored to have been shoplifting, or something—anything—that denies them their innocence. Black people have to be innocent, which ends up meaning they have to be like white people, because Black people are presumed not to be innocent and white people are.

Why should only the innocent children be worthy of care? Of life? Why not adults who may not be pure innocent beings? Wang connects these criteria of innocence to an anxiety about physical safety and demand for comfort:

> The politics of innocence and the politics of safety and comfort are related in that both strategies reinforce passivity.

88

Comfort and innocence produce each other when people base the demand for comfort on the innocence of their location or subject position. Even though I am a queer woman of color, my existence as a person living in the United States is built on violence. As a nonincarcerated person, my "freedom" is understood only through the captivity of people like my brother, who is serving a forty-year sentence.[3]

Bodies that arouse fear, disgust, discomfort, guilt, must be removed from social space. I would add two things to this. The demand for spaces comes from thinking from the point of view of a consumer. One is not a student or a citizen, one has bought an experience and feels entitled to customer service. More charitably, the demand for spaces of safety and comfort may in part stem from feeling precarious and uncertain about one's chances in a volatile world. Both connect to one of Wang's themes: the rise of debt as the dominant social bond, which in turn is part of a broader picture, one that we find in Randy Martin, of the quantitative management of risk and uncertainty.

The liberalism of liberal America is always qualified. Its tendencies to exclusion rarely rise to the level of a concept. It has bad feelings about certain kinds of people. "White civil society has a psychic investment in the erasure and abjection of bodies onto which they project hostile feelings, allowing them peace of mind amidst the state of perpetual violence."[4] This is the condition of possibility for *politics* in the sense that liberal political theory can understand it. Consider, for example, the psychogeography of Zuccotti Park during Occupy Wall Street.[5] The general assembly was as far away as it could be from the drum circle, and its consensus-talk treated the latter-day hobos who gathered at the other end under the category of *problems*.

Where Judith Butler works outward from the bodies assembled in the movements of the squares, Wang asks who is excluded from being there at all and what forces conspire to separate such a them from an us.[6] This leads to a quite different field of concepts, such as *algorithmic governance, municipal plunder, carceral space,* and the *predatory state.* While she corals these new concepts under the old rubric of *biopolitics,* they may actually point beyond these limitations.

In the United States and perhaps elsewhere, the state has evolved from a tax state, to a debt state, to a *predatory state.*[7] Local government in particular is accountable to creditors, not publics. Despite austerity, the police and prison systems continue to be amply financed, even if, as we shall see, policing is tasked with raising its own revenue. Policing protects property, not social relations. Expanding prisons is a popular policy with rural constituencies, for whom prison employment is one of the few new sources of jobs. Spending on prisons has risen much faster than on education. Wang: "incarceration has little to do with 'crime' as such."[8]

Filling prisons requires an expansion of crime, which calls for the criminalizing of populations deemed not to be innocent. Wang follows Huey Newton and the Black Panthers in seeing one of the key developments here: a rise in the automation of labor leading to a surplus population, a mostly Black lumpenproletariat.[9] The Black Panthers thought the tax state would expand welfare to keep a surplus population consuming, but instead what happened was an expansion of credit and mass incarceration.

The predatory state works in part through municipal plunder. Cities (and their taxpayers) end up footing the bill and taking the risk for so-called public–private development projects, meaning that the costs are socialized and the profits privatized. Such schemes are often examples of what David Harvey calls the *spatial fix.*[10] When the property market crashes, cities step in with development projects to restart accumulation. But when these stop working in turn, the city is left with the costs. Something like this happened in New York in 1975 and in Detroit in 2013.

In New York, what resulted was a political *state of exception*.[11] Democratic oversight of the city's finances no longer applied, resulting in an austerity regime aimed at paying back debt rather than running essential services. More recently, the city of Flint, Michigan, has been without clean water for a thousand days and counting. In Detroit, the added wrinkle is that it was a form of high-risk borrowing—interest rate swaps —that caused the fiscal crisis in the first place. With municipal plunder, the city becomes a machine for extracting debt repayments from its citizens. Wang: "the state is no ordinary borrower; it is a borrower endowed with the legal power to loot the public to pay back its creditors."[12]

In cases like the Movement for Black Lives that gathered momentum in the municipality of Ferguson in 2014, police power is deployed in the interests of finance. "In order to remain solvent, municipalities develop a parasitic relation to the people they are supposed to serve."[13] Local governments struggle to raise tax revenue; they turn instead to borrowing and to using the police and the courts to extract fees and fines, particularly from Black populations. In Texas, 650,000 people are locked up for unpaid fines. In New Orleans judges are incentivized to levy fines. An Alabama judge forced people to donate blood to avoid going to jail for unpaid fines.

All of this is in some sense highly irrational, at least from the point of view of reproducing labor-power. It limits Black mobility, making urban space a carceral space. People are often captives in their homes, try to avoiding late fees and fines and unable to show up for work. In some places, there are private collection agencies, alcohol monitoring services, and private probation companies that can also levy court-mandated fees or insist on them even when the courts do not. In Ferguson, municipal fees were at 20 percent of the town budget at the time Black Lives Matter erupted.

Government moves from providing a social infrastructure to surveilling risk and enforcing security. There's a delegitimizing of welfare based on a racism that casts Black people as a whole as deserving of punishment and subject to gratuitous violence. Wang acknowledges the critical force of *Afropessimist* writers such as Frank Wilderson and Jared Sexton, for whom violence against Blackness is foundational, and not merely an exception, to the liberal respect for the individual legal subject.[14] For Afropessimists, Black enslavement is the essential condition of possibility of capitalism. Slaves were brought here to work and die. They were, and remain, a disposable rather than an exploitable population. The predatory state and municipal plunder are merely a wrinkle on primary historical practices and categories. For example, the emancipation of the slaves should in theory have converted chained slave labor into "free" wage labor, but anti-vagrancy laws were widely enacted to restrict Black mobility.

Wang combines this point of view with a Marxist one.[15] She sees Black America as being both disposable and exploitable. She finds W. E. B. Du Bois already trying to negotiate this. After witnessing a lynching, he discovered the sadistic side of racism and moved away from social science. Wang: "How terrible it must have been for W. E. B. Du Bois to realize he had mistaken dusk for dawn."[16] Racial hatred has an irrational core and trumps enlightened reason. One saw this in the Rodney King trial (1993), where white jurors simply could not see a Black man being beaten by multiple cops; they saw instead a Black man "resisting." This pattern repeats over and over in the acquittal of cops for murdering Black people, a situation police bodycams will not solve and may make worse by becoming mobile surveillance devices.

On the other hand, perhaps not everything is explained by the violent maintenance of an irrational division of the population into white civil subjects and a Black population not recognized—and never recognizable—as fully human by even a liberal political order. Wang turns to Cedric Robinson's work on *racial capitalism*.[17] For Robinson, racialism predates capital, and capitalism was not a universal force of modern rationalization. Marx was aware of the complexities within the social formation, including those of race, but he explores this in the political writings, not in *Capital*. There he presents capitalist social relations more or less alone.

Capital gives a one-sided view of social formation that in actuality may include several modes of production and where their interactions cannot be excluded without distorting our view of what the capitalist mode of production is and does. Capitalism appears as a homogenizing social process. What is lost from view is that the social formation is also differentiating. Capital exploits a homogenized class of wage laborers who are formally "free" to sell their labor. But that is just part of a social formation that differentiates free labor from unfree labor and expropriates from the unfree.

One could get the impression from Marx that *primitive accumulation* on the backs of the unfree came first but was rationalized into the exploitation of free labor. For Robinson and for Wang, it is more helpful to see both operating together. Marx wrote as if the expanded reproduction of capital could take place entirely within its own circuits. For Rosa Luxemburg capital always requires an outside.[18] It depends on expropriation. David Harvey reframes Luxemburg's thesis as *accumulation by dispossession*.[19] It's an ongoing, rather than prior, condition. Wang follows Harvey in thinking it may happen in the over-developed world as much as in the colonial and formerly colonial peripheries.

Wang: "Expropriation produces multiple categories of difference."[20] This is a way of avoiding having our own political agency succumb to the very power that works by means of differentiation. There's no advantage in arguing (for example) whether slavery is the sole basis of capitalism or whether it is the theft of indigenous land. Or whether the disposable Black body is what is most excluded by differentiation from humanity, or the rapeable female body. Expropriation fractures the population.

The Afropessimists are right: it is surreal to imagine that Blackness could ever be included in the category of free liberal subject that is based in the first place on its exclusion. It takes nothing away from the specificity of that exclusion to bracket the claim that it is unique. Rather than the (eventual) inclusion of Black America, a more likely future is immiseration for all. Starting with Black populations, more and more marginal populations will be taxed, fined, and garnished into funding the exclusionary urban development that excludes them. Capital as a mode of production may depend not just on prior or parallel modes of production that work by expropriation and dispossession. All I would add is: Maybe a novel mode of production is emerging as well.

This brings us to algorithmic governance. Here the state of predictive policing, municipal fee-farming, racialized subprime mortgage lending, student debt, and much else start to come together in the same analysis. Let's start with predictive policing. Using algorithms to predict where crime will happen appears as a neutral and scientific approach to policing at a time when policing has for a small but growing part of the population lost legitimacy.

Wang looks at PredPol, which grew out of a university research project and became a start-up. It claims to predict where crime will happen through an analysis of past crime frequency by location. There is no way of knowing if it works. The algorithm is proprietary. There's no control test. The contract with the company obliges police to be its advocates if requested. The data on which it is based comes from a history of racialized policing. It is not even clear if more arrests or fewer are the sign of success, and it appears the company has argued that both ways. PredPol does have one outstanding merit: it makes it look as if racism as a factor in policing went away.

Black (and brown) Americans are incarcerated at higher rates than white people. This became "evidence" for higher rates of criminality. This in turn resulted in higher levels of policing of Black neighborhoods: "race is spatially produced."[21] This gets buried in supposedly neutral computation that discreetly finds proxies for race. Where once the politics of space was governed by the free liberal subject and those excluded from being him, now it is also governed by predictive algorithms that take the differentiations and exclusions of that world as if it was just data. "These new forms of power create the illusion of freedom and flexibility while actually being more totalizing in their diffuseness."[22]

This is the case not only with policing but also with access to credit, whether for a home, a car, or an education. As we learned when the market for mortgage-back securities collapsed, many Black borrowers were shunted into subprime lending even when they qualified for lower interest loans. The cruel paradox of student loans is that students borrow to get degrees to get jobs, but employers use credit scores as proxies for good citizenship, and students who have missed payments will have lower credit scores and hence less chance of employment. All of this is poorly regulated, not to mention subject to all sorts of arbitrary fees. My bank once tried to charge me an inactivity fee. Having to do nothing seemed to them an untapped income source!

Algorithmically managed consumer debt becomes a novel form of accumulation by dispossession. It appears as part of a larger pattern of control through information. Wang gathers the strands of her illuminating, high-contrast snapshot of today's America under the concept of *biopolitics*. I'm not a fan of this yoking together of the ancient categories of *bios* and *polis*, but let's see what Wang manages to get out of it.

In Foucault, biopolitics takes the place of sovereign power, the power over life and death.[23] For Giorgio Agamben (after Foucault), biopolitics is the growing inclusion of human life in calculations of power.[24] Robert Esposito adds the concept of *immunization*.[25] One could think of immunity as the other side of community, a sort of *exclusionary inclusion*, an internal separation of what is deemed foreign or other. Just as Cedric Robinson shows expropriation working alongside exploitation, Esposito shows sovereign power working alongside biopolitics. The modern state does not really dispense with arbitrary violence, or what Achille Mbembe calls *necropolitics*, the power to kill, specifically killing in the interests of preserving life (for others).[26]

Wang's example of biopolitics at work is the creation of the category of the superpredator in the nineties. Criminologists glanced at a demographic bulge in young men of color and predicted a crime wave. "The entire social body is diagnosed as being at risk of coming undone if the juvenile crime infection is not rooted out."[27] The response was in part a sentencing regime that included juvenile life imprisonment without parole. Even the NAACP moved away from prison rights and embraced tough-on-crime rhetoric, even though this was connected to such folk devils as the welfare queen, the Black rapist, and the superpredator.

Wang: "The biopolitical construction of juveniles as subjects defined by irrationality marks this subset of the population as a calculable risk that must be pre-emptively managed."[28] This is not that other old standby of political theory: the sovereign politics of friend-enemy. It is a matter of contagion. Criminologists substituted metaphors from biology into thinking about the self-protecting agency of community (as immunity). But these days it seems it is thought just as much through metaphors to do with information. Good citizens are information; bad ones become noise.

For Agamben, the typical space of biopower is not a political space at all, but the camps.[29] These are established in a state of exception when the sovereign suspends the law, and therefore the exception becomes the rule. This category is not limited to concentration camps but might include refugee camps or extraterritorial sites of rendition and torture. There may be a whole spectrum of exceptions become law.

Wang adds to this the juvenile sentenced as an adult. In the past, American law protected juveniles from the full force of the law, on the grounds that they are not fully responsible civic subjects. The juvenile sentenced as an adult has none of the rights of an adult other than the right to be punished as one. Wang: "for the social body to defeat the infection of the juvenile superpredator, the undesirable element must first be incorporated into the body of the law."[30] In this case, biopolitics creates the category of the delinquent youth who is such a threat that he has to be policed and incarcerated to prevent a future (theoretical) explosion of crime. "The emphasis is not on judging specific acts attached to specific persons, but on isolating a type of person that can be identified with abnormality."[31]

As Michel de Certeau saw a long time ago, the thing about Foucault is that he always sees from the point of view of power itself.[32] As a result, Wang has to supplement the top-down biopolitical frame with forms of Black agency. The civic death that is imposed on Blackness may not extend all the way to social death, because that would negate the vitality, legacy, and ingenuity of Black autonomous culture itself.[33] What one could add in between is the critical criminology literature that tried to see from the point of view of the so-called delinquent.

To stick just with the radical criminology I studied before abandoning my law degree: Howard Becker's *Outsiders* asked about the difference between how such people are labeled by those with power over them compared to how they labeled themselves. Stanley Cohen asked about the role of the media in creating folk devils and whipping up moral panics about them.[34] Dick Hebdige asked about the aesthetic and cultural practices by which subcultures create themselves by recoding what received cultural material meant, changing the conversation around the delinquent from pathology to resistance.[35] Stuart Hall and others connected the construction of the British equivalent to the superpredator to the police diffusion of a political crisis.[36]

Wang is properly cautious about seeing political motives behind actions that respond to policing. Riots aren't started by Leninists in the making.[37] But perhaps there's more to be said about subaltern agency, about a whole way of life, a culture, a sociality, that resists or evades civic death. Besides its top-down perspective, biopolitics ends up relentlessly focused on the body perceived at a certain scale. As Paul B. Preciado insists, much of the regulation of bodies these days is chemical as well as corporeal.[38] This applies to prison populations and psychiatric care but also to the maintenance of the contemporary body generally. There may be forms of techno-governance—chemical, informational—not quite captured by the concept of biopolitics at all.

Policing has always been technical. It may be a question of how its technics changes, and here the technics of differentiation and of homogenization, of crime and labor, might evolve in parallel. Wang calls the effect of technics the *intrusive-unseen*: "Do you hear the surveillance camera whisper, your body is not your body, your body is a point on a grid."[39]

Wang: "What those who designed these derivative financial products essentially did was take an underlying asset, hold it between two mirrors so that it appeared to proliferate to infinity, then mistake the multiplied reflection for the creation of new wealth." Wang shows something really very similar at work in the algorithmic production of criminal data: "It is possible that as technologies of control are perfected, carcerality will bleed into society."[40]

Here I'd like to connect Wang's work to that of the late Randy Martin on derivative logic, not just of finance but of political and cultural practices, too.[41] We are all subject to a technics that now manages both differentiation and homogenization algorithmically. Perhaps it's not capitalism any more but something worse—another mode of production growing on top of it, where a vectoralist ruling class controls social space and extracts a surplus through information asymmetries, turning nonknowledge to its advantage.

Against this, Wang wagers on the Black radical imagination, in the spirit of Fred Moten.[42] She writes: "in the interstices of this relentless assault on black life, an insurgent black social-ity exists." She draws strength from the Black Lives Matter protests that started in Ferguson, from resistance to pipelines at Standing Rock and from Occupy Wall Street. But all were temporary. "The fissure was not a place where we could live. We could not hold on to the new social forms we invented in the process of revolt ... We failed to make the revolution our permanent home."[43]

Perversely, such moments weld people together in what Sartre called the *fused group* in the face of police (and private security) harassment and violence.[44] But that external gaze only fuses the group for so long. They dissolve back into seriality and passivity. We're left with the Black Liberation habit of "survival pending revolution."[45] Perhaps we need an alterna-tive technic as well as an insurgent corporeality.

Wang Hui: China's Twenty-First Century

It no longer seems all that persuasive to criticize China for failing to live up to the model of liberal democracy and liberal economy embodied by the United States. On the other hand, it is disabling to concede too much to the claim of China's unique-ness and opacity to the gaze from without. The work of Wang Hui treads a delicate but effective path through this dilemma. In *China's Twentieth Century*, he holds twenty-first century China to account through the prism of its own twentieth century cul-tural and political innovations: "Many show disdain for the political innovations of twentieth-century China, but can China today generate any political processes that can lead to a truly new and different future as it did in 1949?"[46]

Wang's work is not really ethnographic, and not least because the People's Republic of China succeeded in resisting and countering colonial control. China's return to world history in the twentieth century is one of that period's defining events, impossible to capture in mere outline. Both the achievements and the failures of the Chinese Communist Party are on an unprecedented scale.[47] And yet, given that much of the fate of global capitalism now rests in the hands of the Chinese Communist Party, China's twentieth century cannot be left out of the formation of concepts for thinking and acting in and against these times. Hence our lightning tour of ethnographic counterpoints to western-centric aesthetics and technics makes a stop here.

China is one of the main absences in Eric Hobsbawm's magisterial multivolume history of the modern world.[48] Wang neatly grafts on a new line of historical thought to it. In its effort to modernize, China had to transcend two earlier revolutions, bourgeois democracy and the industrial revolution, what Hobsbawm called the *dual revolution*. As the twentieth century began, three of the world's reigning empires came apart: Russia, Austria, and Turkey. It was supposed to be the end of the multiethnic empire and the birth of a modern political form in which state, nation, and people were one—except in China, where the empire did not fall. The 1911 revolution is the start of China's short twentieth century, but it did not break up the empire.[49]

The link between the former Qing Dynasty and the 1911 Republic was the doctrine of a sovereignty that resides in the people. But which people? Was China to be an empire or a nation-state? For Wang, "the continuity of sovereignty was always reconstructed, renewed, and never abandoned."[50] For intellectuals grappling with the problem of change within continuity, this could be parsed as a question of whether China should look more like the expansive Qing Dynasty or the more compact Ming. Overseas Chinese revolutionaries opposed the Qing empire and wanted something like the more compact Ming territory restored, as they saw things through the prism of racial discrimination.[51]

Should China be a multiparty parliament or revolutionary state? The former project did not make much headway, so many thought that integration required strong executive power. Not the kind espoused by Max Weber that was a neutral function, but rather an administration that could be an integrator.[52] But integration could not come from the top-down alone. Modern China had to learn from the people and mobilize them.

When the May Fourth Movement kicked off in 1919, it may have looked to Mr. Science and Mr. Democracy as its heroes, but the Great War had greatly devalued western modernity in Chinese eyes. China's revolution needed to find its own form. Politics could no longer be an extension of history as conceived by western modernizers; it had to rupture from it. What was needed was a new kind of politics, a cultural one. "Radical Chinese politics could not have arisen without the desire to break from the nineteenth-century political and economic model."[53]

Wang uses Antonio Gramsci's figure of the modern prince to describe a new kind of political party that emerged to fill the role of mobilizing a cultural politics.[54] Both the Nationalists and the Communists attempted it and shared an approach that combined political integration, social mobilization, and the confrontational style. After they turned on their Communist allies in 1927, the Nationalists abandoned this strategy, to their cost.

The Communists turned class into a voluntarist, self-making category, nominating the working class as lead agent of a socialist revolution in a multiethnic, agrarian society. This was not just class as structural location—there were comparatively few actual industrial workers in China—but a project of *becoming a class*. Wang: "The existence of the working class as an appendage of capitalist production—namely, a reified form of labor—is not equivalent to the existence of class politics."[55]

The Communists attacked the bureaucratic class composed of state officials left over from previous revolutionary efforts.

They formed a united front for the liberation of China from foreign oppressors, in which the party organized the working class, and the working class led a class alliance among the people. The category of the people implied a friend/enemy relation.[56]

The Chinese Communists succeeded in putting this theory into practice through some unique strategies. Mao (and Zhou Enlai) studied war doctrine and international law during the Japanese occupation.[57] Out of both study and practice came *people's war* as a political concept. War is a situation in which to create a new political subject and a politicized army. The war to liberate China from Japanese occupation had led to a new kind of party and army. In the base areas, land reform and military struggle became a mass movement. War could be won only by mobilizing the masses. The regular army was supported by local militias.

Wang explores these through the unlikely lens of the Korean War. It's a way of keeping China within a geopolitical frame of reference. Mao Zedong linked the Korean War to the Chinese revolution. Its success had revitalized anti-colonial movements, and its gains had to be defended. Mao was keen to disrupt the order outlined at the Yalta and Potsdam Conferences, in which the great powers decided the fate of Asia among themselves. Wang insists on the international as well as the national dimension to the war.

The people's war doctrine even extended to the prospect of the atom bomb. Mao argued that even such a powerful weapon could not be decisive. The obsession with weapons technology is the military view, but for Mao politics is at the heart of war. The high tech army is, in his famous phrase, a paper tiger.[58] The people, not weapons, are decisive in war. Wang thinks that the US understanding of China was shaped by the Korean War, prompting a new discretion. One might add, however, that the United States never grasped the power of people's war and has come to rely on weapons of remote-controlled slaughter—to rather mixed results.[59]

During the Japanese occupation, the people's war was possible because China was neither an imperial nor colonial country and had a weak and divided ruling class. The party could establish soviets in its base areas. Here its main political and cultural innovation was the *mass line*. The party had to create forms of power that solved people's everyday problems, to win trust and recruit soldiers. The key issue was land ownership, but the party also established its own practices regarding gender equality, labor issues, education, trade, even monetary policy. Wang: "The mass line was the basic strategy of people's war ... [I]t was the Party and its mass line under the conditions of people's war that created the self-expression of a class and, thus, a class in the political sense."[60]

The mass line means: all for the masses, all by the masses, from the masses to the masses. The mass line may have connections in Confucian tradition. Attention to rites and music (*liyi*) and not just statutory measures (*zhidu*)[61] helped to create and maintain a kind of regulatory order, what Wang calls *supra-representation*. Cultural movements come first, and political agents try to steer them. In its revolutionary phase, the party generated its own approach to culture and theory.

The era of China as a revolutionary state is over, but the form of the current state bears the marks of its origins, although perhaps as an absence.[62] Wang: "as China's public administration has shifted its role from political integrator to a nonpolitical bureaucratic system, the party-state has inevitably suffered a breakdown of representation."[63] After its victory, the Communist Party tried several times to keep open a path to its renovation through contact with mass politics, but with the catastrophic failure of the Cultural Revolution, this came to an end.

State politics fully displaced mass politics and a corresponding depoliticization of the masses. "The Party has submitted itself increasingly to the logic of the state, depriving itself of its essence, which should be a form of political organization and political movement."[64] Along with the bureaucratization of the party, there's the marriage of party and capital and the abandonment of category of class.

Wang frames this situation in an interesting way, insisting that the separation of the political form from its social form is actually common to formerly socialist and (formerly) liberal states. In both east and west, party politics becomes fully state politics, with political parties losing their heterogeneous quality: "It is the logic of the state that has come to control parties, not political parties that have come to control the state."[65]

Meanwhile, the media lost its public function.[66]

> The large-scale expansion of the media has entailed the contraction of the public sphere, as freedom for the media industry has replaced freedom of speech for the citizens. In China, though the media may appear to be controlled by politics, the political sphere has, in fact, been gradually colonized by the media ... In the political competition between the "partified" media and the traditional party that spawned this media force, the former possesses more political energy and style, and the latter resembles a hapless power apparatus that has lost its ideological function.[67]

Curiously, "today, the forces suppressing citizen's freedom of speech come not only from the traditional political sphere but from media power that has been corporatized and partified as well."[68]

The party still acts as the leading entity but no longer represents anyone. How it might be democratized may yet depend on its distinctive form and history. "Western democracy based on general elections is not the only model of democracy, nor is democracy a merely formal practice."[69] There might be other criteria:

> If a state's political system has a strong capacity to respond to problems, it indicates that the society contains elements of and

a potential for democracy. But because our theories on democracy focus so intently on its political form, they have neglected these substantive potentials.[70]

In China today, the dynamic of reform includes local experiments as well as negotiations between center and region. That might be a positive sign. With the weakening of political power, however, state power surrenders to networks of capital's special interests. "Hence, the crucial problem is not the privatization of state-owned property but freeing state-owned property in China from interest networks centered on capital."[71]

The Chinese Communist Party has frequently used violence to solve internal tensions. When Deng Xiaoping put an end to conflict with the party between competing political lines, he may also have weakened its ability to express and negotiate differences in concert with the people. Wang:

> The cruelty and brutality that appeared during certain line struggles have taught us a heavy lesson—that the [Chinese Communist Party] must resolve problems on the basis of democracy and law ... Today, the suppression of intellectual debate implemented by political and media power also marks the end of politics.[72]

The party no longer has much relative autonomy from the state and little independent theoretical space. Politics becomes management.

Wang: "Contemporary China is undergoing a historical process of class restructuring and the suppression of class politics."[73] This is not to deny the frequency of moments of labor resistance.[74] Worker's struggles today take the form of strikes, self-organization, attempts to shorten contracts, or creation of broader local or provincial associations. There's attention to protecting worker's rights. In situations of labor shortage, workers "fire the boss" and simply take off for another job.

But labor no longer functions as the core of a movement with broad ambitions. The suicide of Foxconn workers in 2010 turned into a discussion about how to reproduce labor power.[75]

The working class used to be a small part of Chinese society, and yet class was the mobilizing form of a revolution. Now China has the largest working class in the world, but it is largely absent from the larger political scene. The objective existence of a working class does not in itself generate a labor movement. "That the working class was the leading class was a political assessment rather than a positivist one."[76]

There are some distinctive features of the working class in China. The rural to urban migration is unusual in that rural workers were supposed to have rights to land from the socialist era. The workers in the state sector were organized in work units (*danwei*) that were not only instruments of surveillance but also of working class everyday life as well as its social life.

What is called the *new poor* is a different category. They have college degrees but make as much as blue collar workers. Wang: "They are products of a capitalist economy's move from manufacturing toward finance capital, from a real economy to a virtual economy."[77] To the extent that they give rise to a political expression, the new poor are not unlike those that generated Occupy and Gezi Park.[78] They are active politically, but within limitations. "Their inability to satisfy their material desires disillusions them, yet they constantly reproduce a logic of action that exactly fits with consumer society."[79] They are roughly analogous to what I call the *hacker class*.

The new poor can be distinguished from the new workers. The latter are mostly rural in origin, although the village home is more a symbol of something lost. They shuttle between dormitory and workshop, human social life reduced to the reproduction of labor power. They lack the security of the old working class. Their struggles as workers take some new forms, such as the foreman system, in which they use labor brokers as the interface with employers.

The old working class linked its fate as a class to that of the whole socialist system, rather than just protecting a class interest or the interests of individual workers. This connection between political and social form is gone. There are two broad approaches to resolving this problem of the crisis of political representation. Wang sees the notion of importing western-style multiparty democracy as the right-wing option. The left-wing option is to reconstruct political representation within the existing Communist Party.

Such a path cannot rely on traditional politics and must include postparty politics. Wang does not explore this, but these would have to include some that rely on a more recent kind of technical and media infrastructure (what Benjamin Bratton calls *the stack*) than the mass print and broadcast infrastructure common to the otherwise rather different eras running from Mao to Deng. If the media seem more powerful than the party, then a renewed party needs its own media form.

One could also phrase this as a distinction between the politics of the citizen and the politics of the people. Wang wants to rethink the politics of the people as one that can include the attention to individual citizen's rights but that does not reduce representation to the representation of the individual. His interest remains in the kind of "universality" central to a class politics in which the working class was supposed to be the leading class in a mobilization of the people.

Wang:

> I believe that as China explores transformations in its political form under these new conditions, it needs to draw on the egalitarian legacy of its revolutionary and socialist history. This would allow it to overcome the crisis of legitimacy that has arisen due to the incongruity of political and social forms.[80]

Could there be a new class politics? Perhaps. Modern class politics was always active in the zone where classes overlap, such as between workers and peasants. A class has to look beyond its own interests. Perhaps one might need to ask whether there are new classes that are potential allies or enemies arising out of novel forces and relations of production.

A revival of class politics might begin (but not end) with the issue of equality. Inequality is connected to a lack of public interest, which corresponds to erosion of public policy. For Wang that politics is more about affect than reason. It has to be felt before it can be thought. However, Wang restricts himself to the more conceptual aspect, looking at some established concepts, such as equality of opportunity, equality of outcome, and equality of capabilities.

The central aim of the labor movement is not to redistribute wealth but to liberate labor. When in power, it pursued the strategies of common property, converting workers into owners, and socialist production to satisfy needs through the production of use values. This was all sidetracked by a return to a developmentalism that favored the productive forces, giving rise to new hierarchies and monopolies within the socialist state.[81] The party shifted its concept of its own mission from being the leading agent of the working class to being the leading agent of the development of the forces of production.

Socialist states sought to overcome four inequalities: between workers and peasants, city and country, physical and intellectual labor, and majorities and ethnic minorities. One could well say that actually existing socialism especially failed to achieve these goals. *But at least it had goals.* Now we have the perverse argument that since socialist states failed to achieve their goals we should abandon socialism for a kind of state that seems to have the opposite aim: increasing inequality so as to accelerate the destruction of its natural conditions of existence.

The difference between Marxists and liberals is that liberals pretend to emerge as innocents from history. Still, for those allergic to thinking about what can be extracted from Chinese Communism, Wang also draws on other sources in modern Chinese theory and practice. The book ends with a tantalizing glimpse at what could be made of the work of Zhang Taiyan (aka Zhang Binglin 1868–1936) on the equality of all things. Zhang drew upon the *Zhuangzi* (aka *Chuang-tzu*), one of the foundational texts of Daoism, and from Mahayana Buddhism. The starting premise is that all things have the same nature and that the goal is the universal liberation from suffering of all beings.[82]

For Zhang, the equality of all things was more an ethical doctrine: each thing in the universe is deserving of respect. This does not negate human action but puts it in continuity with natural forces. Humans exist in both social and natural relations. Nor does it abolish the difference between humans and other things or among nonhuman things, but rather considers differences a prerequisite to equality. Inequality between humans and other things is tied to inequality between humans and other humans. Here Wang hints at how this might connect to Marx's theory of alienation. The exploitation of labor by capital forces a qualitative distinction between two kinds of human, which ramifies throughout all the other relations and things in the world.

Identity politics stays at the level of names and appearances, whereas the equality of all things is a politics of recognition that moves on to singular attributes but where singularity itself is shared. Difference is a prerequisite to equality. Equality is everything being free from appearances. Zhang rejected that modern theory of knowledge in which the relation between person and thing or even person and person is that between self and other, human and alien. He defined differences actively and does not take them as essential.

A consequence for Wang is that ecological and cultural diversity are related. He uses this as a basis for rethinking the question of minorities and their territories in the context of China. A region is a zone of both natural and human difference, shaped by climate as much as by social forces. However, "using a one-sided viewpoint to combat another one-sided force contributes neither to the protection of ecological and cultural diversity, nor to the achievement of equality."[83] The counterpolicy then has to be to absorb differences into equality and recognize them, while negating differences that emerge in the order of appearances. He is opposed to both the market and to identity because he recognizes the equality of all things.

While Wang is mostly concerned with China, to treat his work as speaking only to the local would simply reproduce an inequality in the world republic of letters.[84] He also offers insights relevant to other locations in geopolitics. His skepticism about the western form of democracy is understandable. It hardly stops western states from imperial and colonial actions, nor does it stop the exploitation of labor at home or abroad. Liberal democratic states have not led an effective response to climate change.

Even when focused on China, Wang is careful to put China into a geopolitics and a geo-humanities that extends far beyond its borders. He conceives of China as a civilization rather than a nation-state but is careful not to make the concept of civilization turn on any kind of identity or historical uniqueness. Wang: "Civilization is a social paradigm originating from long term relations from diverse origins developed through various forms of mediation."[85] Here his work can be usefully read alongside Kojin Karatani.[86]

Even the question of class and equality, central to his thinking about China, extends beyond China. "With the international division of labor, disparities between classes and within society as a whole has worsened in China. But these disparities are products of the international division of labor and, as such, aspects of larger systemic contradictions."[87] Nor do geopolitical questions stop with labor.

Climate change, the energy issue, cheap labor and even the mechanisms of state oppression are all integral aspects of the new international division of labor. The transfer of global industry also entails the transfer of social contradictions to developing countries.[88]

Understanding China in the world, and the world including China, "implies a need to analyze anew the internal contradictions and imbalances within contemporary capitalism in order to uncover and change their driving force and logic."[89] But perhaps some attention to the forces of production would help us here, particularly the incorporation of information into global infrastructure, the implementation of which is the condition of possibility of the current form of finance, media, and technology corporation. Information as a force of production also extends into industrial production itself, which is now governed by its protocols. Perhaps it is a matter of bringing together some lessons from the Mao era of putting politics in command and the Deng era of focusing on the forces of production, but thinking both outside the imperatives of developmentalism.[90]

Wang:

> The twentieth century has already become history. Even as China takes up its unprecedented role as factory for the world, what has been called the "post-industrial society" of the West has now reached the "end of the era of production," according to Baudrillard.[91]

But perhaps China is also in a sense postindustrial: It runs on a highly advanced and structurally distinct version of what Benjamin Bratton calls *the stack*, the layered infrastructure. Its algorithmic policing of its population is famously intrusive, although whether it is more so than in the United States is debatable.

If I may be permitted to speculate a little beyond the bounds of Wang's worldview: the so-called neoliberal state of the west is just one version of a more general concept of the information state. With the collapse of the financial markets in 2008 and the erosion of the integrity of the neoliberal state form that enabled it, China turned decisively away from such models, and in its place arose Xi Jinping and a far more state-centric model of the information state, one in which big data, mass surveillance, and market pricing mesh with public property, state control of the commanding heights, and a robust and outward-facing infrastructure development program.

Where the party of Mao focused on class struggle and the party of Deng on the forces of production, the party of Xi is something else altogether. The "thought" of Xi Jinping seems to imagine the party's leading role as being in alignment with world history.[92] Its mission is to work in and against a world order not of its making but within which it has more agency than most states, not least because it is on a far bigger scale than a nation-state. Its mission is to build a global infrastructure for an integrated system of information-driven production and distribution. Whether this can be described as a form of capitalism or not is a complicated question. It may well be time to think of it more as a normative model than an exception.

Occasionally, Wang offers glimpses of the transformation to which these developments respond.

> Finance capital has thrown off the constraints of industrial capitalism ... the high tech industry is parting ways with traditional industry... Even though we live in an age when class relationships are being reorganized, the revolution in electronic communication technology prevents us from interpreting the character of social mobilizations simply from the vantage point of class politics.[93]

Or rather, it calls for renewing the analysis of class itself. The new poor stand in a different relation to commodification than either the old or the new worker. They are the class produced by the commodification of information.

But just as the working class is more than a positivist category, so too is the hacker class, which is what the new poor could become. A class not only in itself but for itself. A class necessarily in alliance with other classes. A class that might point toward a new kind of class dialectic, in that their exploitation is more a matter of surplus information than surplus value. To some extent these are transnational phenomena. But they do have distinctive characteristics in China, where the build-out of the stack is more tightly connected to the economic mission of the state than is the case in the west, even if in both east and west the stack has a surveillance and policing function. The difference is now between China's civilization stack and a western transnational one, as interdependent as they may be.

Anna Lowenhaupt Tsing: Friction in the Universal Joint

To really know much about the big, abstract, universalizing forces at work in the world, Anna Tsing thinks we have to pay attention to what happens when they meet and collide with particular situations. And so in *Friction: An Ethnography of Global Connection,* she focuses on what she calls zones of *awkward engagement* or *cultural friction*: "Capitalism, science, and politics all depend on global connections. Each spreads through aspirations to fulfill universal dreams and schemes."[94]

It is not a question of preferring the local, the different, the marginal, or the specific to the abstract, the global, or the universal. In that sense this is not postcolonial theory.[95] But on the other hand, this is not one of those approaches, such as the Marxist, where the totality is the first and last cause of what happens in local situations.[96] It is more a matter of thinking again about these antimonies through a study of various competing universals as they get mixed up in local situations. Empire isn't total; the marginal isn't magical.

A *universal* here is some kind of knowledge that moves objects and subjects. It is both effective and affective, at least in certain situations. Universals can transcend localities, but they have not taken over the whole world. Tsing: "Why is global capitalism so messy?"[97] Perhaps because the implementation of its universals produces both abstraction and friction at the same time.

> Cultures are continually co-produced in the interaction I call "friction": the awkward, unequal, unstable, and creative qualities of interconnection across difference ... Friction refuses the lie that global power operates as a well-oiled machine ... Friction can be the fly in the elephant's nose.[98]
>
> How might scholars take on the challenge of freeing critical imaginations from the specter of neoliberal conquest—singular, universal, global? Attention to the frictions of contingent articulation can help us describe the effectiveness, and the fragility, of emergent capitalist—and globalist—forms.[99]

Global capitalism, if this is what this still is, might not be something that exists in advance and is simply implemented. "Rather than assume we know exactly what global capitalism is, even before it arrives, we need to find out how it operates in friction."[100] Moreover, it might not be the only thing going on in the world where a universal generates friction in its encounters with situations.

Indonesia provides most of the case studies here. It is the fourth most populous country in the world and the biggest Muslim-majority country. It is a major exporter of fossil fuels, rubber, timber products, metals, and palm oil. Whatever the statistics say, Indonesia is a place where universal commodification seems chaotic and self-destructive, creating uninhabitable landscapes. At the end of the Cold War, many client states of both the Soviet Union and the United States collapsed. That included Indonesia's New Order regime of President Suharto, whose thirty-one-year rule started to unravel in the economic crisis of 1997.

Suharto had "made business a predator."[101] His military-dominated regime was notorious for corruption and cronyism.

Take the example of timber: in the 1970s various political clients received timber concessions with an eye on Japanese markets. In the 1980s the government banned the export of logs to foster a local plywood industry. The fall of the New Order government disrupted the established patronage system and created a free for all, leading to a lot of "illegal" resource extraction. But throughout, economic and political actors viewed the forests as uninhabited zones for resource extraction, in the name of development and prosperity.

Tsing's interest is in what happens at the very edges of such abstract processes as development. Markets are not Platonic forms but are bounded by friction—and perhaps one might also say noise (Terranova) or nonknowledge (Martin). The frontier of capitalism is where soldiers and traders disengage "nature" from its local ecologies, cultures, and customs and treat it as a resource. "The landscape itself appears inert: ready to be dismembered and packaged for export."[102]

The frontier is a travelling concept.[103] It requires translation wherever it goes. In the tropical climate of Kalimantan, the frontier meets local practices of shifting cultivation where it is unclear which land is public or private and which land use is legal and illegal. The frontier doesn't recognize communal property, local custom, or indigenous knowledge. The result is what Tsing calls "the tragedy of the tragedy of the commons."[104]

It's a pattern of state-backed corporate dispossession whose agents may be armed gangs or other kinds of uprooted, masculine adventurers who take what they can and move on.

> Imagine for a moment a contradiction between capital and governance. Governance requires rationalization, clarity and order. Capital, in contrast, thrives where opportunities are just emerging ... In the deregulation zones where government is at the end of its tether, capital can operate with the hyper-efficiency of theft.[105]

And then it recruits agents of the state to enable that theft.

Even kinds of commodity extraction that are more orderly and technically complicated might involve friction. When the currency fell in the late nineties, Indonesian coal became competitive with Australian coal, despite the poor infrastructure. Tsing meets a manager sent from Singapore to speed up the loading of coal barges, which he achieves by purchasing a load of bananas that happens by and distributing it to the workers. The coal is destined for India, on a ship where the Indian officers and Indonesian crew have no common language and communicate with hand signs. "To produce a commodity is the work of the translator, the diplomat, the power-crazed magician."[106]

Where there's muck there's brass; where there's gold there's bullshit. Tsing recounts a story about a lone prospector who finds gold where nobody expects it, sparking all kinds of speculative adventure. The story is more truthlike than true. It is part of a process of an economy of appearances, of "spectacular accumulation." It's a tripartite relation between frontier culture, franchise cronyism, and finance capital. Local rights and land-use habits are waved away, creating objects of speculative desire and potential. Never mind whether the drilling samples are real. "Might deregulation and cronyism sometimes name the same thing—but from different moments of investor confidence?"[107] This is a world where Fordist production has not been superseded by post-Fordism, but rather where capital combines with, and is modified by, all kinds of friction generated out of particular situations.

A central part of Tsing's project is a recognizably ethnographic one, based on fieldwork among the Dayak people of Kalimantan, in the Indonesian part of the island of Borneo. They are an isolated mountain people who keep to themselves. Among other things, they practice what used to be called slash-and-burn agriculture. They grow a very mixed range of crops in a swidden, a cleared plot in the forest for temporary use;

then they move on to another. There is no clear demarcation between what is wild and what is cultivated. Take fruits: there's all kinds of durian, lychee, mango, and rambutan, some planted intentionally, some harvested from the wild. A fruit tree may grow out of a rubbish tip where people threw the seeds, and so on.

On this account the Dayaks blur the boundaries between a cultivated landscape and a wild one. Landscapes are supposed to be wild and untouched if they are going to appear within the frame of the universal language of either development or conservation. Here we have what Tsing calls a *gap*, where certain universalizing distinctions do not travel well. The Dayaks are however quite aware of such universals and put them in a sort of ceremonial place for community leaders to use on occasions that suit their interests.

Indonesian national resource policy goes back to the colonial days of the Dutch East Indies. Development divided the country into settled and wild zones, the latter being for resource exploitation. Planners can't see overlap between field and forest in the form of land use such as that of the Dayaks. To the planners, these forest people are outlaws and trespassers. This landscape inhabited by the Dayaks looks weird to both developers and conservationists.

How are such gaps in the fabric of abstraction to be perceived? Here Tsing creates an opening for an ethnographic practice. Not one that tries to reconstruct a precontact totality; rather, one that opens up the gap between a local practice and the universals that overlay their abstractions upon it. Hence in this case: "Instead of basing rights claims on equivalents to private property, we might train our vision on the overlapping socialities of familiar forests, as these empower and constrain individuals in using forest resources."[108]

When one sees what's in the gap, then maybe one can see forest people everywhere and other forms of nonprivate property claim. For example, it makes an interesting point of comparison to the invisibility of nomads to the Israeli state, about which Eyal Weizman has written. The empty forest and the empty desert are both figures of colonial imagination.

> What work has it taken to repress the social intelligence of the forest? ... Learning both with and against the natives whose territories they had come to occupy, colonial scientists concluded that this profitable-yet-fragile nature was transcendent, beyond the circumscribed knowledge of any given vernacular culture.[109]

And so an ethnography of global connection might work on gaps where the vector strikes against some sort of friction.

> Gaps develop in the seams of universal projects; they are found where universals have not been successful in setting all the terms. While a transcendent, non-social, global "nature" has become a powerful thing worldwide, it is not the only kind of nature on the planet. Whenever we want to trace the limits of hegemony, we need to look for gaps. An ethnography of global connection is impossible without this tool.[110]

This is not, however, one of those stories where the bad universal confronts the good that is local and specific. Tsing is interested in how different kinds of universal come into play. The New Order state succeeded even among its quiet dissenters to the extent that they had to use the language of development to articulate their own interests and needs. After its fall, abstract languages of law and morality, nature and the environment became rather more plural.

Environmental politics was one of the few kinds of agency available during the New Order. Even decades later, many people would remember that the New Order came to power through a wholesale massacre of Communists and many others merely suspected of being Communists.[111] Hence a certain prudence. But some legitimate actors within the state itself favored environmental protection, and so the issue was one that could be discussed.

For some, the environment was a legal and ethical issue. Or if the exploitation was technically legal, it might follow the letter but not the spirit of legality. Law became a way of holding the state accountable on its own terms, even if the abstract moral principles informing the critique sometimes owed more to Islam than to Indonesian nationalism.

A quite different kind of environmentalism arose out of the culture of the nature lovers. There is a long-standing tradition of university students forming clubs for hiking and other outdoor activities. They are young and cosmopolitan in outlook. They may be from the provinces but have gone to an urban center for an education and then experience "nature" from that point of view, as something to discover in its difference from the urban.

Nature lover culture is part scout troop, part woodsy romanticism, and part commercial adventure. It is partly about class formation, as generations of college-educated youth assume positions of relative privilege and authority in Indonesian society. While nature lovers are thought of as hippies, they generally need police permits or army approval for their expeditions. Nature lover culture is an instance of what Tsing calls a *contingent lineage*, or what Martin calls a *derivative*, or what I would call *détournement*.[112]

Before the fall of the New Order, concerns about the ethical integrity of the law and the nature lover tradition of nature appreciation were safe, apolitical, and nonconfrontational ways of creating some distance from state power and its habits of thought. They could be brought to bear on questions of the environment to the extent that the state itself was conflicted about the relative merits of conservation and development. After the fall of the New Order, things get more interesting. Islam, Marx, and Bollywood might all appear through transnational communication vectors as forms of abstract thought and feeling to be adapted for local use.

Tsing is particularly interested in transnational environmental activism after the fall of the New Order. "Regional, religious, and gender initiatives reach out to harvest allegorical packages as they zip around the globe, unmoored from their origins."[113] Jakarta was no longer so central. IMF pressure had reduced the scope for the state to secure consent through subsidies and selective rewards (as Achille Mbembe notes also in the African context). Political agency was in flux.

In this context, Tsing observes activists at work trying to stop logging in Kalimantan and drawing on abstract, affective, transnational forces to do so. "The effect of a new allegory is most striking when it inspires unexpected social collaborations, which realign the social field."[114] She listens to activists trying to motivate Dayaks with the story of Chico Mendes, a Brazilian labor movement organizer who worked with Brazilian rubber tappers and who made an alliance between them and North American environmentalists.

Strikingly, the activist telling this story appears to conflate the story of Chico with the story of Chipko, a very different movement in which Chipko Himalayan women protected their trees by putting their arms around them and refusing to move. The Chico story probably came from the movie *The Burning Season* (1995). The Chipko story has been popularized by the Indian ecofeminist activist Vandana Shiva.[115] Tsing: "Activist packages travel when they are unmoored from the contexts of culture and politics from which they emerged and reattached as allegories within the culture and politics of those with the institutional strength to spread the word."[116]

"Difference within common cause: Perhaps this is more important than we ordinarily think." The alliance of different kinds of universal language brought to bear to fight local issues is not without its complexities. Tsing notes the adjustments women activists have made to appear more "modest," adapting themselves to current Islam-inspired ideas about comportment. But it is refreshing that Tsing nowhere stresses any need for consensus, which became such a focus of activists at the time of

Occupy in the United States. "Progressive activists spend most of their time either searching for consensus or making a point of their irreconcilable differences. My story suggests other political avenues. It also suggests other methods for learning about the world."[117]

A project to which Tsing contributes here is what I might call *comparative universal studies*. Rather than compare different geopolitical units to one another, one could compare the trajectory of different flows of information and what it enables, both good and bad. Thus, it is worth recalling the Bandung Conference of African and Asian States of 1955, a landmark in nonaligned and postcolonial histories.

> In Bandung, the globe was a symbol of what might be possible … Science, modernization, and freedom were simultaneously dream bridges for the development of Third World nations and real life programs within the contingencies of Cold war politics, elite power grabs, authoritarian regimes, religious wars, ecological disasters, and bureaucracies of expertise.[118]

For all its limitations, one might ask how and why that global dream space disappeared.

Tsing is also interested in the universals of conservation and the environment. These she traces to what appears to be a kind of Protestant theology.[119] Nature has to be preserved, as it is where the nature lover can experience God directly. "Only because God was known to be universal could nature be depicted that way."[120] It is about individual and personal contact with the universal, but in the process, the collaborative work of producing nature for the contemplation (or consumption) of the nature lover is spirited out of view. Nature is wilderness, a view that produces particular difficulties in understanding the role of indigenous or local peoples in maintaining a landscape.

A historically novel kind of universal comes from the application of cybernetic techniques to earth system sciences.[121]

Tsing reports on her fieldwork among the climate modelers with an ironic touch. "They simplify and reduce the social and natural world to its geophysical laws." It is the model of the totality that becomes the source of political and moral leverage. The social labor of making the model spills over into modes of thinking and acting. "The global scale takes precedence—because it is the scale of the model." The model makers seem a strange culture to Tsing. The limits of their models breed other models that take account for the problems in the previous models. To be effective, "models must be charismatic and pedagogical."[122]

Rather than see only climate modeling as a product of postwar cybernetic technologies of control, it might be more interesting to see both earth system science and anthropology as produced by much the same historical forces. Both require a vast infrastructure of global vectors—one to collect data, the other to dispatch fieldworkers. Both grew out of projects of imperial resource management—one to extract resources, the other to deal with those pesky natives who got in the way. It is worth asking how the labor practice of making a model-based knowledge starts to shape certain ways of thinking and acting beyond it. But I think we have to acknowledge that anthropology is hardly free of analogous kinds of substitutions, from immediate labor process to the shape of the knowledge and politics it produces. It too is a particular kind of universal.[123]

In any case, the universal that seems always to have the most power these days is that of commodification. It recodes and reorganizes all the others. Tsing tells the sorry tale of the International Tropical Timber Organization and its attempts to create "sustainable" forest management, which mostly meant protecting the industry and timber prices. As Tsing wryly notes, "The organization would be divided into moieties."[124] There were bureaus for producers (such as Indonesia) and consumers (such as the Japanese). The organization ended up settling for spreading the language of "sustainable forest" and was quite impervious to any kind of local knowledge or tactic.

Given the bad record of modern forms of conservation (sustainable or otherwise), Tsing advocates indigenous conservation. She is well aware of the dangers of taking the indigenous to be some utterly other, timeless, or pure social fantasy. The progressive activists she encounters are careful to translate *indigenous* with terms that mean "customary" rather than "of the soil,"' as the latter has problematic connections to anti-Chinese racism. And yet with all those caveats, the indigenous might be the only actor one can put into play with some interests and some methods for living in landscapes without wrecking them.

> The crux of the argument about indigenous peoples and conservation is that the regularizing modern imagination has had *such* a destructive effect on species diversity that almost any other human lifeway is likely to be better at maintaining it.[125]

Interestingly, an indigenous environmental politics is still in some senses a universal or abstract one. Tsing notes in passing that slave labor and forced labor could not be made to do very complicated agricultural labor, and hence farm labor had to be simplified. Such was and remains the plantation system. This relied (and for Jackie Wang still relies) more on coercion than incentive. But as her own Kalimantan fieldwork has shown, indigenous land use can be rather more subtle and complicated.

The question might be as to how such an understanding of the implication of humans into what Haraway calls the *multi-species muddle* can be generalized.[126] Her informants are not necessarily more "spiritual" than other people. Nor are such nonproductive considerations absent. They are not driven by pure need. They might rather pose a challenge to ways of thinking that separate instrumental and the cultural and insist on a hierarchy between them. Thus, arguing that the indigenous rank the spiritual over necessity is to skip over the more interesting question of whether they can be separated or ranked.

Likewise, Tsing wants to put together perspectives from conservation biology and political ecology. The former takes the urges to survive and reproduce as a universal. Everything then becomes a calculus of population dynamics and inter-species competition. In that perspective humans can only be a threat. Political ecology is skeptical of such heteronormative and market-competition-based models of the natural. But they tend not to concede much to the natural sciences and dwell rather obsessively on the human.

Tsing's work is useful for re-engaging theory at more useful and interesting points. It is neither the relentlessly critical style that leaves no space for collaboration, nor is it the postcritical stance of actor network theory, which never met an institution it could fail to like.[127] It's more about a tactic of selective abstraction: "Universal claims allow people to make history, but not under the conditions those claims might lead them to choose."[128]

"Some fragments are able to make themselves look whole." Ripping the mask from this substitution of fragment for whole is not the end of the task. It might also be helpful to creatively make other wholes, as Viveiros de Castro suggests, even if none of them are ever wholly whole. One has to make decisions among which such whole-mimicking fragments can enable practices of collaborative knowing and working. "Despite the power of calls for a singular global science, I discovered environmental knowledge only in the joints of cultural and political encounter. Despite imperial standards for civil society, I have wandered into coalitions built on awkwardly linked incompatibilities."[129]

Collaborations create new interests and new ways of being. "Continued life on earth depends on getting our knowledge into as good a shape as possible." This point need particular stress. Before there can be talk of collaborative labor in the world, it has to exist among forms of knowledge production. "How do we convince people that life on earth is worth saving?"¹³⁰ Certainly not by endless arguments among ourselves about whose methods of knowledge work are best. Challenging the universality of the commodity form is going to take a lot of collaborations among disparate forms of knowing and working in which universals are deployed in local situations.

Achille Mbembe: Africa Contra Hegel

There was once a fantasy, shared by left and right alike, that the states of the underdeveloped world could come, whether by leaps or by steps, to approximate those of the so-called developed world, as if it represented some kind of historical destiny. This idea belongs to what one might call an *imaginary*, or what Chiara Bottici calls the *imaginal*: a world of signification that enables its unity and identity to be thought and enacted.¹³¹

For a long time, I found it helpful to borrow a term used by the Situationists and think rather of an *overdeveloped* world, as if the industrialized states had somehow overshot their historical destiny and ended up in some caricature of futurity. Lately, I've been tempted to reverse the direction and think of postcolonial states not as failed approximations of their colonizers, but to think of those former colonizing states as increasingly coming to resemble the ones they colonized—as Jackie Wang seems to have found.

When one looks at US political and cultural life, it is hard not to see strong similarities with third world states, including failed ones. But this too is merely to play ironically within a geopolitical imaginary in which historical time is at least supposed to have an orientation and a destiny. Perhaps one could go much further in undoing certain fixed contours of the geographic and historical imaginary.

Not the least merit of the writings of Achille Mbembe's *On the Postcolony* is the distance he manages to create, not so much from as within such geopolitical imaginaries. While one cannot claim to be exempt from such an imaginary, one can map its contours from the inside. "Domination consists, for the dominators, and for all others, in sharing the same phantasms."[132]

These are texts about the political-cultural imaginary that is "Africa." This is a place that exists in the colonial imagination and whose effects remain in what he calls the *postcolony*. Neither the discourse of African liberation and national self-determination, nor its neoliberal successor, have truly replaced that colonial imaginary. Furthermore, time isn't linear or cumulative; pasts and presents can have entangled relations with one another.

The Africa that appeared in the colonial imaginary is incomplete, mutilated, not quite human—what Paul Gilroy calls *infrahuman*.[133] It is a place of the strange and monstrous, but also of the familiar and intimate. It is a place for world-historical experiments, just not for Africans. Here Mbembe quotes Hegel to ironic effect:

> Intractability is the distinguishing feature of the negro character. The condition in which they live is incapable of development or culture, and their present existence is the same as it has always been. In the face of the enormous energy of sensuous arbitrariness which dominates their lives, morality has no determinate influence upon them.[134]

One could critique this sort of writing, but Mbembe does something else.[135] He makes Africa the actual location where this imaginary place undoes the self-creation of the very colonizing subject who proclaims and enacts it. The Africa that the west imagines is, among other things, the *locus solus* where that imaginary comes apart.

Colonizing peoples have a hard time with species-being, and as a result Africa has to be the prop of difference of last resort.

There's not much writing about Africa for itself. "More precisely, Africa is the mediation that enables the West to accede to its own subconscious and give a public account of its subjectivity."[136] Africa is where things just are, lacking any justification or logic. Time is time immemorial, lacking dynamics. Rather than having a different being to the west, it lacks being at all.

Africa reveals the problem of writing about the collapse of worlds. It is taken as volatile, unstable, but this instability is read as chaotic. "The upshot is that while we now feel we know nearly everything that African states, societies, and economies *are not,* we still know absolutely nothing about *what they actually are.*"[137] Social theory takes the first industrialization in Europe as a default model. The link between modernity, rationalism, and the west appears as more than contingent. The west remains distinct.

Critical theory has various objections to modernity, against positivism as an excrescence of a rationality of means, or reason as a mask of domination, or the alienation of the direct producer, or technology as metaphysics, or against the teleology and totality of enlightenment, and so on. But the rationality critiqued is still assumed to be western. Starting from conventions that are local, social theory remains provincial. But Mbembe does not particularly want to extend the critical or emancipatory project of the west to the African scene. He is not interested in an African modernity and its claim to an African humanity: "both the asserted denial and the reaffirmation of that humanity now look like the two sterile sides to the same coin."[138] Nor is there a pressing-on to the posthuman in a Black acceleration. Rather, he disrupts the whole spatial and temporal scheme of modernity.

> What distinguishes our age from previous ages, the breach over which there is apparently no going back, the absolute split of our times that breaks up the spirit and splits it into many, is again contingent, dispersed, and powerless existence: existence

that is contingent, dispersed, and powerless but reveals itself in
the guise of arbitrariness and the absolute power to give death
at anytime, anywhere, by any means, and for any reason.[139]

The colonial situation is one in which the colonizer cannot
recognize him or herself in the eyes of the colonized, for
the colonized is not granted the status of a rival subject but
remains a thing. "Colonial discourse is an aberrant product
of the madness that threatens all domination."[140] To the colonizer, the African has no needs or debts, prefers to be lazy
and poor, is untrustworthy and irresponsible, hysterical and
feminine, an animal or a thing. The land itself then appears
without master. The colonizer inherits no responsibility but is
surrounded by a noisy and excessive nature. The colonized is
just what appears, a body to be seized, harassed, compelled, or
as one of a group to be counted, classified, and so on.

In the colonial imaginary, the colonized doesn't really have
being. It just exists, without reason, the way a rock does. It
is nothing, and the colonizer's only action in regard to it is
negation, annihilation, an exhausting violence. And yet the
colonized is also there to be enjoyed. All that matters are the
desires of the colonizer and his *commandment*. Mbembe: "But
what would the colony be, if not a place where the European,
freed not only of inhibitions but of any need to keep watch on
his or her imagination, reveals his or her 'other' self?" Colonial
discourse is an autoerotic incantation. "As a miraculous act,
colonialism frees the conquerors' desires from the prison of
law, reason, doubt, time, measure. Thus, to have been colonized
is, somehow, to have dwelt close to death."[141]

This is the problem of colonial existence for the colonizer:
how to exist in a world where one dominates mere things,
incapable of recognizing that they are dominated? Hence "the
colonizer is only conscious of self in the enjoyment of the
thing that he or she produces and possesses, and the appetite
this brings." The colonizer projects himself outward, becomes

obsessed with hierarchy, counting, judging, eliminating. But it is enervating. "A time has got farther away, leaving behind only a field of ruins, an immense weariness, an infinite distress, and a need for vengeance and rest."[142]

The colonizer produces nothing but an enervated enjoyment of things that don't cohere or point forward.

> As a result of sticking together these bits of the actual, colonial discourse ends up producing a closed, solitary totality that it elevates to the rank of a generality. And so reality becomes enclosed within a pre-ordained madness. How could it be otherwise, since the actual is no longer perceived except through the mirror of a perversity that is, in truth, that of the subject uttering this discourse?[143]

The imaginary of the colonial state makes it the organizer of public happiness. But in practice it had no such extensive power. Sovereignty is arbitrary and cruel, as there is no underlying imaginary covenant. Sovereignty thinks of itself as a gift to the colonized. The native is at best a protégé.

As a consequence, the imaginary of the postcolony appears to inherit that of the colony. But in what sense is it "post"? The postcolony inherits from the colony a time that isn't linear or sequential. It is made up of disturbances, interlocking situations, some reversible. It calls into question the times of social theory, their developmental assumptions, of take-off and take-off failure. There may be nonmodern times that are not anti-modern. But in any case the horizon of the future is closed.

Governing, before and after colonization, is a matter of commandment, which rests on an imaginary of state sovereignty. Sovereignty rests in turn on a founding violence that gives the state the sole power to judge. That founding violence is converted into authority without constraint. To this is joined a kind of everyday violence, in acts and rituals. Anything contesting this violence as law is savage and outlaw. Sovereignty is exercised as an indiscriminate force that disqualifies its own negation.

No questions arise as to the ends of commandment. It is purely a matter of means.

> The lack of justice of the means, and the lack of legitimacy of the ends, conspired to allow an arbitrariness and intrinsic unconditionality that may be said to have been the distinctive feature of colonial sovereignty. Postcolonial state forms have inherited this unconditionality and the regime of impunity that was its corollary.[144]

Commandment acts with impunity because what it commands it treats as animal. This goes back to colonial times. The native is alien to the colonizer. The native is an animal with a bundle of drives but no abilities. There can only be domination. In Hegelian terms, the native cannot be the means through which spirit realizes itself.[145] It is possible to sympathize with the colonized, but only in the same way as the colonizer has affection for animals. The animal can be domesticated and groomed, but it is not human. To the colonizer, the colonized has only animal needs: to drink, eat, fuck.

Commandment crosses a boundary between what elsewhere might be public and private. It shouts its commands at any time. Commandment is outside common law, in a time and place of permanent exception. There is a delegation of rights to companies and colonizers, along with privileges and immunities. Commandment thinks it is both ruling and civilizing, but the latter just means incorporation into production, through coercion and corruption. The colonized are not recognized as having rights.

Civil society presupposes a distinction between public and private power. The colony lacks such distinctions. Nor does it have a distinction between right and force. Civil society presupposes autonomous institutions. Civil society contains a tension between inclusion and equality and exclusion and inequality (on which see Chantal Mouffe).[146] The colony and postcolony lack this doubly: as indigenous social forms and as colonial ones. There is undoubtedly much variation in the combinations of preexisting power and colonial power, and whether the postcolony is about exploiting mineral resources or cash crops. But in none of these various cases was the state formed out of reciprocity of obligations between a state and a people. There is no duty of protection.

The postcolonial state affirms the more despotic aspects of the colonial one, itself resting on indigenous power forms, sometimes reinvented for the occasion. These were often authoritarian regimes. However, for a while, postcolonial states did manage some measure of allocation of enjoyments and utilities. There was no relation between job and salary or salary and wealth produced. Jobs were distributed by the state to secure loyalty and gratitude and to model a form of obedience for the population. Salaries made subjection seem legitimate. They were not based on any imaginary of political equality and equal representation, but quite the opposite. Rather, they were claims through which the state created debts on society. They were about redistribution, not equivalence. "The means of livelihood he or she received were not designed to reward a process of converting energy into wealth, but were helping shape a particular figure of submission and domination."[147]

Economic things were converted into social and political things. It was a triple process: a state takeover of society, a socialization of state power, and a privatization of public prerogatives. Mbembe: "The allocation of utilities and means of livelihood has taken the form of a practically uncontrolled extension of the chain of privileges, material benefits, and enjoyments that the ruling clique has arrogated to itself."[148]

With the end of the Cold War and the rise of global vectors of communication and trade, these states did not do well. It was not possible to turn them into productive combinations for world markets. The salary regime gave way to survival strategies, including quasi-criminal ones among the rank and file of the armed forces, with a culture of raids and booty and an economy that looked more like war. Africa economies went underground. Export growth can't cover debt repayments.

Between the state and the individual was family, kin, and lineage, but these forms were weakening. A generalization of war and of forms of political mobilization are neither transitions to democracy nor disintegration. Casual and informal work becomes the rule. There is a general lack of security. Urban mobs, land shortage, refugee movements, mercenaries, criminalization of the ruling classes, and the militarization of trade become endemic. The implosion of the public sector blocks intracommunal transfers. There is a compensatory rise of Pentacostal religions, Islam, and so on. The withering of the state is also a withering of the market.

The postcolony now offers a form of private indirect government and "novel technologies of domination." Is this the final defeat of the state? Or a deepening of its local form? A weakened sovereignty gives way to the tutelage of creditors, ending the claims of citizens on the state and undermining the fragile claim of the state to legitimacy. The state no longer has the solvency that would enable it to act. It lacks the money and the goods and the administrative order to do its job. In Mbembe words, "the state no longer has credit with the public."[149]

So there is a restructuring of domination on other grounds: "the future of the state will be settled, as has happened previously in the world, at the point where the three factors of war, coercion and capital (formal or informal, material or symbolic) meet."[150] There are sales of public assets, an end to monopolies, the privatization of infrastructure, and a transfer of public resources to private capital, a privatization of sovereignty and of the means of coercion. Mbembe:

> One characteristic of the historical sequence unfolding in Africa is the direct link that now exists between, on the one hand, deregulation and the primacy of the market and, on the other, the rise of violence and the creation of private military, paramilitary, or jurisdictional organizations.[151]

To which one could add the purely privatized enclaves studied by Keller Easterling. "At its most extreme, the very existence of the postcolonial state as a general technology of domination is at risk."[152]

Populations become clienteles managed no longer through state salaries but through controlling access to the parallel economy. Offices are goods to be traded. People are no longer bound in networks of obligation, but subject to extortion and confiscation. Taxation is without representation and even without public utility in exchange. All this with international support, feeding a cascade of rent seekers. As Benjamin Bratton maintains, this may signal the exhaustion of the model of territorial state and the emergence of a new kind of geopolitics. Mbembe:

> As a result of these dynamics of territorial realignment and spatial dislocation, the real map of the continent is in the process of being reshaped along regional and international axes of traffics that both overlap and transcend the historic routes and networks of the nineteenth century trade expansion.[153]

With this comes a resurgence of local identities and of war, but which does not lead to consolidating a state apparatus. Mbembe does not want to put these developments on the old timeline of development or decline: "nothing allows us to say that, in the long run, prosperity and democracy cannot be born out of crime."[154] Perhaps, as in Kojin Karatani, the spread of religious and cult phenomena are signs of new value systems emerging.[155]

What was extended to the colonies was a tradition in which a sovereign is in charge of life, property, and the honor of their subjects. The postcolony has distinctive styles of political improvisation and creates its own imaginary world of meaning. "In the postcolony, the commandment seeks to institutionalize itself, to achieve legitimation and hegemony in the form of the fetish."[156] Or at least it tries to. The fetish is an object that aspires to be made sacred, but the fetish in the form of the body of the autocrat becomes unaccountable, arbitrary, reflecting only on itself.

Everyday life in the postcolony is not about resistance or collaboration, but is convivial, domestic, familiar, and at worst resulting in what Mbembe calls a *zombification* of both the dominant and dominated. But it may also be a ludic world of play. There is a gap between state-projected images and how people play with these.

There are ways people wriggle out of commandment. Commandment is connected not only to play but to the carnivalesque: "the purest expression of commandment is conveyed by a total lack of restraint, a great delight too in getting really dirty. Debauchery and buffoonery go hand in hand."[157] The postcolony is chaotic and lacks a stable sign system. It is a regime of unreality, a hollow simulacrum; the fetish of power is a sham and becomes just a thing again.

"The commandment aspires to act as a total cosmology for its subjects—yet, owing to the very oddity of this cosmology, popular humor causes it, quite often unintentionally, to capsize."[158] Commandment is extravagant; it has to feed itself and its retinue and clients and has to show publicly that it can do so. It is sumptuous, yet has to have both style and harshness, combining sexual subordination and anxious virility: commandment becomes a zombie.

Carnival praxis is hardly blasphemy or sacrilege and is more like a bodily mythology, a theophagy, a god devoured by its worshippers. Commandment is a right to punish, not to make useful. Commandment is a requisitioning of bodies for an economy of death, a necropolitics. It is a permanent public display of grandeur, but also of the loss of limits and of any sense of proportion. It propagates a cant language, implausible but locally intelligible, dogmatic and pseudoreligious.

There is a thirst for prestige, honors, gratitude, and no shortage of middlemen who preach before the fetish of power, rewarding its narcissistic self-gratification. What is central to commandment is the bodies of those commanded, which are used to entertain the powerful. Various cultural remnants from precolonial times are therefore pressed into service.

> Wearing the party uniform, with the image of the head of state printed on it, women have followed the rhythm of the music and swung their torsos forward and back; elsewhere, they have pulled in and thrust out their bellies, their undulating movement evoking as usual the slow, prolonged penetration of the penis and its staccato retreat.[159]

Commandment has a right to enjoy everything.[160]

> To exercise authority is, above all … for the male ruler, to demonstrate publicly a certain delight in eating and drinking well, and … in Labou Tansi's words, to pass most of his time in "pumping grease and rust into the backsides of young girls." The male ruler's pride in possessing an active penis has to be dramatized, through sexual rights over subordinates, the keeping of concubines, and so on. The unconditional subordination of women to the principle of male pleasure remains one pillar upholding the reproduction of the phallocratic system.[161]

The postcolonial imaginary is richly corporeal: "the mouth, the belly, and the penis constitute the classic ingredients of commandment in the postcolony."[162] Commandment is not just control but also conviviality and connivance. Ordinary people are constantly compromised but find ways to deceive and play with power rather than confront it. The commanded body breaks into laughter, which depletes the meaning of commandment. Mbeme:

> the public affirmation of the "postcolonial subject" is not necessarily found in acts of "opposition" or "resistance" to the commandment. What defines the postcolonized subject is the ability to engage in baroque practices fundamentally ambiguous, fluid and modifiable even when there are clear, written and precise rules.[163]

Relation between rulers and ruled becomes simulated in a hierarchy of mock honors and privileges distributed for compliance, creating networks of indebtedness and subordination.

In this imaginary world, everything has gone underground. The autocrat is both remote and close. He is everything at the same time, the all-purpose man, with an endless capacity to multiply identities. He is president "for life." But the autocrat is also a thing, an absolute subjectivity. "Since there is no subject apart from him, he is incapable of seeing himself as mortal." He becomes an arbitrary thing, and so, "voided of what he takes to be his substance, the autocrat, raw power, no longer belongs to the universe of crude, laughable, capricious things." The absolute doesn't exist in reality, so the autocrat's version is a caricature. His fear of mortality perpetuates itself as murder, as a reign of impunity. The autocrat's subjects are made to laugh and dance in spite of themselves. "How then does one live when the time to die has passed, when it is even forbidden to be alive?"[164] In this regard then postcolony might be a generalizable condition.

It is hard to say to what the genre of these extraordinary texts of Achille Mbembe might belong. Like any great work of cultural studies, its object is the truth of the imaginary itself. Mbembe: "I have tried to 'write Africa,' not as a fiction, but in the harshness of its destiny, its power, its eccentricities, without laying claim to speak in the name of anyone at all."[165]

Déborah Danowski and Eduardo Viveiros de Castro: Myth Today

Now that the world most of us have known is ending, it might be time to pay more attention to the experience of those whose world has already ended—indigenous peoples. As Anna Tsing reminds us, the indigenous is a slippery category. Depending on how you count it, there may be three hundred million or more indigenous people still on the planet. Most are survivors of colonialism. Like the rest of us they now have to find forms of life for enduring the Anthropocene.

Creating a relation to indigenous thought and practice is no simple task. The discipline whose job that is—anthropology—is implicated in various colonial projects and has to find ways out of this predicament from within it.[166] Certain self-aware schools of thought within anthropology know this and have various ways of counteracting the discipline's own imperial form. An open question might be how those approaches themselves might adapt, or be adaptable to, life in the Anthropocene.

Which brings us to Eduardo Viveiros de Castro's *Cannibal Metaphysics*, an anthropology on a mission to decolonize thought.[167] It is an anthropology of the concept, although not, as we shall see, so much of the practices from which concepts might be substituted. It might also be a kind of experimental metaphysics, or field geo-philosophy, with an ironic distance from the modern world that is its "natural" home.

Narcissus is the old god of anthropology, for his habit of looking at the other as a reflection that lacks being. As Mbembe reads the colonial imaginary: The other lacks reason, history, writing while Europeans are the supposedly fully realized (or realizable) people. The other reflects us back to ourselves through its lack. Against this, Viveiros proposes a *minor anthropology* that makes differences proliferate: not the narcissism of small differences but rather a bigger world in variation.

Cannibal Metaphysics is not a reflection on a double but rather a triangulation of the classic work of Claude Lévi-Strauss on Amerindian myth and then the encounter of Gilles Deleuze and Félix Guattari with anthropology. Lévi-Strauss once called the set of Amerindian myths he studied a "metaphysics of predation."[168] They map the relative status of predator and prey. He does not interpret these myths so much as translate them, or transform them. His *savage thought* is an image of thought, not of the "savage."[169] It can cast doubt on the categories that organize European mythology, not least the nature–culture distinction that is central to the organization of anthropology itself.

For anthropology, there is one nature, but there can be many cultures, and it sets about documenting and classifying them. Here cultures might be thought of, as Marilyn Strathern does, as specific ways of drawing analogies.[170] The Amerindian world operates quite differently. It is structured by a universality of mind and a diversity of bodies. "Culture" is universal and "nature" is particular.

Viveiros:

> If Western relativism has multiculturalism as its public politics, Amerindian shamanic perspectivism has multinaturalism as its cosmic politics ... Thus if a subject is an insufficiently analyzed object in the modern naturalist world, the Amerindian epistemological convention follows the inverse principle, which is that an object is an insufficiently interpreted subject.[171]

Viveiros is careful not to make this a simple reversal of terms. "When everything is human, the human becomes a wholly other thing."[172]

Myth is a time out of time, before objects and subjects became distinct. Myth is about what Deleuze called the *virtual* and its transformation into the *actual*.[173] "The heterogeneous continuum of the precosmological world thus gives way to a discrete, homogenous space in whose terms each being is only what it is, and is so only because it is not what it is not."[174] Myth is a passage from some sort of primal nature into culture. But Amerinidian myth reverses a western assumption: it is not that the human is differentiated from the animal in myth, it's the reverse. The common condition, the virtual, the primordial—is humanity, not animality.

Amerindian myth has another interesting aspect. Here all beings—the pig, the jaguar, and the human—see the world the same way, but they see different worlds. There is not one nature and multicultural ways of seeing it. To the contrary, there is one way of seeing a *multinaturalism*. There is no thing-in-itself. It may be not so much a variety of natures, so much as nature as variation that the different "species" (as science would call them) perceive.

In addition to being a multinaturalism, Amerindian myth is also a *perspectivism*. The human sees the jaguar as an animal rather than a person; the jaguar sees the human as an animal—but sees itself as a person. "In Amerindian cosmologies, the real world of different species *depends* on their point of view, for the 'world in general' *consists* only of different species, being the abstract space of divergence between them *as* points of view."[175]

Deleuze and Guattari's *Anti-Oedipus* offered an anthropological poststructuralism of flat multiplicities rather than hierarchical totalities, one that collapsed the strata of language and world into one.[176] This meshed with their refusal of any theory of desire as lack. Desire becomes desiring production. It's a monism that refuses any culture–nature divide. It's a baroque multiplicity rather than romantic organic totality or Enlightenment atomization. Amerindian myth may have a special role to play in such a project. "Perspectivism—duality as multiplicity—is what dialectics—duality as unity—has to negate in order to impose itself as universal law."[177]

Apart from a brief mention of Amerindian myth as a metaphysics of predation, there's not much attention to practices that might correspond to them, apart from shamanism. Here, shamanism is a political art. (Viveiros resists the categories of western economics, but art, politics, and the diplomatic get a pass.) Shamanism is a "diplomatic" practice of escaping from the limits of a human perspective, crossing borders into the social worlds of other species, administering relations between natures.

Viveiros draws a contrast between the human sacrifice of *vertical shamanism* and the cannibalism once practiced as part of a *horizontal shamanism* in certain parts of the Amazon basin. There, people would hunt and capture individuals from other groups, treat them with care, ritually kill and eat them. What was ingested is the point of view of the other. "What was eaten was the enemy's relation to those who consumed him, in other words, his condition as enemy."[178] The social body is composed by capturing symbolic resources from without. The material resources of which it might also be composed are not discussed.

There's a remarkable movie by Nelson Pereira dos Santos, *Como Era Gostono o Meu Francês* (1971), that I can't help recalling at this juncture. It stages this situation, of the care and preparation of the captured other, with black humor. In this case, the enemy is a white man. It's not a bad emblem for the alternative relation between Amerindian myth and western anthropology that Viverios is composing here, using the conceptual persona of the enemy.

Anthropology, like so much else in western metaphysics, may depend on the conceptual persona of the *friend*. We are supposed to treat the other as a friend, because the other is really like us, a mirror for ourselves. Others can be rivals, but they are not really different—that is, if they are human. If they are really different, they are not human at all, they are just part of nature and can be treated accordingly. Might it not be better to treat the other as an *enemy*? To Amerindians, other groups of humans are as different as other species. Each appears as an

animal, even though from that animal's point of view, we are
the ones who are animal.

Cannibal metaphysics might be a general method. "Against
the myth of method, then, the method of myth."[179] Maybe
anthropology could be cannibalistic, ingesting the other point
of view in its difference. The world does not become more
rational, but the rational becomes more worldly.

> Indeed, the *Mythologiques*, far from describing a clear, unequiv-
> ocal passage between Nature and Culture, obliges their author
> to map a labyrinth of twisting, ambiguous pathways, transver-
> sal trails, tight alleys, obscure impasses, and even rivers that
> flow in both directions at once.[180]

Which is where Deleuze and Guattari can help. The limit to
Anti-Oedipus is that the human scale is central. Its sequel, *A
Thousand Plateaus,* starts producing concepts that extend
filiation and alliance further into the nonhuman realm.[181]
Instead of desiring production, a concept of *becoming*; what
is produced out of nature is the human, whereas becoming is
a counterproduction, a participation of the human in nature.
"Becoming is the other side of the mirror of production."[182]
Production makes a world that is "like us," as if nature could
be remade as a friendly second nature.

Viveiros:

> So the question is not to unveil the naked truth about pro-
> duction supposedly concealed under the hypocritical cover of
> exchange and reciprocity but, rather, to free these concepts
> from their equivocal functions in the machine of filiative, sub-
> jectivating production by presenting them with their (counter-)
> natural element, which is becoming. Exchange, then, is the
> infinite circulation of perspectives—exchange of exchange,
> metamorphosis of metamorphosis, perspective on perspective:
> again, becoming.[183]

The slippage here is that becoming has only a symbolic dimension. This is a monism achieved by sacrificing any other materiality.

Anti-Oedipus, as is well known, is a text that grows out of the failure of 1968.[184] From that failure, we got the "neoliberal plague" and "the mystical nuptials of Capital and Earth." Here it might be worth revisiting Lévi-Strauss's distinction between hot and cool societies, which Viveiros mentions in passing.[185] The hot societies of the overdeveloped world really are a thermodynamics without equilibrium, using the potential energy of class antagonism or colonial exploitation, or what Raj Patel and Jason Moore call cheap land, cheap food, and indeed cheap nature.[186]

Deleuze and Guattari may or may not want to accelerate capitalism, but Lévi-Strauss had a powerful intuition of its consequences. Viveiros:

> For there are moments where a nostalgia for the continuous appears to be for Lévi-Strauss the symptom of a real illness provoked by what could be called the uncontrolled proliferation of the discontinuous in the West, and not just a simple fantasy or imagined freedom. The global warming of history, the end of cold histories, would in that case be the end of Nature.[187]

This question is taken up in a more recent text, co-authored by Déborah Danowski and Eduardo Viveiros de Castro, *The Ends of the World*, which takes as its starting point "changes in the planet's thermodynamic regime."[188] These might include climate disruption, ocean acidification, ozone depletion, biodiversity loss, nitrogen and phosphorous cycle rifts—in short, the Anthropocene, where we find out that "everything is thermodynamics at bottom."[189]

How does it feel to be human now? To be a human interpellated by this event of the Anthropocene?[190] With its *slow violence* (Rob Nixon), it's *weird hyperobjects* (Timothy Morton), it's *coming barbarism* (Isabelle Stengers), where dystopias become doxa, where there is, as Günther Anders put it when confronting the nuclear age: an absence of the future? It is hard enough to know how to feel when someone dies, let alone when a world dies.[191]

The thing about the Anthropocene is that "although it began with us, it will end without us."[192] To even think it is to find oneself in a space of myth as well as science.

> The semiotic regime of myth, perfectly indifferent to the empirical truth or falsity of its contents, comes into play whenever the relation between humans as such and the most general conditions of existence imposes itself as a problem for reason.[193]

A cannibal metaphysics might come in handy now. If Amerindian myths are also a philosophy, then occidental philosophy might also have the structures and genesis of myths. Even if those myths are passing: "Intriguingly enough, everything takes place as if, of the three great transcendental ideas identified by Kant—God, Soul and World, respectively the objects of theology, psychology, and cosmology—we are now watching the downfall of the last."[194]

In the Anthropocene, humans move from a biological to a geological agent. As such, it's the collapse of a supposedly foundational distinction between the cosmological and the anthropological that might found the myth we call modernity, with its bifurcated and stratified order of the human versus the world.[195] The thought of the end of a world poses a problem of the beginnings of both world and thought. How are world and thought correlated? The terms in play here beg for a semiotic square on which to arrange them.

The myth of Eden is a world before humans that is a world for humans, a world that is providential. Eden persists in the modern idea of wilderness. The word used to mean a barren place but evolved to mean the sublime. Wilderness became a positive version of the world without humans for an environmentalism that thinks of humans as external to it and

denaturing. Interestingly, the Garden of Eden of myth is surrounded by wilderness in the old sense, but for the moderns
the two become the same.

If Eden is a world before the human, there's also a world
after it, perhaps best known from the novel *The Earth Abides*
by George Stewart, or the nonfiction book *The World Without
Us*, by Alan Weisman.[196] There are also versions of the human
after the world. Then there's the modern who does not lose
but abolishes the world by Promethean conquest. The world is
made over as human, clear-felled by labor or industry, producing Heidegger's metaphysical clearing. "For all its openness, the
Clearing cannot but project an inverted image of its external
double, the vast, ferocious wilderness surrounding the Garden
of Eden."[197]

It is strange how the social construction of reality became in
reality the capitalist destruction of the planet.

> Especially in its post-Romantic phase, first with the various
> existentialisms and, later, with post-modern constructionisms,
> the rift between subject and world becomes ... an absolute
> ontological incommensurability that expresses itself in two
> complimentary mythical figures: that of the world's disappear-
> ance, absorbed by the Subject and transformed into his Object
> (a social construction, a projection of language, a phantasm of
> desire); but also that of the Subject's disappearance, absorbed
> by the world and made a thing among things, an organic con-
> traption assembled by a blind watchmaker. The crisis of what
> would come to be known as *correlationism* effectively began
> long before the name was coined.[198]

Against the world of worldless people, Quentin Meillassoux
proposes the (conceptual) erasure of the human from the
world.[199] Meillassoux's world is without a subject, dead,
glacial. It is like Kant in reverse, in that with Kant, losing the
dogmatic world of metaphysical philosophy meant turning
inward, to a marking-out of the limits of the subject. After

Kant, there would be no world other than through the internality of the subject, leading to the loss of the great outdoors. But the detour through the subject gives license to theological temptations. A subject might imagine it knows God. For Meillassoux, the erasure of subject is an erasure of the temptation of the divine.

Danowski and Viveiros would rather follow Steve Shaviro, whose solution is quite the reverse: the world is not only alive but sentient.[200] For Shaviro, Meillassoux's assumption that matter is passive, inert, dead, insentient, indifferent, chaotic only re-introduces human exceptionalism in negative, resulting in "a curious negative idealism, a weird cadaverous subjectalism."[201] It's donut anthropocentrism, empty at the core.

Danowski and Viveiros question the timing of this. Why this quadrant of the mythic universe of western thought, now that the Anthropocene cannot be denied?

> The anti-correlationism of Meillassoux and other materialist metaphysicians of his generation therefore sounds, probably against their explicit intentions, as a pathetic cry of protest, if not a magical formula of exorcism or disavowal, against the forebodingly realizing power of thought, at least in our humble terrestrial abode.[202]

If there is a world without us, then there is also an us without a world. It is perhaps what movies like *Mad Max: Fury Road* (2015) are about, or Cormac McCarthy's reverse passion play, *The Road*.[203] A more Promethean version (found much earlier in JD Bernal) is now called the *singularity*, in which worldless humans overcome species-being and worldly limits: "We will no longer be accountable to the world."[204] Everything will be human, or at least Californian.[205]

A variant of this is *ecomodernism*, with its promise of a good Anthropocene. (Good for whom?) It is basically business as usual and nature once again as providence. Curiously, we are to have no more resentments, but to feel instead a gratitude to the world. It is, as Danowski and Viveiros wryly note, a "marriage of Nietzsche and Pollyanna."[206] If there is not world enough for the commodity, then the production of commodities must continue beyond the world. Capital is to be re-enchanted as a magical agent.

The left wing variant is *accelerationism*. "The accelerationists basic intuition is that a certain world, which has already ended, must finish ending, that is, fully actualize its inexistence." They look forward to the full subsumption of nature into second nature, and then "the only way to conjure an Outside is to produce it from inside by driving the capitalist machine into overdrive."[207] Kodwo Eshun offers perhaps the most satisfying version of this. It was the mythic architecture of my *A Hacker Manifesto*.[208] Nick Srnicek offers a more moderate version that wants to believe again in the state.[209]

Danowski and Viveiros:

> Accelerationists believe that "we" must choose between the animal that we were and the machine that we shall be. In their materialist angelology, what they propose is, in short, a world without us, but made by us. Reciprocally, they imagine a post-human species re-created by a hyper-capitalist "material platform"—but without capitalists. A nature denatured by un-man. A materialism, at long last (!), spiritualized.[210]

It's Hegel for cyborgs. Labor spiritualizes the world. The becoming human of the world is the becoming worldly of the human.

Thus we have so far three quadrants of a semiotic square. The first is the world before humans: Eden (a world for humans) or Meillassoux's world that is indifferent to us. The second is the world after humans: *The World Without Us*, or environmentalists who want to restore some wilderness-Eden somewhere. The third is humans after the world: as excluded from it, as in existentialism, or living on badly after it (*Mad Max*, *The Road*), or living well after it: the ecomodernism (right version), accelerationism (left version). Here too is the Hegelian dream of a future overcoming of the difference.

The quadrant unexplored in this taxonomy might be that of the human as preceding the world. Rather than subtract the human from correlation with the world, subtract the world—but at the beginning. The Amerindian myths Viveiros anatomized in *Cannibal Metaphysics* can now take their place in a larger schema. As we saw, various subsets of the human changed into other species or into things. The part that did not change remained human. If in the west one is inclined to think of humans as the future and animals as the past, here is the reverse: a structure for thought that rather does away with attempts to find what is special in a human development out of the animal, in language, labor, law, desire, culture, history, or futurity.

There might be a corresponding Amerindian concept of time, a nonmodern one lacking modernity's distinctive, non-transitive quality, opening on to an ethnographic present rather than a historical present. This present epoch began when humans ceased becoming-other, ending a mythic, virtual time of transformations. A worldless humanity gives way to a world peopled by multiple peoples. The human is the active principle at the origin of a diverse world. It is a sort of inverse Garden of Eden. Humans came first. Nature separates itself from culture. Amerindian myth is not one with an "environment" that is external to the social. Rather, there are multiple forms of the social, populated by different species, each of which appears to its own kind as human. Every encounter with another species is war and diplomacy, embedded in what Stengers calls a *cosmopolitics.*[211]

Perhaps there's something to be said for such an anthropomorphism over an anthropocentrism, even a negative one like speculative realism where the very subtraction of the human becomes a relentless absent presence. Danowski and Viveiros: "we are of the opinion that anthropomorphism should be granted full philosophical citizenship owing to the as yet unexplored conceptual possibilities it opens."[212] To say that all the others are human is paradoxically a way to remove the specialness of the human.

Danowski and Viveiros press the point against speculative realism even further:

> Each object or aspect of the universe is a hybrid entity, at once human-for-itself and nonhuman-for-an-other, or rather, by-another. In this sense, every existing being, and the world as open aggregate of existing beings, is a being-outside-of-itself, being-qua-being, that does not depend on its being-as-other … Exteriority is everywhere. The Great Outdoors, like charity, starts at home.[213]

The world does not appear as a thing, but as other people. One place it appears vividly is in dreams, in which the reciprocal and exclusive perspectives of different social–animal worlds are permeable. Amerindian dreams are a world of cosmic war and diplomacy, whereas when white people dream they dream of commodities. In contrast, the Amerindian "present us with the politics of dream against the state: not our 'dream' of a society against the state, but dreams as a society against the state dreams them."[214]

Danowski and Viveiros want to confront Eurocentric discourse on the Anthropocene with a structure of myth alien to it, which might reveal its own mythic form. They agree with Dipesh Chakrabarty that it is not enough to redact the Anthropocene into a concept of the Capitalocene, because this leaves out much of what is really challenging about thinking the Anthropocene.[215] I might add this: even if capitalism were to end tomorrow, the problems of the Anthropocene are not then magically solved. I think the Anthropocene returns us to thinking what Marx, after Feuerbach, called *species-being*, but more as a problem than a concept.[216]

Here I agree with Chakrabarty about the need to conceive

of a geologically framed world history of species-being. But for him, this cannot rise to the level of a conscious agent of its own making. It is a universality that cannot subsume the particulars. As Viveiros says in *Cannibal Metaphysics*:

> one of the typical manifestations of human nature is the negation of its own generality. A kind of congenital avarice preventing the extension of the predicates of humanity to the species as a whole appears to be one of its predicates.[217]

But for Danowski and Viveiros, so long as universal history is qualified as *human* it can't really grasp the Anthropocene or understand what, after Stengers, they call the *intrusions of Gaia*.[218] While I would side with Chakrabarty in retaining a distinctive role for science, particularly earth science, as a knowledge of the totality, Danowski and Viveiros (and Stengers) regard this as part of the problem.

Bruno Latour has suggested that since humans are at war with the planet, it might be better if that war was officially declared, so that negotiations for peace could begin.[219] For Latour, Gaia is a common world, one that is perhaps divine but is not a God, more like a hyperobject. It is not transcendent nor an arbiter. There is no God proposition that can steady the partition between nature and the human. Nor can the distinctiveness of the human be assigned to that liminal category between animal and angel, as Giorgio Agamben notes.[220] But so too is the whole separation of human from world. This, for Latour, points to the end of the modern conceit of an exteriority of the human to nature, and the dual constitution that separated the politics of the former from the science of the latter. It is "the multiple organ failure of the cosmopolitical government (nomos) of the Moderns."[221]

Here Danowski and Viveiros are closer to Stengers, for whom Gaia is not earthy or divine but is fundamentally unknowable. Stengers is closer to those who for Alex Galloway point a way forward by refusing metaphysical exchange.[222]

Gaia is discordant, contingent, mutable. It dissolves opposition between an inside and an outside, between an organism and an environment. Gaia is a living and plural world. It's the wilderness in the Eden myth, but not balanced or stable or "ecological" and certainly not Providential.

Where Latour, Stengers, and Danowski and Viveiros are close is in the desire to flatten out a hierarchy of forms of knowing and acting in the world (or perhaps inverting it). They are for little science against big science, a secular, local, and slow science. They take their distance from both Marxists and post-Marxists who still depend on intensified modernity, the cult of nature and reason. For them the Anthropocene preempts any Anthropos, be it class (Andreas Malm), the multitude (Paolo Virno), or the popular (Chantal Mouffe). A multiplicity of peoples must be acknowledged, not all of them human.[223]

If there is a cleavage to think politically, for Danowski and Viveiros it is between *humans* and *terrans*. Humans are still trying to live in the Holocene. Terrans might be a network of Latourian small science people, but they are not a majority and never can be.[224] The indigenous population of South America was larger than Europe at the time of conquest, which eliminated more than 90 percent through war and disease. It was a vast act of extinction. But many survived and went on in a different world.

The genocide of the Amerindians was the beginning of the modern world for Europeans, but the indigenous remain as "veritable end-of-the-world experts." Since they have already survived endings of worlds, they may be better equipped for the Anthropocene. Their project might be a nonmaterial intensification of life, toward a molecular un-civilization, developing "technologies" that may have nothing to do with labor or production. Hacks and exploits are inherent in all forms of life. "The ethnographic present of slow societies contains an image of their future."[225]

Perhaps here we could apply the same fourfold scheme to praxis that Danowski and Viveiros develop for myth. What if we abandoned the narrow model of politics as friend versus enemy and thought as well about what I call the *nonfriend* and the *nonenemy*, a (mythic) structure of the in-*and*-against. Amerindian myth may even have a lot to tell us about this. Even if its core conceptual persona is the enemy rather than the friend, the diplomatic negotiations of its cosmopolitics may have all of these kinds of actor.[226]

Danowski and Viveiros: "the relation between humanity and world can begin to be thought as the relation connecting the one side of a Möbius strip to another." This might require a quite different concept and a myth, adequate to the times. "There are many worlds in the World." That plurality might include ways of thinking and acting on a "political ecology of deceleration."[227]

"Thinking the world as transcendentally heterogeneous to Man, Moderns thought it as empirically 'gratis', inexhaustible and infinitely available for appropriation."[228] Paradoxically, thinking the world anthropocentrically, as made of us, might be one of the few ways to get humans to think like terrans by raising the world's value. In the language of the moderns, I have followed Bogdanov in conceiving of labor as in-*and*-against nature.[229] But one might also, in the language of the nonmoderns, conceive of the hunter as *against-and-in* the human. Maybe there are ways, across the full four quadrants of possible mythic encounters, to be productively nonfriends or diplomatically nonenemies.

That would at least get the humans and terrans talking. Even if it does not quite get to what I have called the *Carbon Liberation Front* or what Elizabeth Povinelli refers to as the *geontology* of powers that structure the relation between life and nonlife.[230] There may be ways of thinking the mediating role of nonhuman technics—a topic quite absent here—in constructing actual relations between life and nonlife besides mythic and symbolic ones, but without excluding them. There are further steps yet to be taken in the collaborative production of knowledge, in and for the Anthropocene.

Eyal Weizman: Climate Colonialism

The climate wars have already started. The "aridity line" is usually considered to be 200 mm of annual rainfall. Below that, you have desert. One could draw lines on a map of Africa, the Middle East, and Central Asia that mark the boundary between desert and conventionally arable land. These lines are moving, as temperatures and rates of evaporation rise, causing all sorts of strife in Eritrea, Ethiopia, Somalia, Sudan, Chad, Niger, Mali, Mauritania, Senegal, Syria, Iraq, Iran, Afghanistan, and Pakistan. As Eyal Weizman notes in *The Conflict Shoreline*:

> Plotting the location of western drone strikes on meteorological maps demonstrates another astounding coincidence: many of these attacks—from South Waziristan through northern Yemen, Somalia, Mali, Iraq, Gaza, and Libya—are directly on or close to the 200 mm aridity line.[231]

In parts of North Africa and the Middle East, modernizing states of the twentieth century tried to push back the aridity line with industrial irrigation infrastructure and farming techniques—akin to what Anna Tsing calls the *plantation system*. This too might be a contributing cause of desertification, as some of these techniques might not be designed to last. Sometimes the expansion of modern agriculture was at the expense of low intensity desert agriculture and pastoral practices, which had endured for centuries. For example, the Bedouin people found themselves subjected to state control through displacement and concentration.

The best-known school of historical thought to take climate into account is that of Ferdinand Braudel.[232] For him, climate was a long-run, mostly stable and periodic layer to historical time. In this he was already clearly a European thinker. Those of us who come from the more capricious world of the Pacific Ocean's El Niño system might not see the old climate quite that way.[233] In any case, Braudel was a Holocene thinker, where climate changed more slowly than historical time. That may not be the case in the Anthropocene. Weizman:

> The climate can no longer be considered a constant ... The current acceleration of climate change is not only an unintentional consequence of industrialization. The climate has always been a project for colonial powers, which have continually acted to engineer it.[234]

Weizman's research methods are from architecture, and among other things show what a kind of architectural research and theory can offer. In *Hollow Land: Israel's Architecture of Occupation,* Weizman argued against the geography of stable places, but rather that "frontiers are deep, shifting, fragmented and elastic territories. Temporary lines of engagement, marked by makeshift boundaries, are not limited to the edge of political space but exist throughout it in depth."[235] The border is in a field of tension with the center.

In situations of conflict about borders, "the mundane elements of planning and architecture have become tactical tools." His key field site was and remains Israel/Palestine, a double territory of "two insular national geographies occupying the same space," a space that includes the volumes of air space above as well as the volumes of mineral rights and so forth below. He introduced a "politics of verticality" into geospatial work.[236]

This was something of a change of direction in architectural research. After the heroic years of modernism, the researcher had turned to *learning from Las Vegas*, from the vernacular, the semiotic, and above all the market.[237] For Weizman and other practicing architects, the new style "involved turning observations into concepts, concepts into tools and tools into design methodologies applied to the construction of building."[238]

But architecture in a zone of conflict, even if it seems far from the border, cannot honestly share in such a program. It has to negotiate a relation between a professional and a political role. Research can't lead to construction. In 2002 Weizman and Rafi Segal collaborated on *A Civilian Occupation*, a project commissioned by the Israeli Association of Architects,[239] who then tried to stop it being shown at the 2002 Berlin Architectural Congress (and destroyed five thousand copies of the catalog). Ironically enough, the resulting controversy made the project famous, which led to a series of commissions worldwide. Here Weizman showed the value of a kind of countermapping, perhaps even a cognitive mapping.[240] This developed into a practice of forensic architecture.[241]

I was fortunate enough to hear Weizman present both the concept and some projects in forensic architecture at the Graduate Institute for Design, Ethnography & Social Thought seminar at The New School.[242] While he was a bit wary of this reading, I proposed that Weizman has opened up a whole fourth quadrant in the practice of architecture. In the old days, architecture was obsessed with the thing itself, the building. Given that fancy architecture schools sometimes think mere building is beneath them, one has to stick up for the humble practice of getting buildings done on time and on budget and that don't leak.

Besides the thing itself, architecture concerns itself with two kinds of sign about it: iconic signs and symbols. Iconic signs resemble the thing itself. They are the plans and elevations and isometrics. The more symbolic architecture is that of language, the word, the logo, and so forth. The postmodern turn shifted the emphasis from the iconic to the symbolic. Weizman has created an architecture about a whole other kind of sign—the index.

Indexical signs are traces of events: where there is smoke, there is fire.[243] Yet the smoke does not resemble the fire; it is not an icon. Nor does it have a code like a symbolic sign system. Forensics is a matter of working backward from the index to the event of which it is the sign, like in a detective story. A forensic architecture takes as its subject events that happen or don't happen in built space, including the destruction of built space.

This seems to me to be a very useful method for what one might call an *ethnography of environments*. Here I am thinking of environments as ground, in relation to the social as figure. The ethnographic, to the extent that it focuses on cultural forms, is good at distinguishing the nuances of how such forms both differ from some putative colonizing standard, while only appearing as such to the ethnographer who is implicated in such a relationship. The ethnographic is not good at technics, at the instrumental form of human social action, in and against nature. This seems to have been left to more "scientific" branches of anthropology.

How then might cultural anthropology expand beyond the social organization of subjective experience? What Weizman offers in this regard is an aesthetics that is focused on media generated by agencies of power or which can be appropriated from them. It is an aesthetics of absence. It tries to find an order for what it finds interesting (in Ngai's sense) about what has been erased or is below the threshold of resolution. What is interesting is what is not directly pictured or is out of the frame. The power of the colonial gaze may very well be one that is othering, classifying, and in particular erasing.[244] But it can't help but leave indexical traces. Even if you erase the other, you leave the mark of the erasing. Weizman finds a positive use for what Steyerl calls the *proxy*.

A fine example of this ethnography of environments is *The Conflict Shoreline*, which contains Weizman's text and magnificent photographs by Fazal Sheikh from his *Erasure Trilogy*.[245] This book was submitted as evidence for the Truth

Commission on Responsibility of Israeli Society for the Events of 1948–1960 in the South. Here, Weizman's focus shifts from Israel's relation to Palestine to its relation to the Bedouin of the Negev desert.

The subject of the book is a small subset of the issues happening all along the line of aridity running across North Africa and the Middle East: the battle over the Negev: "a systematic state campaign meant to uproot the Bedouins from the fertile northern threshold of the desert, concentrate them in purpose-built towns, located mostly in the desert's arid parts, and hand over their arable land for Jewish settlement."[246]

Between 1948 and 1953, about 90 percent of the 100,000 Bedouin were forced out of Negev into Gaza, the West Bank, Jordan, and Egypt. About 12,000 became Israeli citizens but were relocated to an arid and salt afflicted zone of the Negev that was under military rule until 1966. After that, they were relegated to concentration townships. The Bedouin tried repeatedly to return to their land, only to be treated as trespassers and to have their settlements demolished.

What makes this a story about climate and colonialism is that the border of the desert itself is a meteorological fact rather than just a cartographic one. It is marked by the 200 mm annual rainfall isohyet—or rather by a line arrived at by averaging the recorded rainfall for several successive years. Below 200 mm, "farming" is not supposed to be possible. But this all depends on what one thinks constitutes farming. The aridity line is "defined by an interplay between meteorological data (rainfall/temperature), patterns of human use (modern agricultural practices), and plant species (the cereal types used in intensive farming)."[247] But the Bedouin can use much lower rainfall levels to farm. This is an inconvenient fact for a colonial narrative in which settlers make an empty desert bloom with their imported farming methods.

A juridical procedure arose after the founding of Israel to displace Bedouin based on the aridity line. Permanent agricultural settlement was held not to be possible below the aridity line. And so the law could not recognize any Bedouin property rights in the arid zone. Indeed, in 1975 land taken from the Bedouin was declared state land by the Ministry of Justice. It's a version of the doctrine of *terra nullius* familiar to those of us from other parts of the colonial new world.[248] Thus, half of Israel's total land area became an "empty" place, but with the interesting feature that dispossession is coextensive with a meteorological definition of the desert. "The aridity line has become the sharp edge of a legal apparatus of dispossession."[249]

Legal history is always a nuanced and complicated affair, but this ought not to exclude an appreciation of the hard edge of power within it. Before the Negev was under the jurisdiction of Israel, there were the British and before them the Ottoman empire. The 1858 Ottoman land law distinguished between cultivated and uncultivated land. It granted private ownership to those who cultivated barren land and withdrew it if cultivation ceased.

The Bedouin tended to ignore attempts by the Ottomans and later by the British to register their tribal lands and agricultural fields, because they did not want to pay taxes on them to an external power. The Ottomans granted *de facto* autonomy to the Bedouins to maintain their customary land law, and the British continued this practice. Neither power really governed beyond the aridity line. Israel applied the parts of the previous land regulation from Ottoman and British times that suited it. It declared the land uncultivated but did not recognize local land ownership practices. It was "dead land" that Israel would "make bloom." The abstract line of the isohyet began to have real effects.

Weizman details a 2009 court case in which Bedouin tried to reclaim their land, but the courts discounted oral testimony and relied instead on written accounts by European travelers in the Negev. One account is Edward Palmer's 1871 book *Desert of the Exodus*, which Edward Said discussed in his *Oriental-ism*.[250] Palmer had a genocidal hatred of the Bedouin, and yet even his account could be read as offering evidence of settle-ment. The court chose to see how barren the land looked to him rather than that he was witnessing the place in a time of drought.

Another contested source of evidence is aerial photography from 1917. Bavarian pilots surveyed the Negev for the Germans. But then there were the military successes of Auda Abu-Tayeh, working with T. E. Lawrence "of Arabia," and also the arrival of the Egyptian Expeditionary Force, led by the British. The Germans left as the fortunes of war turned against them.

After the war, Winston Churchill promoted air power. The British ruled the desert from the air. They bombed civilian pop-ulations during the Arab revolt of 1936–9. As Sven Lindqvist shows in his remarkable *A History of Bombing*, the systematic bombing of civilian populations happened in colonial wars before being imported to the European theatre.[251] However, the Brits did not get around to an aerial survey again until 1945. Some of this recon was leaked to Zionist paramilitaries and used in their occupation.

Weitzman offers a close reading of both the 1917 and 1945 photographs. "Just like a film, the surface of the earth is a recording device. Just like the terrain, the image has a distinct material topography." The problem for the Bedouin's legal case is that whatever marks they may have left on the ground are below the "threshold of detectability."[252] Their low-impact structures are more or less the size of the film grain. While the 1917 images are from summer, the more detailed 1945 ones are from winter, when the crops are gone.

Photographing the Negev is best after a rainfall, from October to November, which is the start of the rainy season. The optics are at their best, particularly early in the morning, when the shadows are long. These were the conditions under which Fazal Sheikh made his images, flying at 2,000 feet in a Cesna with the door removed. He flew only on weekends when there were no military training flights. The Negev is a cluttered airspace. "This complex volume is an integral part of the architecture of the Negev."[253]

The photographs are not self-evident. They have to be read. You can miss the signs of past habitation. The narrative about the Negev that you bring to the act of interpretation shapes vision. For example, there are two views about what happened to the abandoned ancient cities of the Negev. One theory is that more than two millennia ago, a slow movement of the aridity line northward made them no longer viable. Another theory is that desertification was all caused by Arab neglect, reversed by Israel's energetic policy of making the desert bloom.

In the latter view the Bedouin, and the Arabs in general, are considered the fathers, not the sons of the desert. But as Weizman argues: "Rather than neglecting the Negev, the Bedouins were the only people to have maintained their ancient knowledge of the land and further developed the existing infrastructure of ancient runoff farming."[254] Sometimes they even maintained and built on the ancient systems themselves.

After the explusion of the Bedouin from the better Negev land, the Israelis adopted a different approach. They constructed water pipes underground, for security reasons. The Jewish National Fund planted European style forests as a mode of local climate modification. They were creating "geopolitical facts" in the desert.[255] Place names were changed. The Green Patrol, established in 1977, used the language of nature preservation against indigenous land use. Bedouin settlements are destroyed as interfering with "nature."

But the Negev is still a desert, and desertification is increasing. This may partly be linked to unsustainable farming practices. But it may also be related to anthropogenic climate change. The whole story may be becoming part of the unfolding of the climate wars all along the aridity line. It is possible that climate is one of the drivers of regional instability. In 2013 Israel fenced off its border with Egypt and built detention camps for refugees and migrants. The Bedouin, being stereotyped as "nomads," are suspected of weapons smuggling; they are closely policed. The Jewish National Fund responded to desertification with even more forests, which is part of a general use of "ecology" as a political tool.

While moving the Bedouin away from the arable parts of the Negev, the Israeli state has also established military firing ranges and dangerous industrial facilities close to where they have been settled. As Andrew Ross found in the rather different desert landscape of Phoenix, Arizona, there's a kind of spatial injustice by which the toxic is distributed, and thus one has to be wary of "green" projects that merely displace hazards elsewhere.[256]

In his magnificent novel, *The City & The City*, China Miéville coined the verb to *unsee*.[257] In the novel, the context is two cities interwoven into each other where citizens of each have to unsee the other, even when they are on the same street. It is possible that Weizman's early work on the architecture of Israeli occupation was one of Miéville's sources. But it seems to me that the notion of unseeing has a broader application. One can unsee the history of Bedouin land use. One can unsee the effects of anthropogenic climate change. One can unsee refugees and migrants pouring out of parts of the world that may have been destabilized at least in part by climate change.

Weizman's forensic architecture offers powerful tools for seeing again what has been unseen by certain regimes of visual power. Images can pass through the world and leave little trace, like Hito Steyerl's *poor images*.[258] But architecture leaves traces. It leaves indexical signs even when the architecture is erased. Forensic architecture intervenes in the sensoria of technical images to generate a counteraesthetics that can lead to a counterethnography.

Weizman and his collaborators in Forensic Architecture were nominated for the prestigious Turner Prize in 2018. They did not win it. Work this challenging rarely does win such things. It combines a distinctive aesthetics of the index that pays attention to what is absent with a sensitive ethnographic approach to cultural, social, and political forms of life that questions the myths of development. More than that: it is also a technics of perception that touches on the implications of those specific technics into a larger technical layer.

III

Technics

Cory Doctorow: Information Wants to Be Free, But …

It is hard to imagine anyone better qualified than Cory Doctorow to figure out what is and isn't in the interests of artists and creators in today's media landscape. Doctorow was a Canadian version of a "red diaper baby," born to Trotskyist militants. His parents were schoolteachers, both with advanced degrees in education, his father's in mathematics and computation. Doctorow dropped out of college to program, founded a software company, and then went to work for the Electronic Frontier Foundation.

In 2001 he joined boingboing.net, one of the first successful blog-based online magazines, where a typical headline might read "3D Printer Creates DRM-free DIY Steampunk Unicorn Tattoos." Doctorow is also the author of a series of science fiction novels, both for adult and young adult readerships, including *Little Brother*, which begins in a scarily realistic high school locked down by the most ridiculous surveillance, and *Walkaway*, about the difficult politics and technics of autonomous life.[1]

In his nonfiction book, *Information Doesn't Want to Be Free*, Doctorow has produced an essential primer for navigating the shark-infested waters of today's media, from the point of view of the artist or creator.[2] As such, it can be read alongside similar books by Douglas Rushkoff and Astra Taylor.[3] It has a small amount of very good advice about how to figure out what is in the creator's interests. Most of the book is about what he calls *investors* and *intermediaries* (two competing factions of what I call the *vectoralist* class) and how the ways they advance their interests conflict with those of *creators* (or what I call the *hacker* class).

Doctorow comes closest among recent authors to an auto-ethnography of the interests of creators as a *class* interest. What I mean by that is that while, say, musicians and writers and video-makers might think they are making very different things in different styles, they are all going to need investors and intermediaries who have the resources to realize the idea of the work and the means to get it to that fourth term in our story—*audiences*.

Creators are a bit different from other workers, in a couple of ways. First, a lot of what creators make these days takes the form of information. The product of the labor is a file you can copy, regardless of whether the file is text or sound or images or moving images. Second, where labor makes the same thing over and over, the creator makes different things. The whole point of being a creator, and the value of what the creator makes, is that it's at least a bit different. Third, while creators, like workers, don't own the means of production, they don't usually sell their labor power itself. They sell the rights to reproduce their work and make money from it.

From the point of view of the creator, it can be a tricky business working out what is in one's interests. Audiences, like creators, usually don't own the means of making and distributing creative work beyond a few copies. The overwhelming fact about life in this overdeveloped world of ours is that we don't make our own culture for each other. There's a whole host of culture industries and communication industries in between the creator and the audience.

The relationship of creator to audience is mediated by what Doctorow calls investors and intermediaries, which correspond respectively to the culture industry, or Hollywood, and the internet-based communication industry, or Silicon Valley. The investors and intermediaries are perhaps two aspects of

to capture by the big industry players. For a long time, folk music and the blues were not even considered proper music, and these creators got nothing. Still, in the twenty-first century, we now have pretty good tools to actually track exactly who plays which song or which TV show or what not. A system that was simple enough and that set affordable license fees could probably drive a lot of piracy out of business. As the early days of iTunes showed, a lot of people would happily pay for a convenient kind of intermediary to their music, particularly if they thought the artist got some of the money.

A compulsory license does however involve a trade-off. It's a system where anyone can copy something so long as they pay the license. This is how bands get to cover songs written by other bands. The original songwriter might hate the cover version, but so long as the appropriate fee is paid, there's nothing she or he can do about it. So there's a sacrifice of a so-called *moral right* of the creator here, in the interest of a system were the creator could get paid. Or some creators: this is also how Elvis became famous recording a song he got from Big Mamma Thornton: "Hound Dog."

Doctorow makes a good case for extending the compulsory license model further, to cover the current wave of technological change. You want to remix a recording of a pop song? You want to stream your favorite TV show over a network to watch it while out of town? Sure, why not? Should be easy. It is not hard to imagine a world in which creators can get paid while audiences have a lot of flexibility about how they receive their cultural stuff and what they can do with it.

Both investors and intermediaries hate this. The former are not really in the business of investing in the best culture. The latter are not really in the business of building the best networks. They are in the business of making money for their shareholders through controlling, respectively, stocks or vectors of information. So naturally they want to extract a rent—a super-profit—from that control wherever they can. Investors in information stocks have got it into their head that they can charge for every instance their stock is used, ever, and for all time. Intermediaries who control information flows got it into their heads that they can lock both investors and audiences into their proprietary pipes, thereby gaining an advantage over both and also over their rival intermediaries.

Both investors and intermediaries try to recruit creators and audiences to their respective points of view. The investors will tell creators the intermediaries are evil, that they make the output of creators available for free and steal money that rightly belongs to the creators. The intermediaries will tell creators the investors are evil, acting like monopolists and manipulating prices. The investors will panic audiences into thinking the intermediaries are also channels for child porn or terrorism. The intermediaries will tell audiences that what the investors want is some sort of Chinese police state surveillance of the channels just to stop teenagers uploading videos of themselves dancing to some pop song. All of which, it transpires, is hardly exaggeration. Both investors and intermediaries can be evil. A plague on both their houses and the culture industry they control.[7]

There's a tension between how the culture industry works and how actual culture works.[8] The culture industry wants to make everything about culture a commodity. Everything is to be reduced to exchange. But culture does not entirely work like that. It is also a world of gift giving. I play the record for my friend because I think they might like it, and they do, so I lend it, and so forth. As it actually works between people it's about giving and sharing. Maybe my friend won't give the record back. Maybe the friend forgot about it. And later invited me to the movies—their treat.

In the days of mechanical reproduction of culture, a lot of the sharing stuff was invisible, and the reproducing part was hard. Before home taping on cassette, it was hard to make your own copy. A lot of what went on as a culture of sharing was outside the commodity economy and outside the law. The investors did not have to worry too much about me pressing my own records. That would be a big operation. The law was robust enough to catch people doing that anyway.[9]

Investors don't see the gift part as what culture is all about. Certainly their lawyers don't. Lawyers get paid to read or to listen or to watch. Every minute is billable. The idea that the rest of us share cultural information as a gift to each other, for free, out of love, just doesn't make sense to entertainment lawyers. And so there's an obsession with locking down any and every possible use of a cultural artifact. Everything that is not a sale must be "piracy." It must be a lost sale, at least in their delusional and rather ahistorical world.

Investors thought they were being hard-nosed about this, but it is how the intermediaries managed to play them for suckers. The con was—and is—Digital Rights Management, or what Doctorow calls the *digital lock*. It's a little bit of encryption code that prevents the content of a file from playing on machines that lack the right digital cryptographic key. As Doctorow points out, these locks are hardly unbreakable. The whole point of computation is to move information around. Locking the information up is contrary to the way the whole thing works.

And worse: what's really being locked-in here is the investor, the creator, and the audience to some proprietary channel owned by the intermediary. The song or the book or the movie is now stuck as a useless file, unless you have the special product from Apple or Amazon or whoever, which is the only one on which it can be accessed. The digital lock was a win for intermediaries.

It gets worse: because the locks don't really work, they have to be continually updated. That means the intermediaries have to have control over your computers so that they can remotely change the locks. Needless to say, this is not popular. So they need to outlaw tampering with the locks or even telling other people how to do it. In short: intermediaries can change things on your computer or phone, without you knowing about it. You are not allowed to interfere with this or even know how it actually works. The only winners here are the intermediaries; they have power over investors, creators, and audiences alike.

The intermediaries want everyone in locked channels that they control, and they persuaded investors to go along with this, because—pirates! But the investors have their own ideas about what is in their interests, and it conflicts with that of intermediaries, not to mention creators and audiences. Investors are pretty obsessive protectors of their monopolies over information stocks.

Investors want the intermediaries to be legally liable for every single unauthorized copy that ever gets made over their networks. Now, if I make a copyright-violating copy of something and send it FedEx to someone, FedEx is not in any legal trouble; it is just the common carrier. So long as FedEx agrees not to play favorites and will ship anything for anyone, it isn't responsible for what people ship. (The same applies to the phone company.)

It would appear to make perfect sense to extend this sort of thinking to various forms of internet intermediary services. So long as your internet service provider or your social media site is abiding by certain fair-play rules, why should it not have the same sort of common carrier status? There is already a simple process for dealing with copyright-violating stuff. The owner of the copyright sends a notice, and so long as the infringing information comes down, there's no additional liability on the part of the intermediary.

This is a system open to abuse. If someone puts something about your company on the internet that you don't like, just claim a copyright violation. It is also becoming a favorite tool of authoritarian governments. But the take-down notice system is at least a bit better than what the investors really want.

They want to have access not only to public but also to private communications to look for copyright violations. It is easy to see why investors want the intermediaries to be liable. It really looks bad when some giant media conglomerate takes some impoverished child to court for downloading a few of its pop songs. Besides, the kid probably doesn't have any money anyway—which rather punctures the argument about lost sales. Investors would rather sue intermediaries.

The power to look into private communications is something else. As Doctorow points out, if he wants to use Youtube to send a video of his child in the bath to relatives, how is that any business of the investors? So what if some Taylor Swift song was playing in the background? In short, the investors want the whole communication vector for everything everywhere to be redesigned around their problems.

It might be tempting to buy into all these arguments, to take the side of the investors against the intermediaries or vice versa. But their interests are not our interests. As Doctorow sagely notes:

> The future of the Internet should not be a fight over whether Google (or Apple or Microsoft) gets to be in charge or whether Hollywood gets to be in charge. Left to their own devices, Big Tech and Big Content are perfectly capable of coming up with a position that keeps both "sides" happy at the expense of everyone else.[10]

What's a creator to do? Well, the first thing might be to stop believing that either the investors or the intermediaries have your back. Investors want to treat what you create as their private property to be added to their vast fiefdoms, from which they think they are entitled to a rent in perpetuity. Intermediaries don't really care about the creator's need to make a living, so long as they can charge everyone for information as it passes through their pipes—and gather a lot of additional information about our habits in the process.

Doctorow thinks that as a matter of professional survival, canny creators have to think tactically about when their interests can be aligned with those of investors or those of intermediaries, or neither. Surprisingly, after explaining what a raw deal creators get from investors, he cautions against rushing out of their clutches and going fully independent. Not many creators are really cut out to do all the other work that it takes to bring their art before an audience. Unless you want to spend years of your life studying your branch of the culture industry and learning all its various crafts, going indie might not be for you.

On the other hand, it has become easier than it used to be. The investors have divested themselves of a lot of full-time employees. You too can hire good people to do all the necessary tasks. The actual production costs in many areas have come way down. So it's an option, but not one to be considered lightly, unless you want to sit up late doing the bookkeeping, sending press releases and chasing unpaid invoices. Not to mention storing crates upon crates of the stock in your garage.

With the intermediaries, Doctorow is rather selective about where their interests and those of creators are aligned. Net neutrality is a good example. Internet intermediaries are creatures of government largesse and regulation. And yet they want to claim they should be "free" to charge premiums for actually delivering your information in a timely fashion. If internet intermediaries are to be treated as common carriers, exempt from copyright liability, given right-of-way to lay their cables and so forth, then the least that can be asked of them is that they not discriminate between customers.

On the other hand, Doctorow thinks it is a better tactic to side with the intermediaries who let people have our stuff for free than to advocate either for digital locks or for some Spanish Inquisition–style copyright enforcement regime. It's a question of priorities: the creator has to think first about being known before worrying about being paid. Having information circulate freely at least helps with the first of those obstacles.

As Doctorow points out, creators have had to adjust to technical change before. Musicians who did not particularly want to record but rather to keep touring found themselves outflanked by those who invested time and effort in coming up with a recorded sound. They then got to tour even more because broadcasting made their recorded sound popular. Now things are rapidly going the other way. Musicians who just want to record and don't or can't really play before audiences find it is harder and harder to generate an audience or get paid that way. So things got worse for musicians who just want to record, but things tilted back in favor of those with a great live show.

Doctorow makes a good case that it is generally in the creator's interest for stuff to circulate as a free gift. But then you have to come up with a plan for which part of the art to commodify. You can sell tickets for appearances, like the touring musician. You can sell swag, like t-shirts. There's advertising—which is what has supported boingboing.net since 2003. You can crowd-source. Or you can do special commissions. Doctorow leaves out some other options. One is the art world, where you make bespoke one-off objects for wealthy patrons—on which see Hito Steyerl. Or you can get a day-job in academia—if there still is one.

Frankly, the options aren't great, but that isn't really the fault of free stuff on the internet. The options were never all that great for creators. If the public isn't buying your Great Work, it may not be because they can download it for free. It's more likely they just don't care for it or even know it exists. Things are not much better or worse now, they're just different.

While no techno-utopian, Doctorow does have a political or ethical lodestar that orients his work: "Anything that minimizes the drag on our collective efforts should be celebrated."[11] There are tools out there now that might support common life. As he puts it, information doesn't want to be free, people do.

Those of us who have been keeping up with the whole line of thought about things having "agency" might dispute that.[12]

Once information started to be produced as something relatively autonomous from the material substrate that sustained it, it really did seem to want to be shared like a gift. As I put it in a different riff on the same meme: information wants to be free but is everywhere in chains.[13] It keeps getting stuffed back into the narrow confines of rather old-fashioned models of absolute private property.

As Tiziana Terranova might argue, the fundamental part of the problem has to do with information itself. It is always somewhere in between complete chaos and complete order. It's neither noise nor a constant tone; it's always a pattern with lots of redundancy. Take this book: I made up none of these letters, none of these words. These are all old patterns I am just repeating. I just changed the order of these elements a bit.

It's always rather artificial to call any piece of information someone's property. It's always just a bit of a larger pattern of information that is collectively made and remade. It really does want to be free, but there's a class that interposes itself between us and our information, by controlling stocks or flows of it. This class seems to think everything about its potential for common life has to be sacrificed to its need to keep collecting the rent.

I have etched the outlines of the class conflict between creators (the *hacker class*) versus investors and intermediaries (fractions of the *vectoralist class*) rather more sharply than Doctorow does. Doctorow is one of the finest organic intellectuals among the creators of our time, and he sees things from the creator point of view. From there, we can move on to study the phenomenology of the interfaces creators use more closely (Lev Manovich). We can look at the strange ontological properties of information on which those forces of production are built (Tiziana Terranova). We can investigate those forces of production themselves as a kind of geopolitical agent (Benjamin Bratton). We can study how they shape not only kinds of work but also kinds of city in which to work (Keller

Easterling). We can even investigate how the design of labor process ends up making the whole world available for use as a commodity (Jussi Parikka).

Benjamin Bratton: The Stack to Come

What I like most about Benjamin Bratton's *The Stack: On Software and Sovereignty* is first its close attention to what I would call the forces and relations of production. We really need to know how the world is made right now if it is ever to be remade. Second, I appreciate his playful use of language as a way of freeing us from the prison-house of dead concepts. It is no longer enough to talk of neoliberalism, precarity, or biopower. What were once concepts that granted access to interesting information have become habits. Third, while no friend to bourgeois romantic anti-tech humanism, Bratton has far more sense of the reality of the Anthropocene than today's accelerationist thinkers.[14] "We experience a crisis of 'ongoingness' that is both the cause and effect of our species' inability to pay its ecological and financial debts."[15]

The category of thing that Bratton studies looks a bit like what others call the forces and relations of production, or *infrastructure*, but is better thought of as *platforms*. They are standards-based technical and social systems with distributed interfaces that enable the remote coordination of information and action. They are both organizational and technical forms that allow complexity to emerge. They are hybrids not well-suited to disciplinary study by sociology or computer science on their own. They support markets but can or could enable nonmarket forms as well. They are also about governance and as such resemble states. They enable a range of actions and are to some extent reprogrammable to enable still more.

Platforms offer a kind of generic universality, open to human and nonhuman users. They generate user identities whether users want them or not. They link actors, information, events across times and spaces, across scales and temporalities. They also have a distinctive political economy: they exist to the extent that they generate a *platform surplus*, where the value of the user information for the platform is greater than the cost of providing the platform to those users. Not everything is treated as a commodity. Platforms treat some information as free and can rely on gift as much as commodity economies.

Bratton's particular interest is in stack platforms. The metaphor of the stack comes from computation, where it has several meanings. For example, a *solution stack* is a set of software components layered on top of one another to form a platform for the running of particular software applications without any additional components. All stacks are platforms, but not all platforms are stacks. A stack platform has relatively autonomous layers, each of which has its own organizational form. In a stack, a user might make a query or command, which will tunnel down from layer to layer within the stack, and then the result will pass back up through the layers to the user.[16]

Bratton expands this metaphor of the stack to planetary scale. The world we live in appears as an "accidental megastructure" made up of competing and colluding computational stacks. Computation is planetary-scale infrastructure that transforms what governance might mean. "The continuing emergence of planetary-scale computation as meta-infrastructure and of information as an historical agent of economic and geographic command together suggest that something fundamental has shifted off-center."[17]

The stack generates its own kind of geopolitics, one less about competing territorialities and more about competing totalities. It appears via its symptoms: It both perforates and hardens borders. It may even enable "alien cosmopolitanisms." It's a "crisis of the Westphalian geographic design." "It is not the 'state as a machine' (Weber) or the 'state machine'

(Althusser) or really even (only) the technologies of governance (Foucault) as much as it is *the machine as the state*."[18]

Bratton follows Paul Virilio in imagining that any technology produces its own novel kind of accident.[19] A thought he makes reversible: accidents produce technologies, too. Take, for example, the First Sino-Google War of 2009, when two kinds of stack spatial form collided: Google's transnational stack and the Great Firewall of China.[20] This accident then set off a host of technical strategies on both sides to maintain geopolitical power. Perhaps the stack has a new kind of sovereignty, one that *delaminates* geography, governances, and territory. These might then be candidates for a materialist version of Anna Tsing's comparative universals studies.

In place of Carl Schmitt's *nomos of the earth*, Bratton proposes a *nomos of the cloud*, as in cloud computation, a crucial layer of the stack.[21] *Nomos* here means a primary rule or division of territory, from which others stem. Unlike in Wendy Brown and other theorists of neoliberalism, Bratton thinks sovereignty has not moved from state to market but to the stack.[22] Schmitt championed a politics of land, people and idea versus liberal internationalism, an idea revived in a more critical vein by Chantal Mouffe.[23]

One could read Bratton as a very contemporary approach to the old Marxist methodology of paying close attention to the forces of production.

> An understanding of the ongoing emergence of planetary-scale computing cannot be understood as a secondary technological expression of capitalist economics. The economic history of the second half of the twentieth century is largely unthinkable without computational infrastructure and superstructure ... Instead of locating global computation as a manifestation of an economic condition, the inverse may be equally valid. From this perspective, so much of what is referred to as neoliberalism are interlocking political-economic conditions within the encompassing armature of planetary computation.[24]

The stack could have been the form for the global commons, but instead became an "invasive machinic species."[25] Infrastructures might grow out of the old forms of sovereignty of state and capital but start to produce their own. Code becomes a kind of law.[26] The state ends up running according to code's logic.[27] "This is its bargain: no more innocent outside, now only theoretically recombinant inside ... The state takes on the armature of a machine because the machine, The Stack, has already taken on the roles and register of the state."[28]

Bratton:

> Will the platform efficiencies of The Stack provide the lightness necessary for a new subtractive modernity, an engine of a sustainable counter-industrialization, or will its appetite finally suck everything into its collapsing cores of data centers buried under mountains: the last race, the climate itself the last enemy? [However], It may be that our predicament is that we cannot design the next political geography or planetary computation until it more fully designs us in its own image or, in other words, that the critical dependence of the future's futurity is that we are not yet available for it![29]

Bratton's conceptual object is not just the actually existing stack, but all of its possible variants, including highly speculative ones such as Constant's *New Babylon*.[30] But there are also actual but failed or curtailed ones, such as Ken Sakamura's *TRON*, the Soviet Internet and Soviet cybernetics, and Stafford Beer's *Project Cybersyn*.[31] The actual stack includes such successful technical developments as TCP/IP. This protocol was the basis for a modular and distributed stack that could accommodate unplanned development. It was about packets of information rather than circuits of transmission, about smart edges around a dumb network. TCP/IP was authored as a scalable set of standards.

Bratton thinks of infrastructure as a stack platform with six layers, treated in this order: *earth, cloud, city, address, interface, user*. I think of it more as the four middle layers, which produce the appearance of the user and the earth at either end. I will also reverse the order of Bratton's treatment and start with the sensoria of users, which is where we all actually come to experience ourselves in relation to the stack.

User layer: A user is a category of agent, a position within a system that gives it a role. We like to think we are in charge, but we might be more like the Apollo astronauts, "human hood ornaments."[32] It's an illusion of control. The more the human is disassembled into what Raunig and others think of as *dividual* drives, the more special humans want to feel.[33] "In this, the User layer of The Stack is not where the rest of the layers are mastered by some sovereign consciousness; it is merely where their effects are coherently personified."[34]

For a long time, design thought about the user as a stylized persona. As Melissa Gregg and others show, the scientific measurement of labor produced normative and ideal personas of the human body and subjectivity.[35] Fordism was an era of the design of labor process and leisure-time media for fictional people. But these personas are no longer needed. As Hiroki Azuma shows, the stack does not need narrative fictions of and for ideal users but database fictions that aggregate empirical ones.[36]

The stack not only gives but takes data from its users. "User is a position not only through which we see The Stack, but also through which The Stack sees us."[37] This is the cause of considerable discomfort among users who reactively redraw the boundaries around a certain idea of the human. Bratton is not sympathetic:

> Anthropocentric humanism is not a natural reality into which we must awake from the slumber of machinic alienation; rather it is itself a symptomatic structure powered by—among other things—a gnostic mistrust of matter, narcissistic self-dramatization, and indefensibly pre-Copernican programs for design.[38]

Bratton is more interested in users who go the other way, such as the quantified-self, who want self-mastery through increasingly detailed self-monitoring of the body by the machine. In Maurizio Lazzarato's terms, they are a people who desire their own machinic enslavement.[39] Bratton thinks it is a bit more nuanced than that. There may still be a tension between the cosmopolitan utopias of users and their molding into data-nodes of consumption and labor. "To be sure, the bio-geo-politics of all this are ambiguous, amazing, paradoxical, and weird."[40]

The stack does not care if a user like you is human or not. Bratton is keen to oppose the anthropomorphizing of the machine: "we must save the nonhumans from being merely humans." Making the inhuman of the machine too like the merely human shuts out the great outdoors of the nonhuman world beyond. "We need to ensure that AI agents quickly evolve beyond the current status of sycophantic insects, because seeing and handling the world through that menial lens makes us, in turn, even more senseless."[41] As one learns from Achille Mbembe, commandment that only confronts others that it perceives as lacking autonomous will quickly lose itself in ever more hyperbolic attempts to construct a sense of agency, will, and desire.

Debate about user "rights" has been limited to the human, and limited to a view of the human merely as endowed with property and privacy rights. Rather like Henri Lefebvre's *right to the city*, one needs a right to the stack that includes those without property.[42] One could even question the need to think about information and its infrastructures in property terms at all. Bratton is not keen on the discourse of oedipal fears about the Big Machine spying on us, resulting in users wanting no part in the public, but to live a private life of self-mastery, paranoia, and narcissism. "The real nightmare, worse than the one in which the Big Machine wants to kills you, is the one in which it sees you as irrelevant, or not even a discrete thing to know."[43] Maybe the user could be more rather than less than the neoliberal subject. The stack need not see us as users. To some extent it is an accommodation to cultural habits rather than a technical necessity.

Interface layer: If one took the long view, one could say that the human hand is already an interface shaped over millennia by tools.[44] That ancient interface now touches very new ones. The interface layer mediates between users and the technical layers below. The interface connects and disconnects, telescopes, compresses, or expands layers, routing user actions through columns that burrow up and down through the stack. The Stack turns tech into images and images into tech. "Once an image can be used to control what it represents, it too becomes technology: diagram plus computation equals interface."[45]

Interfaces are persuasive and rhetorical, nodes among the urban flow. "What is open for me may be closed for you, and so our vectors are made divergent."[46] Interfaces offer a kind of protocol or generic threshold. We probe our interfacial condition, being trained through repetition. From the point of view of the interface layer, users are peripheral units of stacks. One could think of the Apple stack, for example, as creating a single distributed user for the "Apple experience."

Interfaces change not only the form of the subject but the form of labor.

> Today, at the withering end of post-Fordism ... we observe logistics shifting from the spatially contiguous assembly line to the radically dis-contiguous assemblage line linked internally through a specific interfacial chain. Contemporary logistics dis-embeds production of things from particular sites and scatters it according to the synchronization and global variance in labor price and resource access.[47]

Interfaces also become more powerful forms of governance over the flows they represent. They have to appear as the remedy for the volatile flows they themselves cause. Their reductive maps become true through use. They may also be the icons of weird forms of experimental religion or ways of binding. They can notate the world with friend/enemy borders. Frantz Fanon once noted that when French colonial power jammed the radio broadcasts of the resistance, Algerians would leave the radio dial on the jammed signal, the noise standing in for it.[48] Bratton wonders how one might update the gesture. Like Paul Gilroy and Kojin Karatani in their different ways, Bratton wonders what new kinds of universality could emerge[49] as a kind of abstraction from of interfacial particularities and their "synthetic diagrammatic total images."[50] Read together with Anna Tsing, one could examine how these emerging universals play with others and generate friction at the stack's peripheries.

However, as Bratton realizes, "We fear a militarization of cognition itself ... Enrollment and motivation according to the interfacial closures of a political theological totality might work by ludic sequences for human Users or by competitive algorithmic ecologies for nonhuman Users." Both human and nonhuman cognition could be assimilated to stack war machines. Or perhaps, one could remake both human and nonhuman users into a new kind of polity, in part through interfaces of a different design. "A strong interfacial regime prefigures a platform architecture built of total interfacial images and does so through the repetition of use that coheres a durable polity in resemblance to the model."[51]

Address layer: Address is a formal system, independent of what it addresses, that denotes singular things through bifurcators such as names or numbers, which can be resolved by a table for routing. Addressing creates generic subjectivity, so why not then also generic citizenship? Address can also give rise to something like fetishism. In Bratton's novel reading of Marx, capitalism obfuscates the address of labor, treating it as a thing and addressing things in labor's place as if those things had magical properties.

If we are all users (humans and inhumans), then a right to the stack is also a right to address, as only that which has an address can be the subject of rights in the "virtual geographic order" of a stack geopolitics.[52] Address is no longer just a matter of discrete locations in a topography. As I put it in *Gamer Theory*, space is now a topology, which can be folded, stretched, and twisted.[53] As Alex Galloway has already shown, the distributed network of TTP/IP is doubled by the centralized DNS, which records who or what is at which address.[54]

Bratton's interest is in what he calls *deep address*, modeled on the intertextuality or *détournement* one sees in the archive of texts.[55] Address designates a place for things and enables relations between things; deep address designates also the relations and then the relations among those relations. Deep address is to address as a derivative is to a contract. It is endless metadata: about objects, then metadata about the metadata about those objects, and so on.

The financialization of who or what is addressed, of much interest to Randy Martin, may also be a kind of fetishism, mistaking the metadata about a relation for a relation. Deep address as currently implemented makes everything appear to a user configured as a uniquely addressed subject who calls up the earth through the stack as if it were only a field of addressable resources. Hence,

> not only is the totality of The Stack itself deeply unstable, it's not clear that its abyssal scope of addressability and its platform for the proliferation of near-infinite signifiers within a mutable finite space are actually correspondent with the current version of Anthropocenic capitalism.[56]

However, deep address has become an inhuman affair. Not only are most users not subjects, so too most of what is addressed may not even be objects. As a result, deep address generates its own accidents. Maybe it is headed toward heat death or maybe toward some third nature. Deep address may outlive the stack. Bratton: "we have no idea how to govern in this context."[57]

City layer: Beneath the address layer is still the old-fashioned topography it once addressed—the city. Only the city now looks more like Archizoom's *No-Stop City* than the static geometries of Le Corbusier.[58] In the city layer absorbed into the stack, mobilization is prior to settlement, and the city is a platform for sorting users in transit. As Virilio noted some time ago, the airport is not only the interface but also the model of the overexposed city.[59]

Like something out of a J. G. Ballard story, the city layer is one continuous planetary city.[60] It has a doubled structure. For every shiny metropolis there's an anti-city of warehouses and waste dumps. The stack subsumes cities into a common platform for labor, energy, and information. Proximity still has value, and the economy of the city layer depends on extracting rents from it. Here one might add that the oldest form of ruling class—the rentier class—has found a future not (or not only) in monopolizing that land which yields energy (from farms and mines) but also that which yields information—the city.[61]

Cities become platforms for users rather than polities for citizens. And as Easterling might concur, their form is shaped more by McKinsey or Haliburton than by architects or planners. Architecture becomes at best interface design, where cement meets computation. It is now a laminating discipline, creating means of stabilizing networks, managing access, styling interfaces, mixing envelopes. Cities are to be accessed through mobile phones, which afford parameters of access, improvisation, syncopation.

The ruin our civilization is leaving does not look like the pyramids. It's a planet wrapped in fiber optic. But perhaps it could be otherwise.

Our planet itself is already the mega-structural totality in which the program of total design might work. The real design problem then is not foremost the authorship of a new envelope visible from space, but the redesign of the program that reorganizes the total apparatus of the built interior into which we are already thrown together.[62]

Ironically, today's pharaohs are building headquarters that simulate old forms, be it Google's campus, Amazon's downtown, or Apple's retro spaceship. They all deny their spatial doubles, whether its Foxconn where Apple's phones are made or Amazon's "logistics plantations." But it is hard to know what a critical practice might be that can intervene now that cities are layers of stacks platforms, where each layer has its own architectural form. "Is Situationist cut-and-paste psychogeography reborn or smashed to bits by *Minecraft*?"[63] Bratton doesn't say, but at least nicely frames the kind of question one might now need to ask.

Cloud layer: Low in the stack, below the city layer, is the cloud. It could be dated from the development of Unix timesharing protocols in the 1970s, from which stems the idea of users at remote terminals sharing access to the same computational power. The cloud may indeed be a kind of power. "As the governing nexus of The Stack, this order identifies, produces and polices the information that can move up and down, layer to layer, fixing internal and external borders and designating passages to and from."[64]

It may also be a layer that gives rise to unique kinds of conflict, like the First Sino-Google War of 2009, where two stacks, built on different kinds of cloud with different logics of territory and different imagined communities of user, collided. That may be a signal moment in an emerging kind of geopolitics that happens when stacks turn the old topography into a topology.

The rights and conditions of citizenship that were to whatever degree guaranteed by the linking of information, jurisdiction and physical location, all within the interior view of the state, now give way perhaps to the riskier prospects of a Google

Grossraum, in which and for which the terms of ultimate political constitution are anything but understood.[65]

The cloud layer is a kind of *terraforming* project.[66] Clouds are built onto, or bypass, the internet. They form a single big discontinuous computer. They take over functions of the state, cartography being just one example. There are many kinds of clouds, however, built into different models of the stack, each with their own protocols of interaction with other layers. Google, Apple, and Amazon are stacks with distinctive cloud layers, but so too are WalMart, UPS, and the Pentagon.

Some cloud types: Facebook, which runs on the captured user graph. It is a rentier of affective life offering a semi-random newspaper and cinema, strung together on unpaid nonlabor, recognition, and social debit. Then there's Apple, which took over closed experience design from Disney, and offers brand as content. As a theology, Apple is an enclave aesthetic about self-realization in a centralized market. It's a rentier of the last millimeter of interface to its walled garden.

On the other hand, Amazon is an agora of objects rather than subjects, featuring supply chain compression, running on its own addressing system, with algorithmic pricing and microtargeting. But even Amazon lacks Google's universal ambition and cosmopolitan mission, as if the company merely channeled an inevitable quant reason. It is a corporation founded on an algorithm, fed by universal information liquidity, which presents itself as neutral platform for humans and nonhumans, offering "free" cloud services in exchange for information.[67] "Google *Großraum* delaminates polity from territory and reglues it into various unblendable sublayers, weaving decentralized supercomputing through increasingly proprietary networks to hundreds of billions of device end-points."[68]

Despite their variety, these clouds are all shaped by the desire of the vectoralist class, which is to extract what Bratton calls "platform surplus value."[69] But perhaps they are built less on extracting rent or profit so much as *asymmetries of information*, or extracting information derivatives. They attempt in different ways to control the whole value chain through control of information. Finance as liquidity preference may be a subset of the vectoralist class as information preference, or power exercised through the most abstract form of relation, and baked into the cloud no matter what its particular form.

Bratton:

> The Cloud polis draws revenue from the cognitive capital of its Users, who trade attention and micro-economic compliance in exchange for global infrastructural services, and it in turn provides each of them with an active, discrete online identity and the license to use that infrastructure.[70]

Maybe this is "algorithmic capitalism"—or maybe it's not capitalism anymore, but something worse, something Bratton's innovations in conceptual language help us perceive, but which could be pushed still further.[71]

The current cloud powers are all built out from accidental advantages or contingent decisions, with a lot of help from human users whose free labor provides the feedback for their constant optimization. We are all guinea pigs in an experiment of the cloud's design. But Bratton is resistant to any dystopian or teleological read on this. The cloud layer was the product of accident as much as design, conflict as much as collaboration. Still, there's something unsettling about the prospect of the *nomos of the cloud*. Bratton: "The camp and the bunker, detention and enclave, are inversions of the same architecture."[72] The nomos of the cloud can switch between them. It is yet to be seen what other topological forms it might enable.

Earth layer: Was computation discovered or invented? Now that the stack produces us as users who see the earth through the stack, we are inclined to substitute from our experience of working and playing with the stack onto the earth itself.[73] It starts to look like a computer, maybe a first computer, from which the second one of the stack is derived. But while earth and stack may look formally similar, they are not ontologically identical. Or, as I speculated in *A Hacker Manifesto*, the forces of production as they now stand both reveal and create an ontology of information that is both historical and yet ontologically real.

Bratton: "The Stack is a hungry machine."[74] It sucks in vast amounts of earth in many forms.[75] Everyone has some Africa in their pocket now—even many Africans, although one should not ignore asymmetries in where extractions from the earth happen and where the users who get to do the extracting happen.

> "There is no Stack without a vast immolation and involution of the Earth's mineral cavities. The Stack terraforms the host planet by drinking and vomiting its elemental juices and spitting up mobile phones ... How unfamiliar could its flux and churn be from what it is now? At the radical end of contingency, what is the ultimate recomposability of such materials? The answer may depend on how well we can collaborate with synthetic algorithmic intelligence to model the world differently.[76]

The stack terraforms the earth, rather like the aesthetics of the avant-garde architects of Superstudio.[77] It terraforms according to a seemingly logical but haphazard geodesign. Bratton:

> As a landscaping machine, The Stack combs and twists settled areas into freshly churned ground, enumerating input and output points and re-rendering them as glassy planes of pure logistics. It wraps the globe in wires, making it into a knotty, incomplete ball of glass and copper twine, and also activating the electro-magnetic spectrum overhead as another drawing medium, making it visible and interactive, limning the sky with colorful blinking aeroglyphs.[78]

Particularly where the earth is concerned, "computation is training governance to see the world like it does and to be blind like it is." But the stack lacks a bio-informational skin that might connect ecological observation to the questioning of resource management. Running the stack now puts more carbon into the atmosphere that the airline industry. If it were a state it would be the fifth largest energy suck on the planet. "Even if all goes well, the emergent mega-infrastructure of The Stack is, as a whole, perhaps the hungriest thing in the world, and the consequences of its realization may destroy its own foundation."[79]

Hence the big question for Bratton becomes: "Can The Stack be built fast enough to save us from the costs of building The Stack?" Can it host computational governance of ecologies? "Sensing begets sovereignty."[80] I pick up this theme in *Molecular Red* in connection with weather and climate.[81] But could it result in new jurisdictions for action? Hence, "we must be honest in seeing that accommodating emergency is also how a perhaps illegitimate state of exception is stabilized and over time normalized." Because so far "there is no one governance format for climates and electrons that the space for design is open at all."[82]

Bratton is reluctant to invite everything into Bruno Latour's *parliament of things*, because this to him is a coercing of the nonhuman and inhuman into mimicking old-fashioned liberalism.[83] But making the planet an enemy won't end well for most of its inhabitants.

Which brings us to the problem of the stack to come and Bratton's novel attempt to write in the blur between what is here but not named and what is named but not really here. For Bratton, geopolitics is a design problem. "We need a geopolitics of design that is comfortable not only with computation but also with vertical systems of designation and decision."[84] But this is not your usual design problem thinking.

The more difficult assignment for design is to compose relations within a framework that exceeds both the conventional appearance of forms and the provisional human context at hand, and so pursuing instead less the materialization of abstract ideas into real things than the redirection of real relations through a new diagram.[85]

Designing the stack to come, like any good design studio, Bratton starts with what is at hand.

Part of the design question then has to do with interpreting the status of the image of the world that is created by that second computer, as well as that mechanism's own image of itself and the way that it governs the planet by governing its model of that planet.[86]

This is not a program of cybernetic closure, but rather of "enabling the world to declare itself as data tectonics ... Can the 'second planetary computer' create worlds and images of worlds that take on the force of law (if not its formality) and effectively exclude worse alternatives?" It might start with "a smearing of the planet's surface with an objective computational film that would construct a stream of information about the performance of our shared socio-natural spaces."[87]

For Bratton (unlike Latour, Haraway, and Tsing) there is no local, only the global.[88] We're users stuck with a stack that resulted from "inadvertent geoengineering." But the design prospect is not to perfect or complete it, but to refashion it to endure its own accidents and support a range of experiments in rebuilding: "the geo-design I would endorse doesn't see *dissensus* as an exception."[89]

It's not a romantic vision of a return to an earth before the stack. Bratton: "the design of food platforms is less about preserving the experiential simulation of preindustrial farming and eating ... and more like molecular gastronomy at landscape scale." But it is not a naïve techno-utopianism either. While I don't think it's a good name, Bratton is well aware of what he calls *cloud feudalism*, which uses the stack to distribute power and vale upwards. And he is fully aware that the "militarized luxury urbanism" of today's vectorialist class depends on super-exploitation of labor and resources.[90] At least one novel observation here, however, is that the stack can have different governance forms at each level. The stack is not one infrastructure, but a laminating of relatively autonomous layers.

The school of thought known as media archaeology would look at the actually existing stack alongside all of the parallel attempts to think and make something like it that fell by the wayside. These might range from the speculations of Alexander Bogdanov to the attempt to computerize the Soviet *Gosplan*—which as Bratton notes does not look completely unlike what Google actually achieved.[91] Hayek may have been right in his time that state planning could not manage information better than a market. But maybe neither could manage information as well as a properly designed stack platform. Perhaps, as some Marxists once held, the capitalist ruling class (and then the vectoralist ruling class) perfected the forces of production that make them obsolete as a ruling class. Perhaps in the liminal space of the stack to come one can perceive technical-social forms that get past both the socialist and capitalist pricing problems.

Bratton:

> We allow, to the pronounced consternation of both socialist and capitalist realists, that some polypaternal supercomputational descendant of Google *Gosplan* might provide a mechanism of projection, response, optimization, automation, not to mention valuation and accounting beholden neither to market idiocracy nor dim bureaucratic inertia, but to the appetite and expression of a curated algorithmic phyla and its motivated Users.[92]

Perhaps there's a way planning could work again, using deep address, but from the edges rather than the center.

This might mean, however, an exit from a certain residual humanism: "the world may become an increasingly alien environment in which the privileged position of everyday human intelligence is shifted off-center." Perhaps it's not relevant whether artificial cognition could pass a Turing test and is more interesting when it doesn't. Here Bratton gestures toward a posthuman accelerationism but with far more sense of the constraints now involved. "The Anthropocene should represent a shift in our worldview, one fatal to many of the humanities' internal monologues."[93]

Bratton: "The Stack becomes our *dakhma*."[94] Perhaps a tower of silence like the raised platforms built by the Zoroastrians for excarnation, where the dead are exposed to the birds. To build stack to come we have to imagine it in ruins:

> design for the next Stack ... must work with both the positive
> assembly of matter in the void, on the plane and in the world,
> and also with the negative maneuver of information as the
> world, from its form and through its air.[95]

To think about, and design, the stack to come means thinking within the space of what Bratton calls the *black stack*, which is a "generic profile of its alternative totalities."[96] It might look more like something out of Borges than out of the oracular pronouncements of Peter Theil or Elon Musk.[97] Bratton: "Could this aggregate 'city' wrapping the planet serve as the condition, the grounded legitimate referent, form which another, more plasmic, universal suffrage can be derived and designed?"[98] Let's find out.

Lev Manovich: At the Coalface of the Interface

I'm sure I'm not the only one annoyed by the seemingly constant interruptions to my work caused by my computer trying to update some part of the software that runs on it. I have it set to require my permission when it does so, at least for those things I can control. This might be a common example that points to one of Manovich's key points about media today: the software is always changing. As Doctorow explains, its often just to change the locks.

Everything is always in beta, and the beta testing will in a lot of cases be done by us, as free labor, for our vendors. As Lev Manovich says in *Software Takes Command*: "Welcome to the world of permanent change—the world that is now defined not by heavy industrial machines that change infrequently, but by software that is always in flux."[99]

Manovich takes his title from the modernist classic, *Mechanisation Takes Command*, published by Sigfried Giedion in 1948.[100] Like Giedion, Manovich is interested in the often anonymous labor of those who make the tools that make the world. It is on Giedion's giant shoulders that many students of actor networks, media archaeology and cultural techniques knowingly or unknowingly stand.[101]

Where Giedion is interested in the inhuman tool that interfaces with nonhuman natures, Manovich is interested in the software that controls the tool. "Software has become our interface to the world, to others, to our memory and our imagination—a universal language through which the world speaks, and a universal engine on which the world runs."[102] If you are reading this, you are reading something mediated by, among other things, dozens of layers of software, including Word v. 14.5.1 and Mac OS v. 10.6.8, both of which had to run for me to write it in the first place.

Manovich's book is limited to media software, the stuff that both amateurs and professionals use to make texts, pictures, videos, and things like websites that combine media. This is useful in that it is the software most of us know, but it points to a much larger field of inquiry that is only just getting going.

Giedion published *Mechanization Takes Command* in the age of General Electric and General Motors. As Manovich notes, today the most recognizable brands include Apple, Microsoft, and Google. The last of whom, far from being "immaterial," probably runs a million servers.[103] Billions of people use software; billions more are used by software. And yet it remains an invisible category in much of the humanities and social sciences.

Unlike Wendy Chun and Friedrich Kittler, Manovich does not want to complicate the question of software's relation to hardware.[104] In Bogdanovite terms, it's a question of training. As a programmer, Manovich sees things from the programming point of view. Chun on the other hand was trained as a systems engineer. And Kittler programmed in assembler language, which is the code that directly controls a particular kind of hardware. Chun and Kittler are suspicious of the invisibility that higher level software creates in relation to hardware, and rightly so. For Manovich this "relative autonomy" of software of the kind most people know is itself an important feature of its effects.

The main business of *Software Takes Command* is to elaborate a set of formal categories through which to understand *cultural software*, that subset of software that is used to access, create, and modify cultural artifacts for online display and communication and for making interactives or adding metadata to existing cultural artifacts, as perceived from the point of view of its users.

The user point of view somewhat complicates one of the basic diagrams of media theory. From Claude Shannon to Stuart Hall, it is generally assumed that there is a sender and a receiver and that the former is trying to communicate a message to the latter, through a channel, impeded by noise, and deploying a code. Hall breaks with Shannon by proposing the startling idea that the code used by the receiver could be different to that of the sender. But he still assumes there's a complete, definitive message leaving the sender on its way to a receiver.[105]

Tiziana Terranova takes a step back from this modular approach that presumes the agency of the sender (and in Hall's case, of the receiver). She is interested in the turbulent world created by multiples of such modular units of mediation. Manovich heads in a different direction. He is interested in the iterated mediation that software introduces in the first instance between the user and the machine itself through software.

Manovich: "The history of media authoring and editing software remains pretty much unknown." There is no museum for cultural software. "We lack not only a conceptual history of media editing software but also systematic investigations of the roles of software in media production." There are whole books on the palette knife or the 16-mm film camera, but on today's tools—not so much. "The revolution in the means of production, distribution, and access of media has not been accompanied by a similar revolution in the syntax and semantics of media."[106]

We actually do know quite a bit about the pioneers of software as a meta-medium, and Manovich draws on that history. The names of Ivan Sutherland, J. C. R. Licklider, Douglas Engelbart, the maverick Ted Nelson, and Alan Kay have not been lost to history. They knew they were creating new things. The computer industry got in the habit of passing off new things as if they were old, familiar things, in order to ease users gently into unfamiliar experiences. But in the process we lost sight of the production of new things under the cover of the old in the cultural domain.

There's a whole rhetoric about disruption and innovation, but successful software gets adopted by users by not breaking too hard with those users' cultural habits. Things happen in what Bratton calls *the blur*. Thus, we think there's novelty where often there isn't: start-up business plans are often just copies of previous successful ones. But we miss it when there's real change: at the level of what users actually do, where the old is a friendly wrapper for the new.

Manovich is interested in Alan Kay and his collaborators, particularly Adele Goldberg, at Xerox Palo Alto Research center, or Parc for short.[107] Founded in 1970, Parc was the place that created the graphic user interface, the bitmapped display, Ethernet networking, the laser printer, the mouse, and windows. Parc developed the models for today's word processing, drawing, painting and music software. It also gave the world the programming language Smalltalk, a landmark in the creation of object-oriented programming. All of these are component bits of a research agenda that Alan Kay called *vernacular computing*.

Famously, it was not Xerox but Apple that brought all of that together in a consumer product, the 1984 Apple Macintosh computer. By 1991 Apple had also incorporated video software based on the Quicktime standards, which we can take as the start of an era in which a consumer desktop computer could be a universal media editor. At least in principle: those who remember computer-based media production of the early 1990s will also recall the frustration.

The genius of Alan Kay was to realize that the barriers to entry of the computer into culture were not just computational but also cultural. Computers had to do things that people wanted to do and in ways that they were used to doing them, initially at least. Hence the strategy of what Bolter and Grusin called *remediation*, wherein old media become the content of new media form.[108]

If I look at the first screen of my iPhone, I see icons. The clock icon is an analog clock. The iTunes icon is a musical note. The mail icon is the back of an envelope. The video icon is a mechanical clapboard. The Passbook icon is old-fashioned manila files. The Facetime icon is an old-fashioned-looking video camera. The Newstand icon looks like a magazine rack. Best of all, the phone icon is the handset of an old-fashioned landline. And so on. None of these things pictured even exist in my world anymore; I have this machine that does all those things. The icons are cultural referents from a once-familiar world that have become signs within a rather different world that I can pretend to understand because I am familiar with those icons.

All of this is both a fulfillment and a betrayal of the work of Alan Kay and his collaborators at Parc. They wanted to turn computers into "personal dynamic media."[109]Their prototype was even called a Dynabook. They wanted a new kind of media, with unprecedented abilities. They wanted a computer that could store all of the user's information, which could simulate all kinds of media, and could do so in a two-way, real-time interaction. They wanted something that had never existed before.

Unlike the computer Engelbart showed in his famous *Demo* movie of 1968, Kay and company did not want a computer that was just a form of cognitive augmentation.[110] They wanted a medium of expression. Engelbart's demo shows many years ahead of its time what the office would look like, but not the workspace of any kind of creative activity. Parc wanted computers for the creation of new information in all media, including hitherto unknown ones. They wanted computers for what I call the *hacker class*—those who create new information in all media, not just code.[111] In a way the computers that resulted make such a class possible and at the same time set limits on its cognitive freedom.

The Parc approach to the computer is to think of it as a *meta-medium*. Manovich: "All in all, it is as though different media are actively trying to reach towards each other, exchanging properties and letting each other borrow their unique features."[112] To some extent this requires making the computer itself invisible to the user. This is a problem for a certain kind of modernist aesthetic for whom the honest display of materials and methods is a whole ethics or even politics of communication. But modernism was only ever a partial attempt to reveal its own means of production, no matter what Benjamin and Brecht may have said on the matter. Perhaps all social labor, even of the creative kind, requires separation between tasks and stages.

The interactive aspect of modern computing is by now well known.[113] Manovich draws attention to another feature, one that differentiates software more clearly from other kinds of media: view control. This one goes back not to Parc but to Engelbart's *Demo*. This was a 1968 live presentation to an audience of engineers of the oN-Line System, which brought together windows, hypertest, graphics, and a mouse, not to mention many other features that would become standard in the computerized workplace—and view control. For example, at the moment I have this document in Page View, but I could change that to quite a few different ways of looking at the same information. If I was looking at a photo in my photo editing software, I could also choose to look at it as a series of graphs and maybe manipulate the graphs rather than the representational picture, and so on.

This might be a better clue to the novelty of software than, say, hypertext.[114] The linky, nonlinear idea of a text has a lot of precursors, not least every book in the world with an index, and every scholar taught to read a book's index first. There are lovely modernist-lit versions of this, from Cortesar's *Hopscotch* to Roland Barthes and Walter Benjamin.[115] Manovich follows Espen Aarseth in arguing that hypertext is not particularly modernist.[116] While Ted Nelson got his complex, linky hypertext aesthetic from William Burroughs, what was really going on, particularly at Parc, was not tail-end modernism but the beginnings of a whole new avant-garde.

Maybe we could think of it as a sort of meta- or hyper-avant-garde that wanted not just a new way of communicating within a media but new kinds of media themselves. Kay and Nelson in particular wanted to give the possibility of creating new information structures to the user. For example, consider Richard Shoup's *Superpaint*, coded at Parc in 1973. Part of what it does is simulate real-world painting techniques. But it also added techniques that go beyond simulation, including copying, layering, scaling, and grabbing frames from video. Its "paintbrush" tool could behave in ways a paintbrush could not.

For Manovich, one thing that makes "new" media new is that additional properties can always be added to it. The separation between hardware and software makes this possible. "In its very structure computational media is 'avant-garde,' since it is constantly being extended and thus redefined."[117] The role of media avant-garde is no longer performed by individual or artist groups but happens in software design. A certain view of what constitutes avant-garde is embedded here, and perhaps it stems from Manovich's early work on the Soviet avant-gardes, understood in formalist terms as constructors of new formalizations of media.[118] It's a view of avant-gardes as means of advancing—but not also contesting—the forward march of modernity.

Computers turned out to be malleable in a way other industrial technologies were not. Kay and others were able to build media capabilities on top of the computer as universal machine. It was a sort of *détournement* of the Turing and von Neuman machine. They were not techno-determinists. It all had to be invented, and some of it was counterintuitive. The Alan Kay and Adele Goldberg version was at least as indebted to the arts, humanities, and humanistic psychology as to engineering and design disciplines. In a cheeky aside, Manovich notes: "Similar to Marx's analysis of capitalism in his works, here the analysis is used to create a plan for action for building a new world—in this case, enabling people to create new media."[119]

Manovich downplays the military aspect of postwar computation.[120] He dismisses SAGE air defense network, even though out of it came the TX-2 computer, which was perhaps the first machine to allow a kind of real-time interaction, if only for its programmer. From which, incidentally, came the idea of the programmer as hacker, Sutherland's early work on computers as a visual medium, and the game *Space War*.[121] The Parc story is nevertheless a key one. Kay and company wanted computers that could be a medium for learning. They turned to the psychologist Jerome Bruner and his version of Jean Piaget's theory of developmental stages.[122] The whole design of the Dynabook had something for each learning stage, which to Bruner and Parc were more parallel learning strategies than stages. For the gestural and spatial way of learning, there was the mouse. For the visual and pictorial mode of learning, there were icons. For the symbolic and logical mode of learning, there was the programming language Smalltalk.

For Manovich, this was the blueprint for a meta-medium, which could not only represent existing media but also add qualities to them. It was also both an ensemble of ways of experiencing multiple media and also a system for making media tools and even for making new kinds of media. A key aspect of this was standardizing the interfaces between different media. For example, when removing a bit of sound, text, picture, or video from one place and putting it in another, one would use standard Copy and Paste commands from the Edit menu. On the Mac keyboard, these even have standard key-command shortcuts: Cut, Copy, and Paste are command-X, C, and V, respectively.

Something happened between the experimental Dynabook and the Apple Mac. It shipped without Smalltalk or any software authoring tool. From 1987 it came with Hypercard, written by Parc alumnus Bill Atkinson. Apple discontinued it in 2004. It seems clear now that Apple's trajectory was away from democratizing computing. Other ways to code on your consumer-grade Apple computer (or elsewhere) came along: Perl, PHP, Python, JavaScript, MaxMSP by Miller Puckette, and the elegant Processing by Casey Reas and Ben Fry.[123] Even before MaxMSP some may remember the amazing nato.0+55+3d (1999) and the provocative antics of its alleged developer Netochka Nezvanova.

Here one could say a little more than Manovich wants to about the tensions involved in the spread of access to media-making and media-tool-making, which pushed against certain political-economic limits in the old business models of the culture industry. In this respect Parc was a bit like Dada or the Situationists in one limited sense: it pushed against received ideas about authorship without quite knowing what the consequences would be. We all collage and *détourn* on our laptops these days. The culture industry had to evolve into what I call the *vulture industry* to keep up. It too had to go meta.

And so Kay's vision was both realized and abandoned. It became cheap and relatively easy to make one's own media tools. But the computer became a media consumption hub. By the time one gets to the Apple iPad, it does not really present itself as a small computer. It's more like a really big phone, where everything is locked and proprietary.

A meta-medium contains simulations of old media but also makes it possible to imagine the new. This comes down to being able to handle more than one type of media data. Media software has ways of manipulating specific types of data, but also some that can work on data in general, regardless of type; view control, hyperlinking, sort, and search would be examples. If I search my hard drive for "Manovich," I get various Microsoft Word documents that are versions of this text, pdfs of his books, video and audio files, and a picture of Lev and me in front of a huge array of screens. Such media-independent techniques are general concepts implanted into algorithms. Other than search, geolocation would be another example. So would visualization, or infovis, which can graph lots of different kinds of data set.

Manovich wants to contrast these properties of a meta-medium to medium-specific ways of thinking. A certain kind of modernism puts a lot of stress on this: think Clement Greenberg and the idea of flatness in pictorial art.[124] Russian formalism and constructivism in a way also stressed the properties of specific media, their given textures. But it was interested in experimentally working in between them on parallel experiments in breaking them down to their formal grammars. Manovich: "The efforts by modern artists to create parallels between mediums were proscriptive and speculative … In contrast, software imposes common media 'properties.'"[125]

One could probably quibble with Manovich's way of relating software as meta-medium to precursors such as the Russian avant-gardes, but I won't; he knows a lot more about both than I do.[126] I'll restrict myself to pointing out that historical thought on these sorts of questions has only just begun. Particular arguments aside, I think Manovich (like Steyerl) is right to emphasize how software calls for a new way of thinking about art history, which as yet is not quite a prehistory to our actual present.

I also think there's a lot more to be said about something that is probably no longer a political economy but more of an aesthetic economy, now that information is a thing that can be property. This connects to Sianne Ngai's tripartite aesthetic of the cute, the zany, and the interesting, aligned with information as a commodity, labor, and circulation, respectively. Software is implicated in the design as design-practice and as circulation but also restriction and protocol. As Manovich notes of the difference between the actual and potential states of software as meta-medium: "Of course, not all media applications and devices make all these techniques equally available—usually for commercial and copyright reasons."[127] The aesthetic of information is shaped by the development of intellectual property.

So far, Manovich has provided two different ways of thinking about media techniques. One can classify them as media independent vs. media specific or as simulations of the old media vs. new kinds of technique. For example, in Photoshop, you can Cut and Paste like in most other programs. But you can also work with layers in a way that is specific to Photoshop. Then there are things that look like old-time darkroom tools. And there are things you could not really do in the darkroom, like add a Wind filter, to make your picture look like it is zooming along at Mach 1. Interestingly, there are also high pass, median, reduce noise, sharpen, and equalize filters, all of which are holdovers from something in between mechanical reproduction and digital reproduction: analog signal processing. There is a veritable archaeology of media just in the Photoshop menus.

What makes all this possible is not just the separation of hardware from software, but also the separation of the media file from the application. The file format allows the user to treat the media artifact on which she is working as "a disembodied, abstract and universal dimension of any message separate from its content."[128] You work on a signal or basically a set of numbers. The numbers could be anything so long as the file format is the right kind of format for a given software application. Thus, the separation of hardware and software, and software application and file, allow an unprecedented kind of abstraction from the particulars of any media artifact.

One could take this idea of separation (which I am rather imposing as a reading on Manovich) down another step. Within PhotoShop itself, the user can work with layers that redefine an image as a content image with modifications conceived as happening in separate layers. These can be transparent or not, turned on or off, masked to effect part of the underlying image only, and so on.

The kind of abstraction that layers enable can be found elsewhere and is one of the non-media-specific techniques. The typography layer of this text is separate from the word-content layer. Geographic Information System (GIS) also uses layers, turning space into a media platform holding data layers. Turning on and off the various layers of Google Earth or Google Maps will give a hint of the power of this. Load some proprietary information into such a system, toggle the layers on and off, and you can figure out the optimal location for the new supermarket. Needless to say, some of this ability, in both PhotoShop and GIS, descends from military surveillance technologies from the Cold War.[129]

So what makes new or digital media actually new and digital is the way software both is, and further enables, a kind of separation. It defines an area for users to work in an abstract and open-ended way.

> This means that the terms "digital media" and "new media" do not capture very well the uniqueness of the "digital revolution." ... Because all the new qualities of "digital media" are not situated "inside" the media objects. Rather, they all exist "outside"—as commands and techniques of media viewers, authoring software, animation, compositing, and editing software, game engine software, wiki software, and all other software "species."[130]

Take the file of a digital photo, for example. The file contains an array of pixels that have color values, a file header specifying dimensions, color profile, information about the camera and exposure, and other metadata. It's a bunch of (very large) numbers. A high-definition image might contain two million pixels and six million RGB color values. Furthermore, any digital image seen on a screen is already a visualization. For the user it is the software that defines the properties of the content. "There is no such thing as 'digital media.' There is only software as applied to media (or 'content')."[131]

New media has always been a bit of a problematic term in media studies.[132] As Wendy Chun suggests, perhaps we are obliged to constantly update to remain the same.[133] Novelty becomes itself repetitive habit. As Cory Doctorow reminds us, a lot of the involuntary updating to which we have to agree is just to maintain existing forms of intellectual property. But for Manovich, new media is new in another sense: software is a meta-medium, both simulating old media tools and adding new ones under the cover of the familiar. Yet a third might be the creation not of new versions of old media or new tools for old media but entirely new media forms—*hybrid media*.[134]

For instance, Google Earth combines aerial photos, satellite images, 3D computer graphics, stills, data overlays. Motion graphics combines still images, text, audio, and so on. Even a simple website combines page description information for text, vector graphics, animation. Or the lowly PowerPoint, able to inflict animation, text, images, or movies on the public.

This is not quite the same thing as the older concept of *multimedia*, which for Manovich is a subset of hybrid media.[135] In multimedia the elements are next to each other. "In contrast, in media hybrids, interfaces, techniques, and ultimately the most fundamental assumptions of different media forms and traditions, are brought together, resulting in new *media gestalts*."[136] It generates new experiences, different from previously separate experiences. Multimedia does not threaten the autonomy of media, but hybridity does. In hybrid media, the different media exchange properties. For example, text within motion graphics can be made to conform to cinematic conventions, go in and out of "focus."

Hybrid media is not the same as convergence, as hybrid media can evolve new properties.[137] Making media over as software did not lead to their convergence, as some thought, but to the evolution of new hybrids. "This, for me, is the essence of the new stage of computer meta-medium development. The unique properties and techniques of different media have become software elements that can be combined together in previously impossible ways."[138]

Manovich thinks about media hybrids in an evolutionary way.[139] Novel combinations of media can be thought of as a new species. Some are not selected or end up restricted to certain specialized niches. Virtual Reality, for example, was a promising new media hybrid at the trade shows of the early 1990s, but it ended up with niche applications. A far more successful hybrid is the simple image map in webdesign, where an image becomes an interface. It's a hybrid made of a still image plus hyperlinks. Another would be the virtual camera in 3D modeling, which is now a common feature in video games.

One might pause to ask, with Alex Galloway, whether such hybrid media help us to map the totality of relations within which we are webbed.[140] But the problem is that not only is the world harder to fathom in its totality; media itself recedes from view.

> Like the post-modernism of the 1980s and the web revolution of the 1990s, the "softwarization" of media (the transfer of techniques and interfaces of all previously existing media technologies to software) has flattened history—in this case the history of modern media.[141]

Perhaps it's a declension of the fetish, which no longer takes the thing for the relation, or even the image for the thing, but takes the image as an image, rather than an effect of software.

Software is a difficult object to study, as it is in constant flux and evolution. One useful methodological tip from Manovich is to focus on formats rather than media artifacts or even instances of software. At its peak in the 1940s, Hollywood made about 400 movies per year. It would be possible to see a reasonable sample of that output. But Youtube uploads something like 300 hours of video every minute. Hence a turn to formats, which are relatively few in number and stable over time. Jonathan Sterne's book on the mp3 might stand as an exemplary work along these lines.[142] Manovich: "From the point of view of media and aesthetic theory, file formats constitute the 'materiality' of computational media—because bits organized in these formats is what gets written to a storage media."[143]

Open a file using your software—say in Photoshop—and one quickly finds a whole host of ways in which you can make changes to the file. Pull down a menu, go down the list of commands. A lot of them have submenus where you can vary some aspect of the file, for example, a color-picker. Select from a range of shades, or open a color wheel and choose from anywhere on it. A lot of what one can fiddle with are parameters, also known as variables or arguments. In a Graphic User Interface (GUI), there's usually a whole bunch of buttons and sliders that allow these parameters to be changed.

Modern procedural programming is modular. Every procedure that is used repeatedly is encapsulated in a single function that software programs can evoke by name. These are sometimes called *subroutines*. Such functions generally solve equations. Ones that perform related functions are gathered in libraries. Using such libraries speeds up software development. A function works on particular parameters—for example, the color picker.

Softwarization allows for a great deal of control of parameters. "In this way, the logic of programming is projected to the GUI level and becomes part of the user's cognitive model of working with media inside applications."[144] It may even project into the labor process itself. Different kinds of media work become similar in workflow. Select a tool, choose parameters, apply, repeat. You could be doing the layout for a book, designing a building, editing a movie, or preparing photos for a magazine. Software becomes sensoria.

Manovich: "Of course, we should not forget that the practices of computer programming are embedded within the economic and social structures of the software and consumer electronics industries." What would it mean to unpack that? How were the possibilities opened up by Alan Kay and others reconfigured in the transition from experimental design to actual consumer products? How did the logic of the design of computation end up shaping work as we know it? These are questions outside the parameters of Manovich's formalist approach, but they are questions his methods usefully clarify. "We now understand that in software culture, what we identify by conceptual inertia as 'properties' of different mediums are actually the properties of media software."[145]

Manovitch's work has a lot of implications for media theory. The intermediate objects of such a theory dissolve in the world of software: "the conceptual foundation of media discourse (and media studies)—the idea that we can name a relatively small number of distinct mediums—does not hold any more."[146] Instead, Manovich sees an evolutionary space with a large number of hybrid media forms that overlap, mutate, and cross-fertilize.

Software studies offer a very different map as to how to rebuild media studies than just adding new subfields, for example, for game studies. It also differs from comparative media studies, in not taking for granted that there are stable media—whether converging or not—to compare. It looks rather for the common or related tools and procedures embedded today in the software that run all media.

Manovich's software studies approach is restricted to that of the user. One might ask how the user is itself produced as a byproduct of software design. *Algorithm plus data equals media*: which is how the user starts to think of it too. It is a cultural model, but so too is the "user." Having specified how software reconstructs media as simulation for the user, one might move on to thinking about how the user's usage is shaped not just by formal and cultural constraints but by other kinds as well. One might think also about who or what gets to use the user in turn.

Tiziana Terranova: The Address of Power

Contrary to certain popular narratives by latecomers, not everybody went gaga over "new media" back in the late twentieth century. In the *cyberculture* period, from the popularization of cyberpunk in 1984 to the death of the internet as a purely scientific and military media in 1995, there were plenty of experimental and critical minds at work on it.[147] I would count Tiziana Terranova as a fine exponent of the constructivist approach, a sober builder of useful theory that might open spaces for new practices in the emerging world of postbroadcast and posttruth media flux. Her book, *Network Cultures: Politics for the Information Age*, is still well worth reading for its keen grasp of the fundamental issues.[148]

Jean-François Lyotard sent everyone off on a bum steer with the idea of the *immaterial*. This was a problem compounded by Fredric Jameson's famous assertion that the technics of late capitalism could not be directly represented, as if the physics of heat engines was somehow clearer in people's heads than the physics of electrical conductivity.[149] Terranova usefully begins again with a concrete image of information as something that happens in material systems and thinks them through the image of a space of fluid motion rather than just as an end-to-end line from sender to receiver.

For Terranova, information is not an essence but a site of struggle:

> I do not believe that such information dynamics simply expresses the coming hegemony of the "immaterial" over the material. On the contrary, I believe that if there is an acceleration of history and an annihilation of distances within an information milieu, it is a creative destruction, that is a productive movement that releases (rather than simply inhibits) social potentials for transformation.[150]

It helps not to make a fetish of just one aspect of media form, whether one is talking about hypertext back then, or big data now.[151] Sometimes these are aspects of more pervasive technological phyla. Terranova: "Here I take the internet to be not simply a specific medium but a kind of active implementation of a design technique able to deal with the openness of systems."[152] This might be a useful interpretive key for thinking how certain now-dominant approaches to tech arose.

To whom is information addressed? Anybody who studied communication late last century would have encountered some version of the sender → encoding → channel → decoding → receiver model, with its mysterious vestigial term *context*. Stuart Hall opened this loop by adding a possible difference between the encoding and the decoding.[153] He made non-identity a function not of noise as something negative but of culture as a positive field of differences. But even so, this way of thinking tended to make a fetish of the single, unilinear act of communication. It ended up as an endless argument over whether the sender's encoding dominated the receiver's decoding, or if the receiver could have a counterhegemonic agency of decoding otherwise. That was what the difference between the Frankfurt school's epigones and the Birmingham school of Hall et al. boiled down to.[154]

Terranova usefully brackets off the whole critical language of domination versus agency, moving the discussion away from the privileged questions of meaning and representation that still dominate critical thinking in the humanities. Like Alex Galloway in *Excommunication*, she insists that a critical perspective need not be hermeneutic.[155] She does so by taking seriously the breakthrough of Claude Shannon's purely mathematical theory of information of 1948.[156] Information actually means three different things in Shannon. It is (1) a ratio of signal to noise, (2) a statistical measure of uncertainty, and (3) a nondeterministic theory of causation. He developed his theory in close contact with engineers working on communication problems in telephony at Bell Labs, one of the key sites where our twenty-first century world was made.[157]

The signal-to-noise problem arose out of attempts to amplify telephony signals for long distance calls, where the additional energy used to amplify the signals also shows up as noise. This, incidentally, is where one sees how the sensoria in which information appears as "immaterial" is actually an effect produced by decades of difficult engineering—not to mention that quite a bit of energy is required to make a signal pass through a copper wire, making the electrons dance in their predictable but nondeterministic way.

What was crucial about Shannon's approach to this problem was to separate out the concept of information from having anything to do with "meaning."[158] Information is just a ratio of novelty and redundancy. "From an informational perspective, communication is neither a rational argument nor an antagonistic experience."[159] It has nothing to with communication as domination or resistance, Habermasian communicative action, or Lyotard's language games.[160]

For information to be transmitted at all, it has to confront the demon of *noise*. In Michel Serres's version, sender and receiver appear as nodes cooperating against noise rather than as differentiated individual entities.[161] Terranova rather follows Gilbert Simondon, who pointed out that Shannon regards the individual sender and receiver as preconstituted addresser and addressee. They just appear, prior to the act of communication. Simondon's approach picks up the vestigial concept of context.[162] For him, the act of communication is also what constitutes the sender and receiver as such. His approach is to think of the context as the site where information produces individuations out of a collective, undifferentiated context.

This is a step toward thinking about the space of information as a more turbulent, metastable system that can be disturbed by very small events: "the informational dimension of communication seems to imply an unfolding process of material constitution that neither the liberal ethics of journalism nor the cynicism of public relations officers really address."[163] The materiality of information is prior to any discussion of "real" reporting or "fake" news or the sender–receiver nodes such flows constitute.

Terranova's work points toward a critical media theory, to thinking about information production and protocols, rather than to second-order questions of meaning. It could be a way of framing a problem of information system design for the whole field of media and culture. Information design could be about more than messages defeating noise, but rather designing fields of possibility beyond click-counting, including problems in the organization of perception and the construction of bodily habits. Like Citton, she points beyond the restricted economy of attention as it has been instrumentalized. A critical media theory could even ask a fundamental question about the power of address—and the address of power.

Information systems tend to be closed systems, defined by the relation between selection (the actual) and the field of possibilities (the virtual), but where that field appears in an impoverished form. "Information thus operates as a form of probabilistic containment and resolution of the instability, uncertainty and virtuality of a process."[164] For Terrannova, what might be a constructive project in the wake of that is some kind of information culture that does not enforce a cut in advance in the fabric of the world, and then reduce its manipulation to a set of predictable and calculable alternatives, addressed to that a priori and unaddressed cut.[165]

Interestingly, Terranova's approach is less about information as a way of producing copies and more about the reduction of events to probabilities, thus sidestepping the language of simulation, although perhaps also neglecting somewhat the question of how information challenged old regimes of private property.[166] Her emphasis is much more on information as a form of control for managing and reproducing closed systems.[167] This then appears as a closure of the horizon of radical transformation. As in Randy Martin, instead of a livable future we have futures markets.

In information systems, the real only ever emerges out of the statistically probable.

> What lies beyond the possible and the real is thus the openness of the virtual, of the invention and the fluctuation, of what cannot be planned or even thought in advance, of what has no real permanence but only reverberations ... The cultural politics of information involves a stab at the fabric of possibility.[168]

The virtual does not arise out of negation, out of a confrontation with techno-power as an-other. It is unquantifiable. It is what an information system does not know about itself.[169]

One of the more powerful features of the theory of information is the way it linked together information and entropy. Thermodynamics, which as Amy Welding shows was a key to the scientific worldview in Marx's era, offered the breakthrough of an irreversible concept of time, one that appeared as a powerful metaphor for the era of the combustion engine.[170] In short: heat leaks, energy dissipates. Any system based on a heat differential eventually "runs out of steam."

Hence the figure of Maxwell's Demon, which could magically sort the hot particles out from the cool ones and prevent an energy system from entropic decline into disorder. But that, in a sense, is exactly what information systems do. The tendency of things might still be entropic: systems dissipate and break down. But there might still be negentropic countersystems that can sort and order and organize. Such might be an information system; as Joseph Needham among many others started to think, it might even be what is distinctive about living systems.[171]

Needham's organicism borrowed from the systems theory of Bertalanffy, which predates Shannon, and was based a lot more on analog thinking, particularly the powerful image of the organizing field.[172] Much more influential was the transposition of the thought-image of the digital to the question of how life is organized as negentropic system, resulting in what for Donna Haraway is a kind of code fetishism.[173] What is appealing to Terranova in the confluence of biological and informaic modes of thinking is the way it bypassed the humanistic subject and thought instead about populations at macro and micro scales.

Where Terranova and Haraway intersect is in the project of understanding how scientific knowledge is both real knowledge and shot through with ideological residues at the same time:

An engagement with the technical and scientific genealogy of a concept such as information ... can be actively critical without dis-acknowledging its power to give expression and visibility to social and physical processes ... Information is neither simply a physical domain nor a social construction, nor the content of a communication act, nor an immaterial entity set to take over the real, but a specific reorientation of forms of power *and* modes of resistance.[174]

While I would want to pause over the word *resistance*, this seems to me a usefully nuanced approach.

One way she does so is by appealing to Henri Bergson's distinction between a quantified and a qualified sense of time.[175] Here time as quality, as duration, retains primacy, offering the promise of a "virtuality of duration."[176] But is this not yet another offshoot of romanticism? And what if it was really quite the other way around? What if the figure of time as quality actually depended on measurable, quantitative time? I'm thinking here of Peter Gallison's demonstration of how the engineering feat of electrically synchronized time, so useful to the railways, enabled Einstein to question the metaphysics of a universal clock time that was the backdrop to Newton's mechanics.[177] As Gallison shows, it is only after you can actually distribute a measure of clock time pretty accurately between distant locations that you can even think about how time might be relative to mass and motion.

It is certainly useful that Terranova offers a language within which to think about a more elastic relation between the information in a network and the topology of that network itself. It isn't always the case that, as with Shannon's sender and receiver, the nodes are fixed and preconstituted as addresser and addressee. "A piece of information spreading throughout the open space of the network is not only a vector in search of a target, it is also a potential transformation of the space crossed that always leaves something behind."[178]

This more elastic space, incidentally, is how I had proposed thinking about the category of *vector*.[179] In geometry, a vector is a line of fixed length but of no fixed position. Thus one could think of it as a channel that has certain affordances but that could actually be deployed not only to connect different nodes, but sometimes to even call those nodes into being. Hence I think of vector as part of a *vector field*, which might have a certain malleable geometry, where what might matter is not some elusive "virtual" dimension but rather the tactics and experiments of finding what it actually affords.

Terranova stresses the way the internet became a more open system, with distributed command functions. It was in this sense not quite the same as the attempts to build closed systems of an early generation of communication engineers: "resilience needs decentralization; decentralization brings localization and autonomy; localization and autonomy produce differentiation and divergence." The network, like empire, is tolerant of differences, and inclusive (up to a point), but also expansionist. As Terranova notes, rather presciently, "There is nothing to stop every object from being given an internet address that makes it locatable in electronic space."[180]

Since 1995, the internet started acquiring the properties of a fully realized vector field, one striated into distinct organization levels, what Benjamin Bratton calls *the Stack*—a useful counterimage to the network, drawing attention to planetary computation's geopolitical and infrastructural qualities. Terranova was a pioneer in understanding that the build-out of this infrastructure, of which information theory was the concept, had significant implications for rethinking the work of culture and politics.

There is no cultural experimentation with aesthetic forms or political organization, no building of alliances or elaboration of tactics that does not have to confront the turbulence of electronic space. The politics of network culture are thus not only about competing viewpoints, anarchistic self-regulation and barriers to access, but also about the pragmatic production of viable topological formations able to persist within an open and fluid milieu.[181]

She notes in passing some of the experiments of the late twentieth century in "network hydrodynamics,"[182] such as the Communitree BBS, Andreas Broeckmann's Syndicate list-serv, Amsterdam's Digital City, the rhizome list-serv, to which I would add the latter's sister-list nettime.org.[183] Some of these fell apart, even if many others lived and mutated. Much of the functionality of today's social media derives from these early experiments. If social media has any "civility" at all, it was invented by trial and error by pioneers in these worlds.[184]

Terranova was also prescient in asking questions about the free labor that was just starting to become a visible feature of stack-life at the time she was writing. She reads this through the Autonomist-Marxist figure of the shift of work processes from the factory to society (the *social factory*).[185] I sometimes wonder if this image might be a bit too limiting. It might be more helpful to think of a dismantling and repartitioning of all institutionalized divisions of labor under the impact of networked communication, more a *social boudoir* than social factory.

Still, it was useful to insist on the category of labor, at a time when it was tending toward invisibility. One has to remember that in cyberculture times, there was a lot more celebration of "playful" fan cultures to the net.[186] Terranova: "The internet does not automatically turn every user into an active producer, and every worker into a creative subject."[187] It also makes plenty of alt-right trolls.[188]

In a 1998 nettime.org post, Richard Barbrook suggested that the cyberculture-era internet had become the site for a kind of poststituationist practice of *détournement*, of which nettime. org itself might not have been a bad example. Before anybody had figured out how to really commodify the internet, it was a space for a high tech gift economy.[189] Terranova thinks Barbrook put too much emphasis on the difference between this high tech gift economy and old-fashioned capitalism. Perhaps it might be helpful to ask whether, at its commanding heights, this still is old-fashioned capitalism. Has the ruling class itself mutated? Does it now draw its power from informatics control, one based in part on capturing the value of information gifted by various forms of what Terranova calls, with her useful oxymoron, free labor? Perhaps the ruling class has changed address and is no longer where we thought it was.

Certainly, the internet became a vector along which the desires that were not recognizable under old-style capitalism chose to flee. Terranova: "Is the end of Marxist alienation wished for by the management gurus the same thing as the gift economy heralded by leftist discourse?" Not so much. Those desires were recaptured again. I don't know who exactly is supposed to have fallen for "naïve technological utopianism"[190]—apart from the Accelerationists, and even there, Kodwo Eshun's Black Accelerationism was a quite canny negotiation between the cramped spaces of both the political and the technical. Among the media activists, artists, and theorists that I met in the struggles of the eighties and nineties, a radical pragmatism of the kind advocated by Geert Lovink prevailed.[191] We were on the internet to do with it what we wanted, for as long as we could make it last, before somebody shut the party down.

Perhaps the worker and the hacker belong to different classes.[192] I think the hacker class is composed of all those whose creations of difference can be captured as intellectual property and commodified. It's a class with no necessary common culture at all, other than what it might make in struggling against the appropriation of its time. But it is not the case that the hacker prefigures new kinds of labor. Rather, both the hacker and worker experience a bifurcation into a secure well-paid elite and a casualized and hyper-exploited—and now global—mass.

This is a perspective from which to attain some critical perspective on attempts to expand the category of labor, to the point where to me it stops making much sense. Terranova's *Network Culture* provided an early introduction in the Anglophone world to the work of Mauritzio Lazzarato, but I always thought that his category of *immaterial labor* was less than helpful.[193] Since I agree with Terranova's earlier dismissal of the notion of information as immaterial, I am surprised to see her reintroduce the term to refer to labor, which if anything is becoming ever more embedded in the material systems of the stack.

For Lazzarato and Terranova, immaterial labor refers to two aspects of labor: the rise of the information content of the commodity and the activity that produces its affective and cultural content. Terranova: "immaterial labor involves a series of activities that are not normally recognized as 'work'—in other words, the kinds of activities involved in defining and fixing cultural and artistic standards, fashions tastes, consumer norms, and more strategically, public opinion." It is the form of activity of "every productive subject within postindustrial societies."[194]

Knowledge is inherently collaborative; hence the tensions in immaterial labor (although other kinds of labor are collaborative, too). "The internet highlights the existence of networks of immaterial labor and speeds up their accretion into a collective entity." This observation would prove to be quite prescient. Immaterial labor includes activities that fall outside the concept of abstract labor, meaning time used for the production of exchange value, or socially necessary labor time. Immaterial labor imbues the production process with desire. "Capital wants to retain control over the unfolding of these vitualities."[195] But at that point one has to wonder if the terms in play here are still capital and labor, or if exploitation might not have new territories and new forms.

Terranova follows those autonomist Marxists who have been interested in the mutations of labor beyond the classic factory form, and like them her central text is Marx's "Fragment on Machines" from the *Grundrisse*.[196] The autonomists base themselves on the idea that the *general intellect*, or ensemble of knowledge, constitutes the center of social production, but with some modification.

> They claim that Marx completely identified the general intellect (or knowledge as the principle productive force) with fixed capital (the machine) and thus neglected to account for the fact that the general intellect cannot exist independently of the concrete subjects who mediate the articulation of the machines with each other.[197]

For the autonomists (Berardi, for example) living labor is always the determining factor, here recast as a mass intellectuality.[198]

The autonomists think that taking the labor point of view means to address labor as subjectivity. Living labor alone acts as a kind of vitalist essence, of vast and virtual capacities, against which capital is always a reactive and recuperative force.[199] This is in contrast to what the labor point of view meant, for example, to Bogdanov, which is that labor's task is not just to think of its collective self-interest, but to think about how to acquire the means to manage the totality of the social and natural world, but using the forms of organizing specific to it as a class.[200]

From that point of view, it might be instructive to look, as Angela McRobbie does, for baby steps toward self-organization among those obliged to do free labor and of how it was recuperated in novel ways.[201]

> Free labor is a desire of labor immanent to late capitalism, and late capitalism is the field which both sustains free labor and exhausts it. It exhausts it by undermining the means through

which that labor can sustain itself: from the burn-out syndromes of internet start-ups to under-compensation and exploitation in the cultural economy at large.[202]

Let's not just assume that this is a "late" iteration of the same "capitalism" as in Marx's era. The internet was the most public aspect of a whole modification of the forces of production, which enabled users to break with private property in information, to start creating both new code and new culture outside such constraints. Those forces of production not only drove popular cyberculture strategies from below but also enabled the formation of a new kind of ruling class from above, one based on extracting not so much surplus labor as surplus information: extracted as content from both labor and nonlabor; extracted as form from the hacker class, the creator of new forms. I have been referring to this new ruling class as the vectoralist class because it owns and controls not the means of production but the vector of information. This class includes those who in Doctorow's terms control the stocks of information (investors) and its flows (intermediaries).

The most interesting part of *Network Culture* is where Terranova extends the Deleuzian style of conceptual constructivism to scientific (and other) languages that are interested in theories and practices of soft control, emergent phenomena, and bottom-up organization.[203] Her examples range from artificial life to mobile robotics to neural networks. All of these turned out to be intimations of new kinds of productive machines.

There is a certain ideological side to much of this discourse, and yet "the processes studied and replicated by biological computation are more than just a techno-ideological expression of market fundamentalism." They really were and are forms of a techno-science of rethinking life, and not least through new metaphors. No longer is the organism seen as one machine. It becomes a population of machines. "You start more humbly and modestly, *at the bottom*, with a multitude of interactions in a liquid and open milieu."[204]

For example, in connectionist approaches to mind, "the brain and the mind are dissolved into the dynamics of emergence."[205] Mind is immanent, and memories are Bergsonian events rather than stored images.[206] These can be powerful and illuminating figures to think with. But maybe they are still organized around what Bogdanov would call a *basic metaphor* that owes a bit too much to the unreflected experience of bourgeois culture.[207] It just isn't actually true that Silicon Valley is an "ecosystem for the development of 'disruptive technologies' whose growth and success can be attributed to the incessant formation of a multitude of specialized, diverse entities that feed off, support and interact with one another," to borrow a rather breathless quote from some starry-eyed urban researchers that Terranova mentions.[208] On the contrary, Silicon Valley is a product of American military-socialism, massively pump-primed by Pentagon money.

Terranova connects the language of biological computing to the Spinozist inclinations of autonomist theory: "A multitude of simple bodies in an open system is by definition acentered and leaderless" and "A multitude can always veer off somewhere unexpected under the spell of some strange attractor."[209] But I am not sure this works as a method. Rather than treat scientific fields as distinct and complex entities, embedded in turn in ideological fields in particular ways, Terranova selects aspects of a scientific language that appear to fit with a certain metaphysics adhered to in advance.

It can be fascinating and illuminating to look at the "diagonal and transversal dynamics" of cellular automata and admire at a distance how "a bottom-up system, in fact, seems to appear almost spontaneously."[210] But perhaps a more critical and radical information theory approach might be the necessary complement. What role does stack infrastructure play in such systems? What role does an external energy source play?

In what ways are these kinds of science homologous with the distinctive forms of commodified information of the vectoralist class?[211] It is quite possible to make a fetish of a bunch of tiny things, such that one does not see the special conditions under which they might appear "self" organizing.

As much as I revere Lucretius and the Epicurians, it seems to me to draw altogether the wrong lesson from him to say that "in this sense, the biological turn entails a rediscovery, that of the ancient clinamen."[212] What is remarkable in Lucretius is how much he could get right by way of a basic materialist theory derived from the careful grouping and analysis of sense impressions. One really can move from appearances, not to Plato's eternal forms, but to a viable theory that what appears is most likely made of a small number of elements in various combinations.[213] But here the least useful part of the Epicurean worldview is probably the famous swerve, or *clinamen*, which does break with too strict a determinism, but at the expense of positing a metaphysical principle that is not testable. Hence, contra Terranova, there can be no "sciences of the clinamen."[214]

This is also why I am a bit skeptical about the overuse of the term *emergence*, which plays something of a similar ideological role to clinamen. It becomes a too-broad term with too much room for smuggling in old baggage, such as some form of vitalism. Deleuze, in his Bergsonian moments, was certainly not free of this defect. A vague form of romantic spiritualism is smuggled in through the back door and held to be forever out of reach of empirical study.

Despite those caveats, I think there are still ways in which Terranova's readings in biological computing are enabling, in opening up new fields from which—in Bogdanovite style—metaphors can be found that can be substituted into other fields and tested there. The key word here is *tested*. When tested against what we know of the history of the military entertainment complex, metaphors of emergence, complexity, and self-organization do not really describe how this new kind of power evolved at all.

More interesting are Terranova's use of such studies to understand Alex Galloway's great early theme: how control might work now.[215] Here we find ways of thinking that actually can be adapted to explain social phenomena:

> The control of acentered multitudes thus involves different levels: the production of rule tables determining the local relations between neighboring nodes; the selection of appropriate initial conditions; and the construction of aims and fitness functions that act like sieves within the liquid space, literally searching for the new and the useful.[216]

That might be a thought-image that leaves room for the deeper political-economic and military-technical aspects of how Silicon Valley, and the military entertainment complex more generally, came into being.

Terranova: "Cellular automata ... model with a much greater degree of accuracy the chaotic fringes of the *socius*—zones of utmost mobility, such as fashions, trends, stock markets, and all distributed and acentered informational milieus."[217] Read through the lens of Bogdanov rather than Deleuze, I think what is useful here is a kind of *tektology*, a process of borrowing (or *détournement*) of figures from one field that might then be set to work in another.[218]

For Bogdanov this is a practical question, a way of experimenting across the division of labor within knowledge production. It isn't about the production of an underlying metaphysics held to have radicalizing properties in and of itself. Hence one need not subscribe either to the social metaphysics of a plural, chaotic, self-differentiating "multitude," upon which "capital" is parasite and fetter and which cellular automata might be taken to describe. The desire to affirm such a metaphysics leads to blind spots as to what exactly one is looking at when one looks at cellular automata.

I agree with Terranova's rejection of the social construction-ism that seemed a default setting in the late twentieth century, when technical questions could never be treated as anything but second order questions derived from social practices. Deleuzian pluralist-monism had the merit at least of flattening out the terrain, putting the social and the asocial on the same plane, drawing attention to the assemblage of machines made of all sorts of things, and managing flows of all kinds, both animate and inanimate. This took a somewhat reactionary turn in the work of Bruno Latour.[219]

The other danger of that approach is that it is a paradoxical way of putting theory in command again, in that it treats its metaphorical substitutions between fields as more real than the fields themselves. What is treated as real is the transversal flows of concepts, affects, and percepts. The distinctive fields of knowledge production within which they arose were thus subordinated to the transversal production of flows between them. And thus theory remains king, even as it pretended to dethrone itself. It falls short of a fully comradely approach to the coproduction of knowledge.

It seems crucial in the age of the Anthropocene that thought take "the biological turn."[220] Never was it more obvious that the "social" is not a distinct or coherent object of thought at all. One of the great struggles has been to simulate how this actual world works as a more or less closed totality, for that is what it is. The metaphorics of the virtual seem far from our current and most pressing concerns. The actual world is rather a thing of limits.

Terranova ends *Network Culture* with a rethinking of the space between media and politics, and here I find myself much more in agreement. Why did anyone imagine that the inter-net would somehow magically fix democracy? This seemed premised on a false understanding from the start: "Communi-cation is not a space of reason that mediates between state and society, but is now a site of direct struggle between the state and different organizations representing the private interests of organized groups of individuals."²²¹

Of all the attempts to think "the political" in the late twentieth century, the most sober was surely Jean Baudrillard's theory of the silent majority.²²² He had the wit and honesty to point out that the masses do not need or want a politics, and they want even less an intellectual class to explain politics to them. The masses prefer spectacle to reason, and their hyperconformity is not passivity but even a kind of power. It is a refusal to be anything but inert and truculent. Hence the black hole of the masses, which absorbs everything without comment or response. Meaning and ideas lose their power there—as even liberal pundits found out in Donald Trump's America.

Keller Easterling: Extrastatecraft and the Digital City

As a kid I was always fascinated by my father's work as an architect. He used to take me to building sites and explain what was going on. But I was particularly interested in how he made the plans. These he drew by hand on a huge drafting table, with a range of geometric tools. Even more amazing was the blueprint machine, which turned the drawings into inky copies, for the client, the builder, and the town clerk's office.

It was an era when an architect still gave form to the world. Buildings were made of standard parts but were not themselves quite standard. As Rem Koolhaas shows in his magnificent book *Delirious New York*, you can date buildings in a city once you know how the building codes change through time, because the codes are a kind of invisible envelope that the actual structures strain up against.²²³ They are almost always as tall and big as the codes would let them be, but each has its own form, shoehorned into the grid.

That era is over. The architect today is no "fountainhead." It is rather sad to watch today's "starchitects" designing their weird-looking signature buildings.[224] These seem now always to be either museums or condos for billionaires. The brand-name architect just builds useless luxury housing and trinkets for the 1 percent. The actual design of the world is now in the hands of other people.

Perhaps the decline of architecture can be mapped onto the design—or rather redesign—of politics. The architect made buildings that carved out private space against the boundary of a public one that was in the shape of some kind of polis. It was not always a democratic one, but it was a polis that formed the platform for modes of political calculation, consensus, and *dissensus*.[225] But does that polis still exist, or do we live only within Randy Martin's derivative power, in which the management of what was formerly the polis is outsourced to financial instruments?

Of particular interest here is Keller Easterling's *Extrastatecraft: The Power of Infrastructure Space*.[226] Following Armand Mattelart's call for a critical history of global infrastructure, Easterling offers three case studies in new forms of built-out power, and some remarkably productive language for thinking about the kinds of built space that might be replacing those of both architecture and politics.[227]

Easterling: "Buildings are no longer singularly crafted enclosures, uniquely imagined by an architect, but reproducible products." Not only buildings and office parks, but whole cities are now constructed according to the formulae of infrastructural technology. And so the object of analysis has to shift toward an understanding of that infrastructure. "Infrastructure space, with the power and currency of software, is an operating system for shaping the city."[228]

Infrastructure is how power deploys itself now, and it does so much faster than law or democracy. Easterling's three case studies are free zones like Shenzhen in China; global broadband networks and their imposition on existing cities such as Nairobi; and International Organizations for Standardization

(ISOs), which "legislate" the design of things and processes.

Of these case studies, the ISOs are perhaps the weirdest: "The whole world now speaks a dialect of ISO Esperanto, one that often resembles the hilarious, upbeat argot of self-help gurus."[229] And to media and communication scholars, the broadband story is perhaps the best known. Here I will concentrate on the first, the free trade zone story.

Easterling's book is aimed at architects, but it deserves a wider audience. Its goal is to redefine the object of analysis so that it might be possible to reconstitute the object of professional intervention for architects and planners. "Exposing evidence of the infrastructural operating system is as important as acquiring some special skills to hack into it."[230] This has implications both for what planning could be, but also for how social movements might engage with questions of scale.

This reconstitution of the object of analysis is a very important step. I am continually frustrated by the way in which scholars in the humanities and social sciences keep trotting out the same old authorities and the same tired languages, which pretty much guarantee that when they look at the present all they will see is how it looks like the past. Easterling: "Well-rehearsed theories, like those related to Capital and Neoliberalism continue to send us to the same places to search for dangers while other concentrations of authoritarian power escape scrutiny."[231]

Sometimes one has to just forget Marx and Foucault in order to see the world afresh, which is after all what both Marx and Foucault were able to do, by selectively forgetting the authorities and languages that preceded them.

So one of Easterling's moves is to see the free trade zone as central rather than peripheral. She shows the long history of such zones, their rapid rise in the postwar years, and their weird proliferation into other kinds of "enclave" form. What they all have in common is their detachment on the one hand from the envelopes of national polities and on the other their connection into a global infrastructure of trade and communication. They are addresses in a stack or nodes in a vector field.

When I was in China in 1987, I visited Shenzhen, famous as Chinese leader Deng Xiaoping's most visible commitment to the "open door policy." When I saw it, it was still a fishing village, overshadowed by a vast, muddy, construction site. It is now a city of more than ten million people. An entire city was built, *in my lifetime*. And it is not the only one. This is an unprecedented fact in human history.[232] Many such cities are some version of free trade zone, set up outside the regulatory envelope of the nation-state, such that labor and environmental law need not apply, and nor do the usual taxes. Such spaces have lately mutated into weird new forms, such as knowledge parks, satellite universities, supply chain cities, super-factory cities, leisure island cities, full-service container ports.

Manuel Castells described a new global spatiality that emerged in the late twentieth century as a space of flows laid over, and circumventing, the old space of places.[233] Where once geography constrained flows to the contours of places, now the virtual geography of comms infrastructure warps that geography of places to that of flows. Or to put it in another a language I have used for this: the second nature of built form is subsumed into a third nature of standardized mediation.

The space of flows is, among other things, a way of routing economic power around the power of labor, of circumventing labor's ability to organize and command space. In the free trade zone, "inexpensive labor is imported from South Asia and elsewhere like machinery or other equipment." And "From its inception, the most overt and routine forms of violence have been aimed at workers."[234] The labor compound may even be cordoned off within the free trade zone, even as it is cordoned off from its "host" country.

To the usual tools of coercion against labor can now be added deportation. Labor can be expelled back to its "home" country, or within a state like China, back to the provinces from whence it came. And while they are maybe not (or not yet) responsible for the majority of labor, these special cities are of enormous size. The notorious Foxconn company alone has about 800,000 workers in Shenzhen.

It is as if cities were engineering their own doppelgangers, which are not always about dirty manufacturing and cheap labor. They can also be about finding ways to aggregate and tap the abilities of what I call the *hacker class*—those whose efforts yield not quantities of product but qualities of novelty that can be turned into copyrights, patents, or other information instruments through which to command a slice of the commodification process. Hence the proliferation of campus cities, IT cities, media cities, and their nonwork doubles—the vacation cities, urban-scale zones like the very strange resort the South Koreans have built in the North, about which Easterling has written elsewhere.[235]

All cities are now branded global products, competing with each other as mediatized simulacra of each other. What is curious is the attempt to create new brands, which might then appeal within the third nature space of flows for both investment and high skill hacker-class populations. Consider here the Technopark Alliance, which includes Luzern, Winterthur, and Skolkovo, which one might think of as niche brands meant to appeal to consumers of quite specialized forms of city.

What makes all this possible is a kind of infrastructure design way, way beyond the scope of the architect's drafting board or even the design software that has replaced it since my father's time. On the one side is technical engineering, on the other a kind of financial engineering, and caught in the squeeze between is old-fashioned architecture. It is being replaced by design systems that establish protocols for the unfolding of cities across greenfield sites, where the unit of design is not the building so much as the zone.

The language in which Easterling talks about this is the language of the interface. As Alexander Bogdanov argues, we get our metaphors for how the world works from our labor processes. We substitute metaphors from labor processes familiar to us into our larger worldview.[236] Easterling ingeniously deploys the point-and-click language, which architects as well as most members of the hacker class are familiar with as a kind of basic metaphor for how the world is now designed. Thus: "The infrastructural operating system is filled with well-rehearsed sequences of code—spatial products and repeatable formulas like zones, suburbs, highways, resorts, malls, golf courses. Hacking into it requires forms that are also like software."[237]

Hence, the metaphor not only for how the world is built but also for how to engage with it shifts into the register of computing as popularly experienced and understood: "the MS Dos of urban software might be productively hacked."[238] But before it can be hacked, it has to be understood. Easterling offers a set of subsidiary metaphors for contemporary infrastructure design: *multipliers*, *switches*, and *topologies*.

The multipliers include cars, elevators, mobile phones. The first, the car, was the multiplier that made possible one of the precursor forms of the greenfields city, the greenfields suburb. But "Levittown was simple software."[239] Its repeated unit-forms were few. Sadly, it may be the case that the United States never quite acquired the higher order practices of building forms at the next scale. Hence the endless attempts to solve spatial problems with yet more versions of the Levittown software.

The switch is something like an interchange highway. The switch is a macro-order feature compared to the multiplier, shaping where the multipliers can circulate.

Topology might designate the art of patterning switches and multipliers into grids and networks for optimal circulation. "Topologies model the 'wiring' of an organization ... Just as an electronic network is wired to support certain activities, so space can be 'wired' to encourage some activities and routines over others."[240]

In *Gamer Theory*, I argued that another way to think about the supersession of second nature by third nature is to think of it as the incorporation of *topography* into *topology*.[241] Comms infrastructure enables spaces to be folded or twisted, so that points that are geographically remote can be brought into close communication with one another, although usually at the expense of the hinterlands around each. Thus, New York City can be right next to London and very remote from upstate New York.

Easterling finds a remarkable precedent for today's urban infrastructure design in James Oglethorpe's 1733 protocol for the growth of Savannah, Georgia. It was not a master plan, imagining how the city might fill out the topography around it. Rather, it was a kind of growth protocol that imagined a kind of unit-addition model, each unit having a certain configuration of public and private space, amenities and services.

Jackson Heights, my home in New York City, is a little version of this protocol approach, where the code involved doubling the size of blocks and enclosing the land in the middle of blocks as a shared space for the rows of buildings on each side. This is a quite different way of thinking about what "planning" might be, as the unit takes precedence, nested within macro-scale switches.[242]

Easterling is not interested only in new cities but also the refashioning of existing ones. Here what is of interest is how third nature, or topology, not only creates new spaces but reconfigures old ones. This Easterling calls *broadband urbanism*, and her case study is Nairobi: "For broadband urbanism the object of interplay is to maximize access to information."[243] It is a way of reformatting existing cities, by bolting on an infrastructure that is light and distributed but pervasive and which makes any and every asset, whether human or not, a resource that can be assessed, mobilized, combined, and marketed.

Perhaps the most interesting intervention in Easterling's book is when it starts to touch on geopolitics. From the infrastructure engineering point of view, geopolitics is a complicated field of state and nonstate actors. It is a picture that does not neatly resolve into either realpolitik or liberal internationalism. The world is not an all-against-all conflict of state actors. Nor is it really something that could ever be tamed by international agreement. Various attempts to rethink it by adding nonstate actors don't really address the real drivers of global infrastructural space.

Easterling wants to get away from the "chessboard" metaphor for geopolitics.[244] Of course, if one pays attention to infrastructure, one's first question would be: *who made the board in the first place?* Even the "smooth" spaces imagined by Deleuze and Guattari are premised on their difference from the striated or chessboard ones.[245] In any case, all these modes of thinking tend to take militarized space as primary, as if we really did live in Clausewitz's world, only where politics was just war by other means.

What I find really refreshing about Easterling's book is the way it both shows forms that are outside of conventional concepts and narratives such as the free trade zone and then also offers new conceptual tools for understanding those forms. If one rethinks what architecture actually is, it turns out to be one of the most, not least, important levels of analysis.

Interestingly, the binary warlike approach might not be much worse than what descends from liberal internationalist rhetorics of cooperation. Easterling:

> More disturbing than a binary competitive stance is its cooperative reciprocal stance. It is not a means by which nations attack each other, but a means by which both state and nonstate actors cooperate at someone else's expense—usually the expense of labor.[246]

Current global trade treaty negotiations are aimed not just at labor, either, but at putting the genie of free information back in the intellectual property bottle.

So the world might be run not by statecraft but at least in part by *extrastatecraft*. Easterling: "Avoiding binary dispositions, this field of activity calls for experiments with ongoing forms of leverage, reciprocity, and vigilance to counter the violence immanent in the space of extrastatecraft."[247] She has some interesting observations on the tactics for this. Some exploit the informational character of third nature, such as gossip, rumor, and hoax. She also discusses the possibilities of the gift or of exaggerated compliance and of mimicry and comedy.[248]

Can the planet be usefully hacked? That might be the question for these times. Can the infrastructure being built out, one that precludes by design old-fashioned "politics," yield to new kinds of engagement? These would seem to be very timely questions. Everybody knows the current infrastructure is not one that can last. In a way, it does not even exist, given that on the longer time frames of the Anthropocene it will flicker like an image and be gone—to be replaced, one hopes, by a more habitable one.

Easterling: "Laissez-faire was planned; planning was not."[249] Perhaps neither markets nor plans are adequate metaphors for organization at scale any more. Hayek was right about the limits of planning as an information and organization system. We now know that the geo-engineering of freedom, where market signals are legislated and architected into primacy, has not worked much better. Some keys and tools for thinking otherwise are offered in Easterling's book, and that is what makes it so timely and interesting.

Jussi Parikka: Geology of Media

Once you start digging beyond the idea that media is about interpreting signs, there's no end to how deep the rabbit hole can become. Behind the system of signs is the design of the interface that formalizes them (Manovich). Behind the interface is the volatility that the interface manages (Terranova). Behind that volatility is the stack of levels that produces and processes it (Bratton). Behind the stack is a strange architecture of spatial and geopolitical forms (Easterling).

The rabbit hole keeps going, becoming more of a mineshaft. For some the chemical and mineral dimension is also a big part of what appears when one looks behind the sign.[250] Which brings us to Jussi Parikka's *A Geology of Media*, which tunnels down into the bowels of the earth itself: "Geology of media deals with the weird intersections of earth materials and entangled times."[251]

In this perspective, "Computers are a crystallization of [the] past two hundred to three hundred years of scientific and technological development, geological insights, and geophysical affordances."[252] One could also reverse this perspective. From the point of view of the rocks themselves, computers are a working-out of the potentials of a vast array of elements and compounds that took billions of years to make but only decades to mine and commodify—and discard.[253]

History is a process in which collective human labor transforms nature into a second nature to inhabit. On top of which it then builds what I call a *third nature* made of information, which not only reshapes the social world of second nature but which instrumentalizes and transforms what it perceives as a primary nature in the process.[254] There's no information to circulate without a physics and a chemistry. "The microchipped world burns in intensity like millions of tiny suns."[255]

Perhaps the best way into this perspective is to go through some of the materials whose extraction is necessary to make information something that can appear as if it were for us.[256] As Anna Tsing reminds us, a considerable amount of friction happens at the point of extraction. Parikka picks up the vector at the other end—where geology becomes media artifact. Let's take a periodic table approach to media possibilities.

Coltan is a famous example. It's an ore containing the elements niobium and tantalum, which along with antimony are used in making microcapacitors; a lot of it comes from the Congo. Then there's lithium, used in the batteries of phones, laptops, and hybrid cars, major deposits of which are in Afghanistan. Cobalt is also used in making batteries. Platinum is for hard drives, liquid crystal displays, and hydrogen fuel cells. Gallium and indium for thin-layer photovoltaics; neodynium for lasers; germanium for fiber-optic cable; palladium for water desalination. Aluminum, tantalum, tungsten, thorium, cerium, manganese, and chromium are all part of twentieth century industrial culture but now have extended uses.

Media materiality is still also very metallic: 36 percent of tin, 25 percent of cobalt, 15 percent of palladium, 15 percent of silver, 9 percent of gold, 2 percent of copper, 1 percent of aluminum are for media tech uses. There can be sixty different elements on a computer chip. There's a whole place and a whole industry named after an element: Silicon Valley. Very pure silicon is used to make semiconductors.

We're used to thinking about a geopolitics of oil, but perhaps there's a more elaborate Great Game going on these days based on access to these sometimes rare elements.[257] Reza Negarestani's *Cycolonpedia* is an extraordinary text that reverses the perspective and imagines oil as a kind of sentient, subterranean agent of history.[258] One could expand that imaginary to other elements and compounds. For instance, one could imagine aluminum as an agent in the story of Italian Fascism. Since bauxite was common in Italy but iron was rare, aluminum rather than steel became a kind of "national metal," with both practical and lyrical properties. The futurist poet Marinetti even published a book on aluminum pages.

What aluminum was to twentieth century struggles over second nature, maybe lithium will be to twenty-first century struggles over third nature. It might make sense, then, to connect the study of media to a speculative inquiry into geology, the leading discipline of planetary inquiry (a connection I approached in a different way in *Molecular Red*, by looking at climate science). Parikka: "Geology becomes a way to investigate the materiality of the technological media world."[259]

James Hutton's *Theory of the Earth* (1778) proposed an image of the temporality of the earth as one of cycles and variations, erosion and deposition. Hutton also proposed an earth driven by subterranean heat. By a process of substitution, he took metaphors from the technics of his time and applied it to his object of study: His earth is an engine, modeled on the steam engines of his time. It's a useful image in that it sees the world outside of historical time. But rather than having its own temporality, Hutton saw it as oscillating around the constants of universal laws. This metaphysic inspired Adam Smith. Hence, while usefully different and deeper than historical time, Hutton's geology is still a product of the labor and social organization of its era.

Still, thinking from the point of view of the earth and of geological time is a useful way of getting some distance on seemingly fleeting temporalities of Silicon Valley and the surface effects of information in the mediated sphere of third nature. It also cuts across obsolete assumptions of a separate sphere of the social outside of the natural. "The modern project of ruling over nature understood as resource was based on a division of the two—the Social and the Natural—but it always leaked."[260] One could rather see a first, second, and third nature as equally material in the deepest sense.

Parikka's project includes a bringing together of media materialism and historical materialism: "media structure how things are in the world and how things are known in the world."[261] I was after something similar in *Molecular Red* in turning to Karen Barad's *agential realism*, a project in which materialism is extended toward materiality in the geological, chemical, and physical sense, without entirely losing sight of the category of labor.[262]

Parikka's approach grows out of the work of Friedrich Kittler, "the Goethe scholar turned synth-geek and tinkerer."[263] For Kittler, "man" is an after-image of media-technology. One could think of this as a much-needed update on Foucault's anti-humanism, which at least drags it into the twentieth century.[264] Where Foucault looked to architectural forms, such as the prison or clinic, the structuring of visibility, the administrative ordering of bodies, Kittler takes the next step and examines media as more contemporary practices that form the human.[265] Parikka: "Media work on the level of circuits, hardware, and voltage differences, which the engineers as much as the military intelligence and secret agencies gradually recognized before the humanities did."[266]

Like Douglas Kahn, Parikka wants to extend this work further in the direction of what for us vulgar Marxists would constitute its base.[267] He finds a useful ally in earth artist Robert Smithson, whose "abstract geology" paid close attention to the materiality of art practice.[268] Smithson was an anti-McLuhan, in that he saw media not as extensions of man but as extensions of the earth.

But besides the intriguing spatial substitution, bringing the depths of geology into view, Parikka is also interested in changing temporal perspectives. German media theorist Wolfgang Ernst has written of media as a temporal machine, paying close attention to the shift from narrative to calculative memory.[269] Also of interest here is Siegfried Zielinski's project of a media studies of deep time.[270] Zielinski was trying to escape the teleological approach to media, where the present appears as a progressive development and realization of past potentials. He explores instead the twists and cul-de-sacs of the media archive. Parikka takes this temporal figure and vastly expands it toward nonhuman times, past and present.

Parikka proposes a double-sided relation of media to earth. On the one hand, "the geophysical that becomes registered through the ordering of media reality. And conversely, it is the earth that provides for media and enables it."[271] This double articulation might have its problems, as we shall see later. The goal is to think of a *medianature* as one continuum, rather like Haraway's natureculture.[272] "Medianatures ... is a concept that crystallizes the 'double-bind' of media and nature as co-constituting spheres."[273]

The third nature of information flows does not run on silicon alone. It also runs on fossil fuels. The Anthropocene, which Parikka recodes as the *Anthrobscene*, is "a systematic relation to the carboniferous."[274] For Jason Moore, we might as well call the present epoch the Capitalocene, given the intimate connection between the historic rise of capitalism as a mode of production and the exploitation of resources on a short-term basis, including the millennia's worth of past photosynthetic activity locked away in layers of coal seams.[275] Parikka: "Capitalism had its necessary (but not sufficient) conditions in a new relation with deep times and chemical processes of photosynthesis."[276]

Perhaps we could make the contribution of the nonhuman elements to historical materialism more visible. This might go beyond the rather speculative geology of morals in Deleuze and Guattari.[277] Like Jane Bennett, Parikka is interested in their celebration of the craft of metallurgy, a kind of experimental labor that wants to explore what a material can do. But it might not be the case that this is neatly separable from science.[278] As one learns in JD Bernal's *Science in History*, science and craft, which is to say science and social labor, are always intimately connected.[279]

Still, there is something refreshing about an approach that does not build on Deleuze's "Postscript on Control Societies," which was after all only an occasional piece, but on *Anti-Oedipus* instead.[280] In this perspective, "media history conflates with earth history; the geological materials of metals and chemicals get deterritorialized from their strata and reterritorialized in machines that define our technical media culture."[281] But I am wary of extending the category of "life" to the nonorganic, because there is a danger of merely porting an unexamined vitalism into new fields where it will function yet again as an unexamined first principle.[282]

Here we might learn more from natural scientists trying to reach into the humanities than from philosophers trying to reach into the natural sciences. Parikka usefully draws on Stephen Jay Gould's model of evolutionary time as a *punctuated equilibrium*, as a succession of more or less stable states in variation alternating with moments of more rapid change.[283] There's no sense of progress in this version of deep time, no necessary evolution from lower to higher, from simple to complex.

One can then approach the earth as an archive of different temporal blocks, each with its own rate and variability of change. "What we encounter are variations that define an alternative deep time strata of our media culture ... It offers an anarcheology of surprises and differences."[284] Starting with Hutton's heat-engine earth, but seeing it as passing through shifts as well as cycles and not necessarily on a teleological path anywhere, a vast spatial and temporal panorama opens up, within which media can operate as both very brief but also surprisingly long temporalities. A Youtube video may be fleetingly short when put against the temporality of the earth, but the afterlife of the device that played it may turn out to be moderately long.

Marx saw the machinery into which living labor was accumulated as dead labor, but perhaps it makes more sense to think of it as *undead labor*, for our machines, including media machines, may outlive us all in fossil form.[285] Parikka:

> The amount of operational electronics discarded annually is one sort of geologically significant pile that entangles first, second and third nature: the communicational vectors of advanced digital technologies come with a rather direct link to and impact on first natures ... Communicational events

are sustained by the broader aspects of geology of media. They include technologies abandoned and consisting of hazardous material: lead, cadmium, mercury, barium, and so on.[286]

In this manner, the mediasphere of third nature returns to the lithosphere. China, being short of certain key metals, imports them as scrap and mines some of its minerals now from second nature rather than from nature as such.[287] But Parikka is keen not to lose sight of labor as a category here. Rather than think of third nature as a realm of immaterial labor, he wants to emphasize hard work and hardware and the constitutive role of the geological and chemical in both.

Here it is worth recalling Marx's interest, late in life, in questions of soil chemistry, which led him toward the concept of *metabolic rift*.[288] Second nature got out of synch with nature when minerals extracted from the soil by crops grown to produce food to fuel industrial labor did not return to the soils, thereby depleting them. This led to soil science and to practices of "culturing" soil with nitrogen and potassium and so forth. Thus, there's a prehistory to third nature's dependence on a vast array of mineral inputs, and its dumping of the resultant waste, in second nature's dependence on mineral inputs to sustain—in the short term—commodified agriculture. Parikka: "A deep time of the planet is inside our machines, crystallized as part of the contemporary political economy."[289]

A manifesto-like text in *Mute Magazine* once proposed we move on from psychogeography to a *psychogeophysics*.[290] Drawing on the rogue surrealist Roger Caillois, the new materialism of Rosi Braidotti, and Timothy Morton's studies of hyperobjects, Parikka develops psychogeophysics as a low-theory approach to experimentally perceiving the continuities of medianatures.[291] "Perhaps the way to question these is not through a conceptual metaphysical discussion and essays but through excursions, walks, experiments, and assays? ...

Instead of a metaphysical essay on the nonhuman, take a walk outside."[292]

Parikka pushes back against the limits of psychogeography (not least in my formulation of it) as restricted to the interactions of the ambling human and the urban milieu.[293] A psychogeophysics might be able to detect and map a much deeper and broader field of vortexes, flows and eddies. "Psychogeophysics aims for planetary scale aesthetics." It pushes on from the opening toward the animal in posthumanities writing, toward the earth itself. "Psychogeophysics performs the continuums across the biological, the nonorganic, and the social."[294]

Here it might come up against, and have to work through, the history of nature aesthetics, in which the Grand Canyon went from being seen as beautiful to becoming sublime.[295] Both mapping and landscape painting have an intimate connection to geology (and as Bernard Smith shows, also to maritime exploration[296]). Psychogeophysics might work as a minor concept or practice of a low theory, of variation and deviation, experimenting with ways of perceiving other times and spaces. For example, the work of media artist Joyce Hinterding explores natural electromagnetic fields. The open earth circuit predates closed tech circuits.

A Geology of Media is structured around a passage from the interior of the earth (mining) to its surface (soils) to the air above (dust) and beyond. A psychogeophysics of dust might begin with Marcel Duchamp's Large Glass and his other experiments in "dust breeding." Dust, Parikka suggests, rather troubles our notions of what matter is. A case in point: I'm typing this on an Apple laptop encased in a smooth, polished aluminum shell. But the polishing of the case creates aluminum dust, which is a major health hazard. "There is a bitter irony that the residue of the utopian promise is registered in the soft tissue of a globally distributed cheap labor force."[297]

"We need to attend to the material soul. Made of lungs and breath—and the shortness and time management of breath."[298]

Here Parikka focuses on the human lung as a media that absorbs dust, some of it toxic. Workers make Apple products, imparting their labor to the product, but inhale the aluminum dust, in exchange. Where Franco Berardi proposes the soul as a new site of exploitation, exhaustion, and depression, it's worth paying attention to a more material aspect of the breath–soul relationship.[299] The soul of the hacker class toiling in the overdeveloped world might be inspired, but the lungs of the worker elsewhere may well be respiring toxic dust. Here one might examine Soviet writer Andrei Platonov's materialist theory of the soul, which sees soul as a kind of surplus over bodily subsistence.[300]

In Platonov's terms, bodies don't have souls unless they have surplus energy to expend on growing one (and in his world it is not always a good thing when they do). One could think here of all the soul-restraining features of laboring to produce third nature: Lead damages the nervous system, cadmium accumulates in the kidneys, mercury affects the brain, barium causes brain swelling and liver damage, and so on.

"Mines are a central part of this picture of cognitive capital."[301] Here I agree with Parikka that the rather ethereal theories of semio-capitalism or cognitive capitalism, let alone their acceleration, could do with contact with perspectives such as those of Jason Moore.[302] The latter stresses the material shortcuts on which commodification is based, such as cheap nature, cheap labor, and cheap energy—but which leave long-term debts unpaid. Something like 81 percent of the energy used in the life cycle of computers is to make them, and much of that still comes from burning coal. It is ironic that the dust-free clean rooms of high tech industry are fueled by a process that throws ton after ton of coal dust into the air. "Dust does not stay outside us but is a narrative that *enters* us."[303]

The race for resources that colonizes the planet is continually throwing off waste that will far outlive the cycles of production and consumption in which they are consumed. Parikka: "Any extended understanding of the cultural techniques and technologies of the cognitariat needs to be able to take into account not just souls but where breath comes from."[304]

It is strange that we use the word *fossil* in two such difference senses: fossils are treasured artifacts of the past; fossil *fuels* are artifacts from the deep past to be burned up for energy, their waste cast into the atmosphere with abandon. Parikka teases out two other senses of the word *fossil*: fossil futures and future fossils. What are the potential futures that are now fossil relics in the archive? What fossils are we making now that we can imagine being discovered in some future time, by some other sentient species, after our human-species being has gone the way of the dinosaurs?[305]

The figure of the fossil provides a useful way of thinking and experimentally practicing a psychogeophysics. Fossils are a strange kind of "media" artifact, preserving information across deep time. Certainly the media technology of recent times will make an interesting fossil layer of the Anthropocene for future robot or alien archaeologists.[306] And imagining them as such helps us think about the third nature of information vectors, hurtling information around the world through fiberoptic cable at the speed of light, as something other than a world of super-fast temporalities.

Parikka:

> We need to address how fossils, whether of humans, dinosaurs, or indeed electronics, infuse with the archaic levels of the earth in terms of their electronic waste load and represent a "third nature" overlapping and entangling with the first and second ... The third nature is the logistical vector of information through which production of second nature takes a new informational pace. But as we see from the existence of media fossils, the spheres of two and three are as entangled with "first nature" as they are with each other. They are historically codetermining in a way that defies any clear cut differences between the modern

era of industrialization and the postmodern era of information. In addition, the material residue of the third nature is visible in the hardware and waste it leaves behind, despite its ability to reach abstract informational levels.[307]

Paolo Virno dispenses with the category of second nature in Marx, arguing that Marx only ever used it to denote the false sense of "naturalness" of bourgeois life.[308] But where Parikka and I differ from Virno is in trying to show the paradoxical "real-falseness" of the second nature that bourgeois culture celebrated. It was false in being utterly dependent on cheap labor, cheap nature, and cheap energy, as Patel and Moore would put it. It was doomed from the start to a temporary existence, given the metabolic rift it opened up with its own conditions of existence.

And the solution was not to reverse course, to try to find a way to value what socially organized production takes from, and gives back, from second nature to nature. On the contrary, the solution was to build out a third nature that would deploy the information vector to extract even more resources out of nature, from deeper, from further. And excrete even more waste into the rapidly closing system of planetary metabolism. As Adorno and Debord insisted in their different ways: the whole is the false.[309] It's a second nature and now a third nature that commodified relations of production have extruded out of social labor, like shiny but very temporary soap bubbles.

Media artists play a key role throughout this book, but particularly in opening up the question of the fossil. Worth mentioning is Grégory Chanosky's work on *telofossils*, which posits an alternative teleology to the accelerationist one. In accelerationist thinking, the future extrudes as a linear intensification of the present. For Chanosky, today's tech is tomorrow's fossils, dead and extinct yet preserving their now useless form.

Particularly affecting is Trevor Paglen's *The Last Pictures*, an intentional fossil.[310] Paglen created a photo archive to be attached to a satellite and boosted into space, as satellites are likely to be among the longest living fossils of the era of third nature. Thus, Parikka's movement throughout the book from underground to surface to atmosphere terminates in what for Lisa Parks is our orbital culture.

Besides its spatial imagination, *A Geology of Media* opens up a usefully nonhuman way of thinking about temporalities. The accelerationist view only perceives human time speeding into an inhuman one in which artificial intelligence supersedes us. It seems unable to think the deep, nonhuman times that get produced along the way, as the accelerating juggernaut of third nature throws off waste products, some of which may outlast life itself.

However, one limit to Parikka's project is suggested by this very figure of the fossil, particularly if we think of what Quentin Meillassoux calls the *arche-fossil*.[311] How is it possible to have knowledge of a rock that existed before humans existed? How can there be knowledge of an object that existed in the world before there could be a correlative subject of knowledge? I'm not sure Parikka's double articulation of media and geology really addresses this proposition.

Meillassoux's approach is to abolish the subject of knowledge and restore a speculative and pre-Kantian philosophy of the object, the essential and primary properties of which are mathematical and hence allegedly prior to any sensing and knowing subject. The problem with this is that Meillassoux has to bracket off the complex of scientific labor and apparatus through which the fossil is known at all. His is a contemplative realism that takes the fossil as simply given to thought. What he takes to be its primary qualities, mathematically described, are really the product of tertiary qualities, produced by an inhuman apparatus of scientific instrumentation that mediates a knowledge of this nonhuman object to the human.

Here I find Karen Barad's *agential realism* to be most helpful as a genuinely Marxist theory of science, in that it concerns itself with the means of production of knowledge.[312] The nonhuman world of the fossil is mediated through the inhuman world of an apparatus, one that can sense things beyond the secondary qualities of objects detectable to the merely human senses. Rather than expand the category of object, as Meillassoux's speculative realism does, or attribute life or consciousness to the inorganic and nonhuman as the new materialism does, one can expand the middle, the mediating term, which in this case is the inhuman apparatus of undead labor mixed with living labor.

The inhuman apparatus can perceive beyond the merely subjective time of the human, for it too, like the fossil, is a product of deep time. There is no mystery of correlation to account for, as knowledge is not a matter of a subject contemplating an object. Rather, the appearance of objects and subjects as entities with specific boundaries and temporalities is itself a product of an inhuman process engaging many agents with many temporalities, some of them very deep indeed.

Hence I agree with Parikka here: "We need carefully to refine what we mean by media and communication in the noncorrelationist as well as new materialist contexts of contemporary media culture."[313] But one does not achieve this by extending the category of "life" or "thought" into the deep time of the nonhuman, because this is simply the mirror image to speculative realism's erasure of the subject under the weight of its vision of a chaotic and collapsing objective-real. Both approaches want to assign to a high theory a power it does not have, to define the whole field of being and becoming by itself.

This latent tendency in the book seems contrary to its main achievement, which is to show the power of a more collaborative approach to knowledge, in which a low theory of psychogeophysics wanders between fields or burrows under them, rather than flying like Icarus above them.[314]

While it was a magnificent achievement, the problem with Friedrich Kittler's media theory, the thing that really dates it, is that it had still not given up on the imperial ambitions of a high theory.[315] By pushing this field-colonizing theory as far as it will go, beyond the media apparatus toward the geology from which it is extruded, Parikka makes a step forward in the direction of a new organization of knowledge, toward a "post-colonial" media theory, in the limited sense of not attempting to colonize other fields of knowledge.

Parikka:

> Media materiality is not contained in the machines, even if the machines themselves contain a planet. The machines are more like vectors across the geopolitics of labor, resources, planetary excavations, energy production, natural processes, from photosynthesis to mineralization, and the aftereffects of electronic waste.[316]

Such a perspective calls for a mediating of the various kinds of knowledge of the component parts of that totality to one another without the pretentions to mastery of any one field or discipline over all the others—which is, in brief, the methodological and political principle this book has tried to embody.

Notes

Introduction

1 Jean-François Lyotard, *The Postmodern Condition: A Report on Knowledge*, Minneapolis: University of Minnesota Press, 1984.

2 Bill Reading, *The University in Ruins*, Cambridge, MA: Harvard University Press, 1997.

3 Cathy Davidson, *The New Education*, New York: Basic Books, 2017.

4 Stefano Harney and Fred Moten, *The Undercommons: Fugitive Planning and Black Study*, London: Minor Compositions, 2013.

5 Alexander Bogdanov, *The Philosophy of Living Experience: Popular Outlines*, Chicago, IL: Haymarket Books, 2017.

6 Such might be the disability studies perspective here. See Dan Goodley, *Disability Studies: An Interdisciplinary Introduction*, Thousand Oaks, CA: Sage Publications, 2016.

7 David F. Noble, *The Religion of Technology: The Divinity of Man and the Spirit of Invention*, New York: Knopf, 1997.

8 Here disability studies has a lot to teach us: Lennard J. Davis, ed., *The Disability Studies Reader*, New York: Routledge, 2016.

9 McKenzie Wark, *Molecular Red: Theory for the Anthropocene*, New York: Verso, 2015, 213ff.

10 I am happy to report there is scholarship on this: K. P. Sreekumar and G. P. Nirmalan, "Estimation of Total Surface Area in Indian Elephants," *Veterinary Research Communications* 14, 1, 1990, 5–17. That paper develops a formula for estimating surface area from weight. I do not know if the paper supports the eighty-eight-meters-squared number, because it is behind a paywall. The parable is based on the Coastline Paradox, first noted by Lewis Fry Richardson and made famous by Benoit Mandelbrot.

11 Jack Halberstam, *The Queer Art of Failure*, Durham, NC: Duke University Press, 2011.

12 Janet Roitman, *Anti-Crisis*, Durham, NC: Duke University Press, 2012.

13 McKenzie Wark, *General Intellects*, New York: Verso, 2017.

I. Aesthetics

1 Sianne Ngai, *Our Aesthetic Categories: Zany, Cute, Interesting*, Cambridge, MA: Harvard University Press, 2015.

2 Ibid., 14.

3 Limor Schifman, *Memes in Digital Culture*, Cambridge, MA: MIT Press, 2013.

4 Ngai, *Our Aesthetic Categories*, 238.

5 McKenzie Wark, *Capital is Dead: Is This Something Worse?*, New York: Verso, 2019.

6 Jack Halberstam, *The Queer Art of Failure*, Durham, NC: Duke University Press, 2011; Justin Vivian Bond, *Tango*, New York: Feminist Press at City University of New York, 2011.

7 Hugh Kenner, *Chuck Jones: A Flurry of Drawings*, Berkeley: University of California Press, 1994.

8 Paolo Virno, *A Grammar of the Multitude*, Los Angeles: Semiotext(e), 2004; Angela McRobbie, *Be Creative*, Cambridge, UK: Polity, 2016; see McKenzie Wark, *General Intellects*, New York: Verso, 2017, chapters 3 and 7.

9 Paul B. Preciado, *Testo Junkie*, New York: Feminist Press at City University of New York, 2013; see Wark, *General Intellects*, chapter 15.

10 Celeste Olalquiaga, *The Artificial Kingdom: On the Kitsch Experience*, Minneapolis: University of Minnesota Press, 2002.

11 Karl Marx and Frederick Engels, *Collected Works, Vol. 35. Capital, Vol. 1*, New York: International Publishers, 1996, 81ff.

12 Ngai, *Our Aesthetic Categories*, 79.

13 Keston Sutherland, *Stupefaction*, Calcutta: Seagull Books, 2011.

14 Ngai, *Our Aesthetic Categories*, 100.

15 Walter Benjamin, "The Mimetic Faculty" and "Some Remarks on Folk Art," *Selected Writings Vol. 2: 1927–1934*, Cambridge, MA: Harvard University Press, 1999.

16 Gertrude Stein, *Tender Buttons*, San Francisco: City Lights, 2014.

17 Ngai, *Our Aesthetic Categories*, 93.

18 Francis Ponge, "Orange," *Laurel Review* 49, 1, 2016.

19 Ngai, *Our Aesthetic Categories*, 96.

20 Louis Althusser, *On the Reproduction of Capitalism*, London: Verso, 2014.

21 Theodor Adorno, *Minima Moralia*, London: Verso, 2006.

22 Isabelle Stengers, *Power and Invention*, Minneapolis: University of Minnesota Press, 1997; see Wark, *General Intellects*, chapter 20.

23 Ngai, *Our Aesthetic Categories*, 116.

24 Dashiell Hammett, *The Thin Man*, New York: Vintage Books, 1989.

25 T. J. Clark, *The Painting of Modern Life*, Princeton, NJ: Princeton University Press, 1999.

26 Ngai, *Our Aesthetic Categories*, 122, 129, 132.

27 Raymond Williams, *Keywords*, Oxford: Oxford University Press, 1985, 172–3.

28 Susan Sontag, *On Photography*, New York: Picador, 2001; Roland Barthes, *Camera Lucida*, New York: Hill & Wang, 2010; Vilém Flusser, *Towards a Philosophy of Photography*, London: Reaktion Books, 2000.

29 Tom McCarthy, *The Remainder*, London: Alma Modern Classics, 2015.

30 Franco Moretti, *Graphs, Maps and Trees*, London: Verso, 2007.

31 McKenzie Wark, "Digital Provenance and the Artwork as Derivative," *eflux journal*, no. 77, November 2016.

32 Ngai, *Our Aesthetic Categories*, 158.

33 Ibid., 171.

34 Jean-François Lyotard, *The Postmodern Condition*, Minneapolis: University of Minnesota Press, 1984; Nick Land, *Fanged Noumena*, Falmouth, UK: Urbanomic, 2011.

35 Ngai, *Our Aesthetic Categories*, 13.

36 Ibid., 237.

37 Although perhaps the *pretty* could function as a minor aesthetic in relation to the beautiful. That's the conceit of Jessie Rovinelli's film *So Pretty* (2019). See McKenzie Wark, "Femme as in Fuck You," *eflux journal*, no. 102, September 2019.

38 Ngai, *Our Aesthetic Categories*, 241.

39 Ibid., 242.

40 Hiroki Azuma, *Otaku: Japan's Database Animals*, Minneapolis: University of Minnesota Press, 2009; see Wark, *General Intellects*, chapter 14.

41 McKenzie Wark, *A Hacker Manifesto*, Cambridge, MA: Harvard University Press, 2004; McKenzie Wark, *Gamer Theory*, Cambridge, MA: Harvard University Press, 2007.

42 Raymond Queneau et al., *Oulipo Laboratory*, London: Atlas Press, 1996.

43 Mark Fisher, "Terminator versus Avatar: Notes on Accelerationism," markfisherblog.tumblr.com, 2013

44 Karl Marx, "The Eighteenth Brumaire of Napoleon Bonaparte," in *Surveys From Exile: Political Writings, Volume 2*, London: Verso, 2010, 146.

45 Kodwo Eshun, *More Brilliant Than the Sun*, London: Quartet, 1996, 96.

46 Robin MacKay, ed., *#Accelerate: The Accelerationist Reader*, Falmouth, UK: Urbanomic, 2014.
47 Aria Dean, "Blacceleration," *eflux journal*, no. 87, December 2017.
48 Fredric Jameson, *A Singular Modernity*, London: Verso, 2013.
49 Greg Tate, *Flyboy 2*, Durham, NC: Duke University Press, 2016; Mark Dery, "'Black to the Future'": Interviews with Samuel Delany, Greg Tate and Tricia Rose," in Mark Dery, ed., *Flame Wars: The Discourse of Cyberculture*, Durham, NC: Duke University Press, 1994.
50 Jenna Worthham, "How Janelle Monáe Found Her Voice," *New York Times Magazine*, April, 29, 2018.
51 These are documented in the volume The Otolith Group, *A Long Time Between Suns*, Berlin: Sternberg Press, 2009.
52 Michel Foucault, "Of Other Spaces," *Diacritics* 16, 1, 1986, 22–7.
53 Eshun, *More Brilliant Than the Sun*, 6.
54 Doug Millard, *Cosmonauts: Birth of the Space Age*, London: Science Museum, 2014.
55 Abhrajyoti Chakraborty, "When Satjayit Ray Came to Hollywood," *Hazlitt*, May 2, 2017.
56 Roger Zelazny, *Lord of Light*, New York: Harper, 2010.
57 Brian Aldis, *Trillion Year Spree*, New York: Atheneum, 1986.
58 Samuel Delany, *About Writing*, Middletown, CT: Wesleyan University Press, 2006.
59 Rosi Bradiotti, *The Posthuman*, Cambridge, UK: Polity, 2013.
60 JD Bernal, *The World, the Flesh & the Devil: An Enquiry into the Future of the Three Enemies of the Rational Soul*, 1929, https://www.marxists.org/archive/bernal/works/1920s/soul/.
61 Preciado, *Testo Junkie*; see Wark, *General Intellects*, chapter 15.
62 Eshun, *More Brilliant Than the Sun*, 1, 7, 89, 5.
63 See Hari Kunzru, *White Tears: A Novel*, New York: Vintage, 2018.
64 Eshun, *More Brilliant Than the Sun*, 85 (emphasis mine).
65 Patrice Khan-Cullors, *When They Call You a Terrorist: A Black Lives Matter Memoir*, New York: St Martin's Press, 2018.
66 Eshun, *More Brilliant Than the Sun*, 6.
67 Paul Gilroy, *The Black Atlantic*, Cambridge, MA: Harvard University Press, 1993; see Wark, *General Intellects*, chapter 8.
68 Eshun, *More Brilliant Than the Sun*, 5.
69 Tina Richardson, ed., *Walking Inside Out*, London: Rowman & Littlefield, 2015.
70 Jean-François Lyotard, *Libidinal Economy*, London: Bloomsbury, 2015.
71 Eshun, *More Brilliant Than the Sun*, 4.
72 Ibid., 3.
73 Azuma, Otaku; see Wark, *General Intellects*, chapter 14.

74 Dan Sicko, *Techno Rebels*, New York: Billboard Books, 2010.

75 Saidiya Hartman, *Scenes of Subjection*, New York: Oxford University Press, 1997.

76 Sun Ra, *The Immeasurable Equation: Collected Poetry and Prose*, Wartaweil, Germany: Waitawhile, 2006.

77 Lisa Nakamura, *Digitizing Race*, Minneapolis: University of Minnesota Press, 2008.

78 Eshun, *More Brilliant Than the Sun*, 69, 71.

79 Ibid., 76–7.

80 Ibid., 95.

81 Jim Fricke and Charlie Ahearn, *Yes Yes Y'all*, New York: Da Capo Press, 2003; Jeff Chang, *Can't Stop Won't Stop*, New York: Picador, 2005.

82 Paul Virilio and Sylvère Lotringer, *Pure War*, Los Angeles: Semiotext(e), 2008, 76.

83 Gerald Raunig, *Dividuum*, Los Angeles: Semiotext(e), 2016.

84 Eshun, *More Brilliant Than the Sun*, 38.

85 W. E. B. Du Bois, *The Souls of Black Folk*, New York: Oxford University Press, 2014.

86 Eshun, *More Brilliant Than the Sun*, 54.

87 Rachel Kaadzi Ghansah, "De origine actibusque aequationis," *Los Angeles Review of Books*, October 10, 2013.

88 Quoted in Eshun, *More Brilliant Than the Sun*, 34.

89 Ibid., 197 n14.

90 Eshun, *More Brilliant Than the Sun*, 19.

91 Ibid., 20.

92 Wark, *Gamer Theory*, chapter 2.

93 Although this geneology could be disputed. See DeForrest Brown jr, *Assembling a Black Counter-Culture*, New York: Primary Informaiton, forthcoming.

94 Eshun, *More Brilliant Than the Sun*, 101–2, 29.

95 Ibid., 103.

96 L. H. Stallings, *Funk the Erotic*, Bloomington: University of Illinois Press, 2015.

97 Eshun, *More Brilliant Than the Sun*, 107 (emphasis in the original), 114.

98 Donna Haraway, *Manifestly Haraway*, Minneapolis: University of Minnesota Press, 2016; see Wark, *General Intellects*, chapter 21.

99 Eshun, *More Brilliant Than the Sun*, 112.

100 Gilles Deleuze and Felix Guattari, *Anti-Oedipus*, London: Penguin, 2009.

101 Eshun, *More Brilliant Than the Sun*, 131.

102 Ibid., 66.

103   Ibid., 150, 151.

104   Ibid., 4–5, 6.

105   R. Murray Schafer, *The Soundscape*, Rochester, VT: Destiny Books, 1993.

106   See Txgen Meyer, *The Thirst for Acceleration*, Trans Women Writer's Collective, Los Angeles, 2019.

107   Or perhaps one could think otherwise about what cognition is: Katherine Hayles, *Unthought: The Power of the Cognitive Nonconscious*, Chicago, IL: University of Chicago Press, 2017.

108   Eshun, *More Brilliant Than the Sun*, 182.

109   Ibid., 26.

110   Louis Chude-Sokei, *The Sound of Culture*, Middletown, CT: Wesleyan, 2015.

111   Filippo Tommaso Marinetti, *Mafarka the Futurist*, London: Middlesex University Press, 1998.

112   Samuel Butler, *Erewhon*, London: Penguin Classics, 1979; Angela Davis, *Blues Legacies and Black Feminism*, New York: Vintage, 1999.

113   Giorgio Agamben, *The Open: Man and Animal*, Stanford, CA: Stanford University Press, 2003.

114   Lisa Nakamura, *Cybertypes*, New York: Routledge, 2002.

115   Janet Abbate, *Inventing the Internet*, Cambridge, MA: MIT Press, 2000.

116   Nicholas Mirzoeff, ed., *The Visual Culture Reader*, New York: Routledge, 2012.

117   Nakamura, *Digitizing Race*, 5.

118   Lisa Parks, *Cultures in Orbit*, Durham, NC: Duke University Press, 2005.

119   Chela Sandoval, *Methodology of the Oppressed*, Minneapolis: University of Minnesota Press, 2000; Paul Gilroy, *Darker Than Blue: On the Moral Economies of Black Atlantic Culture*, Cambridge, MA: Harvard University Press, 2011; Haraway, *Manifestly Haraway*; see Wark, *General Intellects*, chapter 21.

120   Nicholas Mirzoeff, *How to See the World*, New York: Basic Books, 2016.

121   Azuma, Otaku; see Wark, *General Intellects*, chapter 14.

122   Nakamura, *Digitizing Race*, 27.

123   For instance, Joshua Clover, *The Matrix*, London: BFI Modern Classics, 2007. For a transgender reading, see Cael M. Keegan, *Lana and Lily Wachowski*, Urbana: University of Illinois Press, 2018.

124   Nakamura, *Digitizing Race*, 104.

125   Eugene Thacker, *Biomedia*, Minneapolis: University of Minnesota Press, 2004.

126 Nakamura, *Digitizing Race*, 94, 96.

127 Ibid., 100, 101.

128 Coco Fusco, *The Bodies That Were Not Ours*, New York: Routledge, 2001.

129 Ruha Benjamin, *Race After Technology*, Cambridge, UK: Polity Press, 2019.

130 Nakamura, *Digitizing Race*, 148.

131 Ibid., 116.

132 Ibid., 116, 117.

133 Steven Brown, *Tokyo Cyberpunk*, London: Palgrave, 2010.

134 Asada Akira, "Infantile Capitalism and Japan's Postmodernism: A Fairy Tale," in Masao Miyoshi and Harry Harootunian, eds, *Postmodernism and Japan*, Durham, NC: Duke University Press, 1989, 273–8.

135 Gilroy, *Darker than Blue*.

136 Nakamura, *Digitizing Race*, 30–1.

137 Ibid., 33.

138 Whitney Phillips, *This Is Why We Can't Have Nice Things*, Cambridge, MA: MIT Press, 2011.

139 Henry Jenkins, *Convergence Culture*, New York: New York University Press, 2008.

140 Hito Steyerl, *The Wretched of the Screen*, New York: eflux, 2013.

141 Eric Michaels, *Bad Aboriginal Art*, Minneapolis: Minnesota University Press, 1994; Svetlana Boym et al., *RAQS Media Collective: Casebook*, Toronto: Art Gallery of York University, 2014.

142 See for example, Brian Larkin, *Signal and Noise: Media, Infrastructure and Urban Culture in Nigeria*, Durham, NC: Duke University Press, 2008.

143 Yuk Hui, *The Question Concerning Technology in China*, Falmouth, UK: Urbanomic, 2016.

144 Maria Fernandez and Faith Wilding, *Domain Errors! Cyberfeminist Practices*, New York: Autonomedia, 2003.

145 Nakamura, *Digitizing Race*, 160.

146 Ibid., 161.

147 Donna Landry and Gerald MacLean, eds, *The Spivak Reader: Selected Works of Gayatri Chakravorty Spivak*, New York: Routledge, 1995.

148 Dick Hebdige, *Subculture: The Meaning of Style*, London: Routledge, 1979.

149 Nakamura, *Digitizing Race*, 168.

150 Ibid., 96.

151 Raunig, *Dividuum*; Maurizio Lazzarato, *Signs and Machines*, Los Angeles: Semiotext(e), 2014: see Wark, *General Intellects*, chapter 5.

152 Adorno, *Minima Moralia*, 57.

153 Hito Steyerl, *Duty Free Art: Art in the Age of Planetary Civil War*, London: Verso, 2017, 185.

154 Ibid.

155 Ibid., 3, 15.

156 Joseph Schumpeter, *Capitalism, Socialism and Democracy*, New York: Harper Perennial, 2008.

157 Yves Citton, *The Ecology of Attention*, Cambridge, UK: Polity, 2017.

158 Steyerl, *Duty Free Art*, 24.

159 Stewart Home, *The Art Strike Papers*, Stirling, UK: AK Press, 1991.

160 Steve Anderson, *Technologies of Vision*, Cambridge, MA: MIT Press, 2017.

161 Astra Taylor, "The Automation Charade," *Logic: A Magazine About Technology*, no. 5, 2018.

162 Steyerl, *Duty Free Art*, 34.

163 Jacques Rancière, *Hatred of Democracy*, London: Verso, 2014.

164 Steyerl, *Duty Free Art*, 38.

165 Ibid.

166 Finn Brunton, *Spam: A Shadow History of the Internet*, Cambridge, MA: MIT Press, 2015.

167 McKenzie Wark, *The Spectacle of Disintegration*, London: Verso, 2013.

168 A term put in circulation by a program of that name at the Strelka Institute, Moscow, 2016.

169 Steyerl, *Duty Free Art*, 44, 44.

170 Ibid., 47.

171 Eyal Weizman, *Forensic Architecture*, Cambridge, MA: MIT Press, 2017.

172 McKenzie Wark, *Virtual Geography*, Bloomington: Indiana University Press, 1994.

173 Steyerl, *Duty Free Art*, 63.

174 Ibid., 71.

175 Ibid., 57.

176 Jonathan Beller, *The Message is Murder*, London: Pluto Press, 2018.

177 Philip Mirowski, *Machine Dreams*, Cambridge: Cambridge University Press, 2002.

178 Steyerl, *Duty Free Art*, 158.

179 Ibid., 157.

180 Wark, *Gamer Theory*, chapter 1.

181 Steyerl, *Duty Free Art*, 159.

182 Ibid., 68–9.

183 Harold Innis, *The Bias of Communication*, Toronto: University of Toronto Press, 1999.

184 Steyerl, *Duty Free Art*, 81.

185   Peter Osbourne, *Anywhere or Not at All*, London: Verso, 2013.

186   Steyerl, *Duty Free Art*, 97.

187   Peter Bürger, *Theory of the Avant-Garde*, Minneapolis: University of Minnesota Press, 1994.

188   Gregory Sholette, *Dark Matter*, London: Pluto Press, 2011.

189   Thomas Elsaesser, *Melodrama, Trauma, Mind-Games*, London: Routledge, 2008.

190   Steyerl, *Duty Free Art*, 130.

191   Ibid., 145.

192   Ibid., 59.

193   Fredric Jameson, *Postmodernism, or, The Cultural Logic of Late Capitalism*, London: Verso, 1992.

194   Steyerl, *Duty Free Art*, 150.

195   Ibid., 181.

196   Stuart Hall, *Cultural Studies 1983: A Theoretical History*, Durham, NC: Duke University Press, 2016.

197   Steyerl, *Duty Free Art*, 178.

198   Christina Kiaer, *Imagine No Possessions: The Socialist Objects of Russian Constructivism*, Cambridge, MA: MIT Press, 2008.

199   Mark Fisher, *Capitalist Realism*, Winchester, UK: Zero Books, 2009.

200   Bernard Stiegler, *Acting Out*, Stanford, CA: Stanford University Press, 2008.

201   Steyerl, *Duty Free Art*, 177.

202   Ibid., 18.

203   Ibid., 24.

204   McKenzie Wark, *The Beach Beneath the Street*, London: Verso, 2011, chapter 11.

205   Mark Wigley, *Constant's New Babylon*, Rotterdam: 010 Press, 1999.

206   Gabriel Tarde, *On Communication and Social Influence*, Chicago: University of Chicago Press, 2011.

207   Kathleen Welsch, *Electric Rhetoric: Classical Rhetoric, Oralism and a New Literacy*, Cambridge, MA: MIT Press, 1999.

208   Lazzarato, *Signs and Machines*: see Wark, *General Intellects*, chapter 5.

209   Stuart Hall, "Encoding and Decoding," in Meenakshi Gigi Durham and Douglas Kellner, eds, *Media and Cultural Studies: Keyworks*, Hoboken, NJ: Wiley-Blackwell, 2012.

210   Marshall McLuhan, *Understanding Media*, Berkeley, CA: Ginko Press, 2003. That technology isn't shaped toward a final form is a way of thinking about it contra Heidegger.

211   Karen Barad, *Meeting the Universe Halfway*, Durham, NC: Duke University Press, 2007. See McKenzie Wark, *Molecular Red: Theory for the Anthropocene*, New York: Verso, 2015, 152ff.

212 Melissa Gregg and Greg Seigworth, eds, *The Affect Theory Reader*, Durham, NC: Duke University Press, 2010.

213 Citton, *The Ecology of Attention*, 5.

214 Stiegler, *Acting Out*.

215 Paolo Virno, *Multitude Between Innovation and Negation*, Los Angeles: Semiotext(e), 2008.

216 Wark, *Molecular Red*, 40ff.

217 The four regimes of attention come from Dominique Boullier, "Les industries de l'attention," *Réseaux*, no. 154, 2009.

218 Guy Debord, *Society of the Spectacle*, New York: Zone Books, 1994; Vilém Flusser, *Into the Network of Technical Images*, Minneapolis: University of Minnesota Press, 2011.

219 Baudrillard, *Seduction*, London: Palgrave, 1991.

220 Dominic Pettman, *Love and Other Technologies*, New York: Fordham University Press, 2006.

221 Citton, *The Ecology of Attention*, 50.

222 Jean Baudrillard, *In the Shadow of the Silent Majorities*, Los Angeles: Semiotext(e), 2007.

223 Debord, *Society of the Spectacle*.

224 Matteo Pasquinelli, *Animal Spirits: A Bestiary of the Commons*, Amsterdam: nAI Publishers, 2009.

225 Nicholas Mirzoeff, *The Right to Look*, Durham, NC: Duke University Press, 2007.

226 Bernard Stiegler, *For a New Critique of Political Economy*, Cambridge, UK: Polity, 2010.

227 Siva Vaidhayanathan, *Antisocial Media*, New York: Oxford University Press, 2018; Siva Vaidhayanathan, *The Googlization of Everything*, Berkeley: University of California Press, 2012.

228 Citton, *The Ecology of Attention*, 71.

229 Ibid., 77.

230 Ibid., 78.

231 Paul Edwards, *A Vast Machine*, Cambridge, MA: MIT Press, 2010.

232 Jean-Paul Sartre, *Being and Nothingness*, New York: Washington Square Press, 1996.

233 Cathy Davidson, *The New Education*, New York: Basic Books, 2017.

234 Jacques Rancière, *The Ignorant Schoolmaster*, Stanford, CA: Stanford University Press, 1991.

235 Kojin Karatani, *The Structure of World History*, Durham, NC: Duke University Press, 2014; see Wark, *General Intellects*, chapter 2.

236 Chiara Bottici, *Imaginal Politics*, New York: Columbia University Press, 2014.

237 See Alexander Galloway's contribution to *Excommunication*, Chicago, IL: University of Chicago Press, 2013.

238 Walter Benjamin, *The Work of Art in the Age of Technological Reproducibility*, Cambridge, MA: Harvard University Press, 2008.

239 Lauren Elkin, *Flâneuse*, New York: Farrar, Strauss & Giroux, 2018.

240 Cited in Citton, *The Ecology of Attention*, 125.

241 Steven Shapin, *A Social History of Truth: Civility and Science in Seventeenth Century England*, Chicago: University of Chicago Press, 1994.

242 Donna Haraway, *Modest_Witness*, New York: Routledge, 1997.

243 Jonathan Crary, *Suspensions of Perception*, Cambridge, MA: MIT Press, 2001.

244 Katherine Hayles, *My Mother Was a Computer*, Chicago: University of Chicago Press, 2005.

245 Félix Guattari, *Three Ecologies*, London: Bloomsbury, 2014.

246 Chris Kraus, *I Love Dick*, Los Angeles: Semiotext(e), 2006.

247 Alexander Galloway, *The Interface Effect*, Cambridge, UK: Polity, 2012; see Wark, *General Intellects*, chapter 17.

248 McKenzie Wark, *The Spectacle of Disintegration*, London: Verso, 2013, chapter 17.

249 Jean Baudrillard, *Fatal Strategies*, Los Angeles: Semiotext(e), 2008.

250 For example, see the Youtube videos of Natalie Wynn, aka Contrapoints.

251 Randy Martin, *Knowledge LTD: Towards a Social Logic of the Derivative*, Philadelphia, PA: Temple University Press, 2015.

252 Ibid., 51.

253 Amy Wendling, *Karl Marx on Technology and Alienation*, London: Palgrave, 2009; see Wark, *General Intellects*, chapter 1.

254 Wark, *A Hacker Manifesto*, chapter 1.

255 Ivan Asher, *Portfolio Society: On the Capitalist Mode of Prediction*, New York: Zone Books, 2016.

256 Martin, *Knowledge LTD*, 75.

257 Hall, *Cultural Studies 1983*.

258 Jameson, *Postmodernism*; Lyotard, *The Postmodern Condition*; Arthur Kroker, *Panic Encyclopedia*, New York: St Martin's Press, 1989; Jean Baudrillard, *Simulations*, New York: Semiotext(e), 1983; Azuma, *Otaku*; see Wark, *General Intellects*, chapter 14.

259 Michael Hardt and Antonio Negri, *Multitude: War and Democracy in the Age of Empire*, New York: Penguin, 2005.

260 Walter Mignolo, *The Darker Side of Western Modernity*, Durham, NC: Duke University Press, 2011.

261 Judith Butler, *Notes Toward a Performative Theory of Assembly*, Cambridge, MA: Harvard University Press, 2018; see Wark, *General Intellects*, chapter 13.

262 Martin, *Knowledge LTD*, 206.

263 Virno, *A Grammar of the Multitude*; see Wark, *General Intellects*, chapter 3.

264 Martin, *Knowledge LTD*, 146.

265 Raymond Williams, *The Long Revolution*, Cardigan, UK: Parthian, 2012.

266 Although there have been some instances of dancers on strike: "Strictly Dancers to Go On Strike?," *The Week*, September 20, 2018.

267 Randy Martin, *Critical Moves: Dance Studies in Theory and Politics*, Durham NC: Duke University Press, 1998.

268 Ramsay Burt, *Judson Dance Theater*, New York: Routledge, 2007.

269 Martin, *Knowledge LTD*, 172.

270 Jed Rasula, *Destruction Was My Beatrice: Dada and the Unmaking of the Twentieth Century*, New York: Basic Books, 2015.

271 Martin, *Knowledge LTD*, 173.

272 Trica Rose, *Black Noise*, Middletown, CT: Wesleyan, 1994; Glen Friedman, *Dogtown: The Legend of the Z-Boys*, New York: Burning Flags, 2002.

273 Martin, *Knowledge LTD*, 189.

274 Azuma, *Otaku*; see Wark, *General Intellects*, chapter 14. Here I would also like to acknowledge the work of my New School Liberal Studies program student Michael Smaczylo.

275 Jackie Wang, *Carceral Capitalism*, Los Angeles: Semiotext(e), 2018.

276 Martin, *Knowledge LTD*, 210.

277 Angela McRobbie, *Be Creative*, Cambridge, UK: Polity, 2016; see Wark, *General Intellects*, chapter 7.

278 Randy Martin, *An Empire of Indifference*, Durham, NC: Duke University Press, 2007.

279 Martin, *Knowledge LTD*, 82.

280 Incite! *The Revolution Will Not Be Funded*, Durham, NC: Duke University Press, 2017.

281 Martin, *Knowledge LTD*, 91–2.

282 Maurizio Lazzarato, *The Making of Indebted Man*, Los Angeles: Semiotext(e), 2012.

283 Martin, *Knowledge LTD*, 100.

284 Ibid., 102.

285 Ibid., 115.

286 Nate Silver, *The Signal and the Noise*, New York: Penguin, 2015. He had become famous for predicting elections using aggregated polling data—until the 2016 Presidential election.

287 Martin, *Knowledge LTD*, 115–16.

288 Yann Moulier Boutang, *Cognitive Capitalism*, Cambridge, UK: Polity, 2012; see Wark, *General Intellects*, chapter 4.

289 Richard Dyer, *Stars*, London: BFI, 1998.

290 Martin, *Knowledge LTD*, 120.

291 Ibid., 121.

292 Chantal Mouffe, *The Democratic Paradox*, London: Verso, 2009; see Wark, *General Intellects*, chapter 11.

293 Martin, *Knowledge LTD*, 126.

294 Ibid., 123.

295 Ibid., 141.

296 Ibid., 123.

297 Ibid., 54.

298 Mirowski, *Machine Dreams*.

299 Martin, *Knowledge LTD*, 132.

300 Ibid., 47.

301 Elie Ayache, *The Blank Swan: The End of Probability*, London: Wiley, 2010.

302 Martin, *Knowledge LTD*, 55.

303 Ibid., 56.

304 Ibid.

305 Ibid., 60, 60, 14.

306 McKenzie Wark, *Capital is Dead: Is This Something Worse?* London: Verso, 2019.

307 Martin, *Knowledge LTD*, 60.

308 Ibid., 62.

309 Ibid., 61.

310 Ibid., 63.

311 Randy Martin, *Financialization of Daily Life*, Philadelphia, PA: Temple University Press, 2002.

312 Martin, *Knowledge LTD*, 78.

313 Ibid., 143.

314 Ibid., 68.

315 Ibid., 74.

316 Brian Massumi, *99 Theses on the Revaluation of Value*, Minneapolis: University of Minnesota Press, 2018.

317 Christopher Lebron, *The Making of Black Lives Matter*, New York: Oxford University Press, 2017.

318 Wark, *Gamer Theory*, chapter 9.

319 Paolo Virno, *When the Word Becomes Flesh*, Los Angeles: Semiotext(e), 2015.

320 John Bellamy Foster, Brett Clark, and Richard York, *The Ecological Rift*, New York: Monthly Review Press, 2011.

II. Ethnographics

1 Jackie Wang, *Carceral Capitalism*, Los Angeles: Semiotext(e), 2018, 193.
2 Ibid., 218–23.
3 Ibid., 286.
4 Ibid., 287.
5 On the psychogeography of Zuccotti Park and the innocent occupier: McKenzie Wark, *Spectacles of Disintegration*, London: Verso, 2013, 200–4; on innocence as it applies to the construction of the deserving (and undeserving) in the case of refugees, see McKenzie Wark, *Telesthesia*, Cambridge, UK: Polity Press, 2012, chapter 7.
6 Judith Butler, *Notes Toward a Performative Theory of Assembly*, Cambridge, MA: Harvard University Press, 2018.
7 Wang, *Carceral Capitalism*, 17.
8 Ibid., 62.
9 Huey Newton, *The Huey P. Newton Reader*, New York: Seven Stories Press, 2011.
10 David Harvey, *The Condition of Postmodernity*, Oxford: Blackwell, 1990.
11 Giorgio Agamben, *State of Exception*, Chicago, IL: University of Chicago Press, 2005.
12 Wang, *Carceral Capitalism*, 173.
13 Ibid., 175.
14 See *Afropessimism: An Introduction*, Minneapolis: Wracked and Dispatched, 2017, a free ebook that collects the key texts: https://racked anddispatched.noblogs.org.
15 See also Asad Haider, *Mistaken Identity: Race and Class in the Age of Trump*, New York: Verso, 2018.
16 Wang, *Carceral Capitalism*, 309.
17 Cedric Robinson, *Black Marxism*, Chapel Hill, NC: University of North Carolina Press, 2000.
18 Rosa Luxemburg, *The Accumulation of Capital*, London: Routledge Classics, 2003.
19 David Harvey, *New Imperialism*, New York: Oxford University Press, 2005; David Harvey, *Rebel Cities*, New York: Verso, 2013.
20 Wang, *Carceral Capitalism*, 118.
21 Ibid., 184.
22 Ibid., 53.
23 Michel Foucault, *The Birth of Biopolitics*, New York: Picador, 2010.
24 Giorgio Agamben, *Homo Sacer*, Stanford, CA: Stanford University Press, 1998; Giorgio Agamben, *State of Exception*, Chicago, IL: University of Chicago Press, 2005.

25 Roberto Esposito, *Immunitas: The Protection and Negation of Life*, Cambridge, UK: Polity, 2011.

26 Achille Mbembe, "Necropolitics," *Public Culture* 15, 1, 2003.

27 Wang, *Carceral Capitalism*, 203.

28 Ibid., 197.

29 Giorgio Agamben, *Remnants of Auschwitz*, New York: Zone Books, 2002.

30 Wang, *Carceral Capitalism*, 213.

31 Ibid., 212.

32 Michel de Certeau, *Heterologies: Discourse on the Other*, Minneapolis: University of Minnesota Press, 1986.

33 Saidya Hartman, *Lose Your Mother: A Journey Along the Atlantic Slave Route*, New York: Farrar, Straus and Giroux, 2008, might be a text from which to learn both about the erasure and the creation.

34 Howard Becker, *Outsiders*, New York: Free Press, 1997; Stanley Cohen, *Folk Devils and Moral Panics*, London: Routledge Classics, 2011.

35 Dick Hebdige, *Subculture*, London: Routledge, 1979; Stuart Hall et al., *Policing the Crisis: Mugging, the State and Law and Order*, London: Palgrave, 2013; Stuart Hall and Tony Jefferson, eds, *Resistance Through Rituals*, London; Routledge, 2006.

36 Stuart Hall et al., *Policing the Crisis*.

37 Gerald Horne, *Fire This Time: The Watts Uprising and the 1960s*, New York: Da Capo Press, 1997.

38 Paul B. Préciado, *Testo Junkie*, New York: Feminist Press at City University of New York, 2013.

39 Wang, *Carceral Capitalism*, 257.

40 Ibid., 145, 39.

41 Randy Martin, *Knowledge LTD: Towards a Social Logic of the Derivative*, Philadelphia, PA: Temple University Press, 2015.

42 Fred Moten, *Black and Blur*, Durham, NC: Duke University Press, 2017.

43 Wang, *Carceral Capitalism*, 191, 301–2.

44 Jean-Paul Sartre, *Critique of Dialectical Reason*, London: Verso, 2004.

45 Wang, *Carceral Capitalism*, 62.

46 Wang Hui, *China's Twentieth Century*, London: Verso, 2016, 152.

47 Martin Jacques, *When China Rules the World*, London: Penguin, 2012.

48 McKenzie Wark, "Undeletable Text: Eric Hobsbawm," *boundary2* 43, May 2016.

49 Wang Hui, *China from Empire to Nation State*, Cambridge, MA: Harvard University Press, 2014.

50 Hui, *China's Twentieth Century*, 13.

51 Rebecca Karl, *Staging the World*, Durham, NC: Duke University Press, 2002.

52 Max Weber, *Essays in Sociology*, Oxford: Oxford University Press, 1958.

53 Hui, *China's Twentieth Century*, 44.

54 Antonio Gramsci, *The Modern Prince and Other Writings*, New York: International Publishers, 1959.

55 Hui, *China's Twentieth Century*, 162.

56 Chantal Mouffe, *The Return of the Political*, London: Verso, 2006; see McKenzie Wark, *General Intellects*, New York: Verso, 2017, chapter 11.

57 Mao Tse Tung, *Selected Military Writings,* Beijing: Foreign Languages Press, 1967.

58 Mao Tse Tung, *Selected Works, Vol. IV,* Beijing: Foreign Languages Press, 1961, 98–100

59 Eyal Weizman, *Forensic Architecture*, Cambridge, MA: MIT Press, 2017.

60 Hui, *China's Twentieth Century*, 140.

61 Hui, *China from Empire to Nation State.*

62 Arif Dirlick, *Complicities: The People's Republic of China in Global Capitalism*, Chicago, IL: Prickly Paradigm Press, 2017.

63 Hui, *China's Twentieth Century*, 39.

64 Ibid., 155.

65 Ibid., 156.

66 On media in the cultural revolution period, see Pang Laikwan, *The Art of Cloning: Creative Production During the Cultural Revolution,* London: Verso, 2017.

67 Hui, *China's Twentieth Century*, 157–8.

68 Ibid., 167.

69 Ibid., 160.

70 Ibid., 300.

71 Ibid., 167.

72 Ibid., 168.

73 Ibid., 171.

74 Ching Kwan Lee, *Against the Law: Labor Protests in China's Rustbelt and Sunbelt*, Berkeley: University of California Press, 2007.

75 Brian Merchant, "Life and Death in Apple's Hidden City,'" *The Guardian*, June 18, 2017.

76 Hui, *China's Twentieth Century*, 161.

77 Ibid., 188.

78 Butler, *Notes Toward a Performative Theory of Assembly*; see Wark, *General Intellects*, chapter 13.

79 Hui, *China's Twentieth Century*, 189.

80 Ibid., 227.

81 Rebecca Karl, *The Magic of Concepts*, Durham, NC: Duke University Press, 2017.

82 Young-tsu Wong, *Beyond Confucian China*, London: Routledge, 2015.
83 Hui, *China's Twentieth Century*, 273.
84 Pascale Cassanova, *The World Republic of Letters*, Cambridge, MA: Harvard University Press, 2007.
85 Hui, *China's Twentieth Century*, 279.
86 Kojin Karatani, *The Structure of World History*, Durham, NC: Duke University Press, 2014; see Wark, *General Intellects*, chapter 2.
87 Hui, *China's Twentieth Century*, 289.
88 Ibid., 292.
89 Ibid., 164.
90 Adrian Chan, *Chinese Marxism*, London: Bloomsbury, 2003.
91 Hui, *China's Twentieth Century*, 180.
92 Xi Jinping, *The Governance of China, Vol.* 2, Shanghai: Shanghai Press, 2018.
93 Hui, *China's Twentieth Century*, 224–5.
94 Anna Lowenhaupt Tsing, *Friction: An Ethnography of Global Connection*, Princeton, NJ: Princeton University Press, 2005, 1.
95 Gayatri Spivak, *Critique of Postcolonial Reason,* Cambridge, MA: Harvard University Press, 1999.
96 Martin Jay, *Marxism and Totality*, Berkeley: University of California Press, 1986.
97 Tsing, *Friction*, 11.
98 Ibid., 4, 6.
99 Ibid., 77.
100 Ibid., 12.
101 Ibid., ix.
102 Ibid., 29.
103 James Clifford, *Routes: Travel and Translation in the Late Twentieth Century*, Cambridge, MA: Harvard University Press, 1997.
104 Tsing, *Friction*, 35.
105 Ibid., 44–5.
106 Ibid., 52.
107 Ibid., 75, 54.
108 Ibid., 200.
109 Weizman, *Forensic Architecture*, 201–2.
110 Ibid., 202.
111 Benedict Anderson and Ruth McVey, *A Preliminary Analysis of the October 1, 1964 Coup in Indonesia*, Singapore: Equinox, 2009.
112 Using the language of the Situationists. See McKenzie Wark, *The Beach Beneath the Street*, London: Verso, 2011, chapter 3.
113 Tsing, *Friction*, 215.
114 Ibid., 228.

115 Vandana Shiva, *The Vandana Shiva Reader*, Lexington: University Press of Kentucky, 2014.

116 Tsing, *Friction*, 234.

117 Ibid., 246, 262.

118 Ibid., 84–5.

119 Margret Grebowicz, *The National Park to Come*, Stanford, CA: Stanford University Press, 2015.

120 Tsing, *Friction*, 88.

121 Paul Edwards, *A Vast Machine*, Cambridge, MA: MIT Press, 2010.

122 Ibid., 102, 103, 105.

123 Alexander Bogdanov, *The Philosophy of Living Experience*, Chicago, IL: Haymarket Press, 2017.

124 Tsing, *Friction*, 108.

125 Ibid., 160 (emphasis in the original).

126 Donna Haraway, *Staying With the Trouble*, Durham, NC: Duke University Press, 2016; see Wark, *General Intellects*, 132ff.

127 Bruno Latour, *Facing Gaia*, Cambridge, UK: Polity Press, 2017.

128 Tsing, *Friction*, 270.

129 Ibid., 271, 267.

130 Ibid., 81, 211.

131 Chiara Bottici, *Imaginal Politics*, New York: Columbia University Press, 2014.

132 Achille Mbembe, *On the Postcolony*, Berkeley: University of California Press, 2001, 231.

133 Paul Gilroy, *Against Race*, Cambridge, MA: Harvard University Press, 2002; see Wark, *General Intellects*, chapters 8.

134 Spivak, *Critique of Postcolonial Reason*.

135 Ibid.

136 Mbembe, *On the Postcolony*, 3.

137 Ibid., 9 (emphasis in the original).

138 Ibid., 12.

139 Ibid., 13.

140 Ibid., 181.

141 Ibid., 185, 189.

142 Ibid., 189, 199.

143 Ibid., 178.

144 Ibid., 26.

145 Alexandre Kojève, *Introduction to the Reading of Hegel*, Ithaca, NY: Cornell University Press, 1980.

146 Chantal Mouffe, *The Democratic Paradox*, London: Verso, 2009; see Wark, *General Intellects*, chapter 11.

147 Mbembe, *On the Postcolony*, 45.

148 Ibid., 49.

149 Ibid., 67, 76.
150 Ibid., 77.
151 Ibid., 78.
152 Ibid., 79.
153 Ibid., 86.
154 Ibid., 93.
155 Karatani, *The Structure of World History*; see Wark, *General Intellects*, chapter 2.
156 Mbembe, *On the Postcolony*, 103.
157 Ibid., 108.
158 Ibid., 109.
159 Ibid., 123.
160 Mbembe is here offering a commentary on the work of Labou Tansi. See for example, *Life and a Half: A Novel*, Bloomington: Indiana University Press, 2011.
161 Mbembe, *On the Postcolony*, 110.
162 Ibid., 110.
163 Ibid., 129.
164 Ibid., 163, 164, 201.
165 Ibid., 17.
166 James Clifford, *The Predicament of Culture*, Cambridge, MA: Harvard University Press, 1988.
167 Eduardo Viveiros de Castro, *Cannibal Metaphysics*, Minneapolis, MN: Univocal, 2017.
168 Ibid., 46.
169 Claude Levi-Strauss, *The Savage Mind*, Chicago, IL: University of Chicago Press, 1966.
170 Marilyn Strathern, *Partial Connections*, Walnut Creek, CA: Altamira Press, 2004.
171 Viveiros, *Cannibal Metaphysics*, 60, 62.
172 Ibid., 63.
173 Gilles Deleuze, *Difference and Repetition*, New York: Columbia University Press, 1995.
174 Viveiros, *Cannibal Metaphysics*, 68.
175 Ibid., 90 (emphasis in the original).
176 Gilles Deleuze and Felix Guattari, *Anti-Oedipus*, London: Penguin, 2009.
177 Viveiros, *Cannibal Metaphysics*, 118.
178 Ibid., 142.
179 Ibid., 215.
180 Ibid., 213.
181 Gilles Deleuze and Félix Guattari, *A Thousand Plateaus*, Minneapolis: University of Minnesota Press, 1987.

182 Viveiros, *Cannibal Metaphysics*, 162.
183 Ibid., 162.
184 Kristin Ross, *May 68 and its Afterlives*, Chicago, IL: University of Chicago Press, 2004.
185 Viveiros, *Cannibal Metaphysics*, 97, 146.
186 Raj Patel and Jason Moore, *A History of the World in Seven Cheap Things*, Berkeley: University of California Press, 2017.
187 Viveiros, *Cannibal Metaphysics*, 215.
188 Déborah Danowski and Eduardo Viveiros de Castro, *The Ends of the World*, Cambridge, UK: Polity Press, 2017, 1.
189 Ibid., 14.
190 Louis Althusser, *On the Reproduction of Capitalism*, London: Verso, 2014.
191 Timothy Morton, *Hyperobjects*, Minneapolis: University of Minnesota Press, 2013; see Wark, *General Intellects*, chapters 18 and 20; Isabelle Stengers, *In Catastrophic Times*, London: Open Humanities Press, 2015; Rob Nixon, *Slow Violence and the Environmentalism of the Poor*, Cambridge, MA: Harvard University Press, 2013; Christopher John Müller, *Prometheanism*, London: Rowan and Littlefield, 2016.
192 Danowski and Viveiros, *The Ends of the World*, 5.
193 Ibid., 6.
194 Ibid., 9.
195 Bruno Latour, *We Have Never Been Modern*, Cambridge, MA: Harvard University Press, 1993.
196 George R. Stewart, *The Earth Abides*, New York: Del Ray, 2006; Alan Weisman, *The World Without Us*, London: Picador, 2008.
197 Danowski and Viveiros, *The Ends of the World*, 29.
198 Ibid.
199 Quentin Meillassoux, *After Finitude*, London: Bloomsbury, 2010; see Wark, *General Intellects*, chapter 19.
200 Steven Shaviro, *The Universe of Things*, Minneapolis: University of Minnesota Press, 2014.
201 Danowski and Viveiros, *The Ends of the World*, 35.
202 Ibid., 36.
203 Cormac McCarthy, *The Road*, New York: Knopf, 2006.
204 Danowski and Viveiros, *The Ends of the World*, 47.
205 JD Bernal, *The World, the Flesh, and the Devil*, London: Verso, 2018.
206 Danowski and Viveiros, *The Ends of the World*, 48.
207 Ibid., 51, 51
208 McKenzie Wark, *A Hacker Manifesto*, Cambridge, MA: Harvard University Press, 2004.

209 Nick Srnicek, *Platform Capitalism*, Cambridge, UK: Polity Press, 2016.
210 Danowski and Viveiros, *The Ends of the World*, 57.
211 Isabelle Stengers, *Cosmopolitics I*, Minneapolis: University of Minnesota Press, 2010; see Wark, *General Intellects*, chapter 20.
212 Danowski and Viveiros, *The Ends of the World*, 71.
213 Ibid., 72.
214 Ibid., 74.
215 Dipesh Chakrabarty, *Climate and Capital: On Conjoined Histories*, Barcelona: Centre de Cultura Contemporània, 2015.
216 Ludwig Feuerbach, *The Fiery Brook: Selected Writings*, London: Verso, 2014.
217 Viveiros, *Cannibal Metaphysics*, 51.
218 Stengers, *In Catastrophic Times*; see Wark, *General Intellects*, chapter 20.
219 Latour, *Facing Gaia*.
220 Giorgio Agamben, *The Open: Man and Animal*, Stanford, CA: Stanford University Press, 2003.
221 Danowski and Viveiros, *The Ends of the World*, 86.
222 Alexander Galloway, *Laruelle: Against the Digital*, Minneapolis: University of Minnesota Press, 2014.
223 Andreas Malm, *Fossil Capital*, London: Verso, 2016; Paolo Virno, *A Grammar of the Multitude*, Los Angeles: Semiotext(e), 2004; see Wark, *General Intellects*, chapters 3 and 11; Mouffe, *The Return of the Political*.
224 Latour, *Facing Gaia*.
225 Danowski and Viveiros, *The Ends of the World*, 108, 104.
226 Stengers, *Cosmopolitics I*; see Wark, *General Intellects*, chapter 20.
227 Danowski and Viveiros, *The Ends of the World*, 113, 120, 114.
228 Ibid., 117.
229 McKenzie Wark, *Molecular Red: Theory for the Anthropocene*, London: Verso, 2015, chapter 1.
230 Elizabeth Povinelli, *Geontologies*, Durham, NC: Duke University Press, 2017.
231 Eyal Weizman and Fazal Sheikh, *The Conflict Shoreline*, Göttingen, Germany: Steidl, 2015, 12.
232 Ferdinand Braudel, *A History of Civilizations*, London: Penguin, 1995.
233 Mike Davis, *Ecology of Fear*, New York: Vintage, 1991.
234 Weizman and Sheikh, *The Conflict Shoreline*, 12.
235 Eyal Weizman, *Hollow Land*, London: Verso, 2017, 4.
236 Ibid., 5, 15, 12.

237 Robert Venturi, Steven Izenour, and Denise Scott Brown, *Learning from Las Vegas*, Cambridge, MA: MIT Press, 1977.

238 Weizman, *Hollow Land*, 259.

239 Rafi Segal, David Tartakover, and Eyal Weisman, *A Civilian Occupation*, London: Verso, 2003.

240 Alberto Toscano and Jeff Kinkle, *Cartographies of the Absolute*, Winchester, UK: Zero Books, 2015.

241 Weizman, *Forensic Architecture*.

242 Graduate Institute for Design, Ethnography & Social Thought, http://www.gidest.org.

243 James Hoopes, ed., *Pierce on Signs*, Chapel Hill: University of North Carolina Press, 1991.

244 Nicholas Mirzoeff, *The Right to Look*, Durham, NC: Duke University Press, 2011.

245 Fazal Sheikh, *Erasure Trilogy*, Göttingen, Germany: Steidl, 2010–15.

246 Weizman and Sheikh, *The Conflict Shoreline*, 9.

247 Weizman and Sheikh, *The Conflict Shoreline*, 10.

248 Sven Lindqvist, *Terra Nullius*, New York: The New Press, 2007.

249 Weizman and Sheikh, *The Conflict Shoreline*, 50.

250 Edward Said, *Orientalism*, New York: Vintage, 1979, 223ff.

251 Sven Lindqvist, *A History of Bombing*, New York: The New Press, 2003.

252 Weizman, *Hollow Land*, 77.

253 Ibid., 14.

254 Ibid., 23.

255 Ibid., 24.

256 Andrew Ross, *Bird on Fire*, New York: Oxford University Press, 2011.

257 China Miéville, *The City & The City*, New York: Random House, 2010.

258 Hito Steyerl, *The Wretched of the Screen*, Berlin: Sternberg Press, 2013.

III. Technics

1 Cory Doctorow, *Little Brother*, New York: Tor Books, 2010; Cory Doctorow, *Walkaway*, New York: Tor Books, 2015.

2 Cory Doctorow, *Information Doesn't Want to Be Free*, San Francisco: McSweeney's, 2014.

3 Douglas Rushkoff, *Program or be Programmed*, New York: Soft Skull, 2011; Astra Taylor, *The People's Platform*, New York: Picador, 2015.

4 Siva Vaidhayanathan, *Copyrights and Copywrongs*, New York: New York University Press, 2003.

5 Doron Ben-Atar, *Trade Secrets: Intellectual Piracy and the Origins of American Industrial Power*, Stanford, CT: Yale University Press, 2004.

6 Phillip Kalantzis-Cope, *The Work and Play of the Mind*, London: Palgrave, 2017.

7 Theodor Adorno, *The Culture Industry: Selected Essays*, New York: Routledge, 2001.

8 John Frow, *Time and Commodity Culture*, Oxford: Oxford University Press, 1997, chapter 3.

9 The actual history of American popular music as a business is a bit messier. See Murray Kempton, *Boogaloo*, New York: Random House, 2003.

10 Doctorow, *Information Doesn't Want to Be Free*, 105.

11 Ibid., 159.

12 Jane Bennett, *Vibrant Matter: A Political Ecology of Things*, Durham, NC: Duke University Press, 2010.

13 McKenzie Wark, *A Hacker Manifesto*, Cambridge, MA: Harvard University Press, 2004, chapter 1.

14 Robin Mackay and Armen Avanessian, eds, *#Accelerate: The Accelerationist Reader*, Cambridge, MA: Urbanomic, 2014.

15 Benjamin Bratton, *The Stack: On Software and Sovereignty*, Cambridge, MA: MIT Press, 2015, 303.

16 Kate Crawford and Vladan Doler, "Anatomy of an AI System," AI Now Institute and Share Lab, September 2018.

17 Bratton, *The Stack*, 5, 3.

18 Ibid., 5, 7, 8 (emphasis in the original).

19 Paul Virilio, *The Original Accident*, Cambridge, UK: Polity Press, 2007.

20 Margaret Roberts, *Censored: Distraction and Diversion Inside China's Great Firewall*, Princeton, NJ: Princeton University Press, 2018.

21 Carl Schmitt, *The Nomos of the Earth*, Candor, NY: Telos Press, 2006.

22 Wendy Brown, *Undoing the Demos*, New York: Zone Books, 2017; see McKenzie Wark, *General Intellects*, New York: Verso, 2017, chapter 11.

23 Chantal Mouffe, *The Democratic Paradox*, London: Verso, 2009; see Wark, *General Intellects*, chapter 12.

24 Bratton, *The Stack*, 56.

25 Ibid., 35.

26 Lawrence Lessig, *Code: And other Laws of Cyberspace*, New York: Basic Books, 2006.

27 Sandra Braman, *Change of State: Information, Policy and Power*, Cambridge, MA: MIT Press, 2009.

28 Bratton, *The Stack*, 38, 40.

29 Ibid., 12, 15.

30 On Constant, see McKenzie Wark, *The Beach Beneath the Street*, New York: Verso, 2011, chapter 11.

31 Francis Spufford, *Red Plenty*, Minneapolis, MN: Greywolf Press, 2012; Benjamin Peters, *How Not to Network a Nation*, Cambridge, MA: MIT Press, 2017; Eden Medinas, *Cybernetic Revolutionaries: Technology and Politics in Allende's Chile*, Cambridge, MA: MIT Press, 2014.

32 Bratton, *The Stack*, 251.

33 Gerald Raunig, *Dividuum*, Los Angeles: Semiotext(e), 2016.

34 Bratton, *The Stack*, 252.

35 Melissa Gregg, *Work's Intimacy*, Cambridge, UK: Polity Press, 2011.

36 Hiroki Azuma, *Otaku: Japan's Database Animals*, Minneapolis: University of Minnesota Press, 2009; see Wark, *General Intellects*, chapter 14.

37 Bratton, *The Stack*, 256.

38 Ibid.

39 Maurizio Lazzarato, *Signs and Machines*, Los Angeles: Semiotext(e), 2014: see Wark, *General Intellects*, chapter 5.

40 Bratton, *The Stack*, 269.

41 Ibid., 274, 278.

42 David Harvey, *Rebel Cities,* New York: Verso, 2013.

43 Bratton, *The Stack*, 364.

44 André Leroi-Gourhan, *Gesture and Speech*, Cambridge, MA: MIT Press, 1993.

45 Bratton, *The Stack*, 220.

46 Ibid., 222.

47 Ibid., 231.

48 Frantz Fanon, *A Dying Colonialism*, New York: Grove Press, 1994.

49 Kojin Karatani, *The Structure of World History*, Durham, NC: Duke University Press, 2014; Paul Gilroy, *Against Race*, Cambridge, MA: Harvard University Press, 2002; see Wark, *General Intellects*, chapters 2 and 8.

50 Bratton, *The Stack*, 297.

51 Ibid., 297, 339.

52 Ibid., 191.

53 McKenzie Wark, *Gamer Theory*, Cambridge, MA: Harvard University Press, 2007, chapter 3.

54 Alexander Galloway, *Protocol*, Cambridge, MA: MIT Press, 2003.

55 Christopher Alexander et al., *A Pattern Language,* New York: Oxford University Press, 1977.

56 Bratton, *The Stack*, 213.

57 Ibid.
58 Pier Vittorio Aureli, *The Project of Autonomy*, New York: Princeton Architectural Press, 2008.
59 Paul Virilio, "The Overexposed City," in Neil Leach, ed., *Rethinking Architecture: A Reader*, London: Routledge, 1997.
60 Simon Sellars, *Applied Ballardianism: Memoirs of a Parallel Universe*, Falmouth, UK: Urbanomic, 2018.
61 Matteo Pasquinelli, *Animal Spirits: A Bestiary of the Commons*, Amsterdam: NAI Publishers, 2009.
62 Bratton, *The Stack*, 182.
63 Ibid., 185, 180.
64 Ibid., 111.
65 Ibid., 114.
66 Benjamin Bratton, *The Terraforming*, Moscow: Strelka Press, 2019; see also McKenzie Wark, *Molecular Red: Theory for the Anthropocene*, London: Verso, 2015, 183ff.
67 Siva Vaidhayanathan, *The Googlization of Everything*, Berkeley: University of California Press, 2012.
68 Bratton, *The Stack*, 295.
69 Ibid., 137.
70 Ibid., 295.
71 Ibid., 81.
72 Ibid., 368.
73 On substitution, see Alexander Bogdanov, *The Philosophy of Living Experience*, Chicago, IL: Haymarket Press, 2017.
74 Bratton, *The Stack*, 82.
75 Sean Cubitt, *Finite Media*, Durham, NC: Duke University Press, 2017.
76 Bratton, *The Stack*, 83.
77 Peter Land and William Menking, *Superstudio: Life Without Objects*, Geneva: Skira, 2003.
78 Bratton, *The Stack*, 87.
79 Ibid., 90, 94.
80 Ibid., 96, 97.
81 Wark, *Molecular Red*, 166ff.
82 Bratton, *The Stack*, 103, 104.
83 Bruno Latour, *We Have Never Been Modern*, Cambridge, MA: Harvard University Press, 1993.
84 Bratton, *The Stack*, xix.
85 Ibid., 210.
86 Ibid., 301.
87 Ibid., 302, 301.
88 Burno Latour, *Facing Gaia*, Cambridge, UK: Polity Press, 2017; Donna Haraway, *Staying with the Trouble*, Durham, NC: Duke University

Press, 2016; Anna Tsing, *The Mushroom at the End of the World*, Princeton, NJ: Princeton University Press, 2017.

89 Bratton, *The Stack*, 306, 306 (emphasis in the original).

90 Ibid., 306, 311.

91 Jussi Parikka, *What is Media Archaeology?* Cambridge, UK: Polity Press, 2012.

92 Bratton, *The Stack*, 333.

93 Ibid., 338, 353.

94 Ibid., 354.

95 Ibid., 358.

96 Ibid., 363.

97 Tiziana Terranova, "Red Stack Attack!," *Euronomade*, March 8, 2014.

98 Bratton, *The Stack*, 10.

99 Lev Manovich, *Software Takes Command*, London: Bloomsbury, 2013, 2.

100 Sigfried Giedion, *Mechanization Takes Command*, Minneapolis: University of Minnesota Press, 2014.

101 Bruno Latour, *Reassembling the Social*, Oxford: Oxford University Press, 2007; Bernard Seigert, *Cultural Techniques*, New York: Fordham University Press, 2015; Parikka, *What is Media Archaeology?*

102 Manovich, *Software Takes Command*, 2.

103 Ibid., 24.

104 Friedrich Kittler, *Gramophone, Film, Typewriter*, Stanford, CA: Stanford University Press, 1999; Wendy Hui Kyong Chun, *Programmed Visions*, Cambridge, MA: MIT Press, 2011; see Wark, *General Intellects,* chapter 16.

105 Stuart Hall, *Essential Essays, vol. 1*, Durham, NC: Duke University Press, 2009.

106 Manovich, *Software Takes Command*, 39, 41, 56.

107 Michael Hiltzik, *Dealers in Lightning: Xerox Parc and the Dawn of the Computer Age*, New York: Harper, 2000.

108 David Jay Bolter and Richard Grusin, *Remediation*, Cambridge, MA: MIT Press, 2000.

109 Manovich, *Software Takes Command*, 61.

110 Engelbart's film can readily be found online, usually under the title "The Mother of All Demos."

111 McKenzie Wark, *Capital Is Dead*, London: Verso, 2019.

112 Manovich, *Software Takes Command*, 65.

113 Janet Murray, *Hamlet on the Holodeck*, 2d ed., Cambridge, MA: MIT Press, 2017.

114 George Landow, *Hypertext 3.0*, Baltimore: Johns Hopkins University Press, 2006.

115 Peter Krapp, *Déjà Vu: Aberrations of Cultural Memory*, Minneapolis: University of Minnesota Press, 2004.

116 Espen Aarseth, *Cybertext*, Baltimore: Johns Hopkins University Press, 1997.

117 Manovich, *Software Takes Command*, 93.

118 Lev Manovich, *The Language of New Media*, Cambridge, MA: MIT Press, 2000.

119 Manovich, *Software Takes Command*, 97.

120 David Golumbia, *The Cultural Logic of Computation*, Cambridge, MA: Harvard University Press, 2009.

121 Steven Levy, *Hackers*, Sebastopol, CA: O'Reilly Media, 2010.

122 Jerome Bruner, *Acts of Meaning*, Cambridge, MA: Harvard University Press, 1990.

123 Casey Reas and Ben Fry, *Processing*, Cambridge, MA: MIT Press, 2014.

124 Clement Greenberg, *Art and Culture*, Boston: Beacon Press, 1965.

125 Manovich, *Software Takes Command*, 121.

126 Alla Efimova and Lev Manovich, eds, *Tekstura: Russian Essays on Visual Culture*, Chicago, IL: University of Chicago Press, 1993.

127 Manovich, *Software Takes Command*, 123.

128 Ibid., 133.

129 Paul Edwards, *Closed World*, Cambridge, MA: MIT Press, 1997.

130 Manovich, *Software Takes Command*, 149.

131 Ibid., 152.

132 Terry Flew, *New Media*, 4th edition, New York: Oxford University Press, 2014.

133 Wendy Chun, *Update to Remain the Same,* Cambridge, MA: MIT Press, 2017.

134 Andrew Chadwick, *The Hybrid Media System*, Oxford: Oxford University Press, 2017.

135 Of the extensive writing on multimedia, let me pick just one: Adam J. Banks, *Digital Griots: African American Rhetoric in a Multimedia Age*, Carbondale: Southern Illinois University Press, 2011.

136 Manovich, *Software Takes Command*, 167 (emphasis in the original).

137 Henry Jenkins, *Convergence Culture*, New York: New York University Press, 2008.

138 Manovich, *Software Takes Command*, 176.

139 Franco Moretti, *Maps, Graphs and Trees*, London: Verso, 2007.

140 Alexander Galloway, *The Interface Effect*, Cambridge, UK: Polity Press, 2012; see Wark, *General Intellects*, chapter 17.

141 Manovich, *Software Takes Command*, 180.

142 Jonathan Sterne, *MP3: The Meaning of a Format,* Durham, NC: Duke University Press, 2012.

143 Manovich, *Software Takes Command*, 215.

144 Ibid., 222.

145 Ibid., 223, 225.

146 Ibid., 234.

147 Maria Fernandez, Faith Wilding and Michelle M. Wright, eds, *Domain Errors! Cyberfeminist Practices*, New York: Autonomedia, 2003; Josephine Bosma et al., eds, *Readme! ASCII Culture and the Revenge of Knowledge*, New York: Autonomedia, 1999; Arthur Kroker and Marilouise Kroker, eds, *Life in the Wires: The CTheory Reader*, Montreal: New World Perspectives, 2004; Aditya Nigam et al., *Sarai Reader* no. 1, Delhi: CSDS, 2001.

148 Tiziana Terranova, *Network Cultures: Politics for the Information Age*, London: Pluto Press, 2004.

149 Jean-François Lyotard, "Les Immatériaux," *Art & Text*, 1985; Jean-François Lyotard and Thierry Chaput, *Les Immatériaux: Epreauves d'écriture*, Paris: Center Georges Pompidou, 1985; Fredric Jameson, *Postmodernism, or, the Cultural Logic of Late Capitalism*, London: Verso, 1992.

150 Terranova, *Network Cultures*, 2–3.

151 Kate Crawford, "Anxieties of Big Data," *The New Inquiry*, May 30, 2014.

152 Terranova, *Network Cultures*, 3.

153 Hall, *Essential Essays*.

154 Lawrence Grossberg, *Bringing It All Back Home: Essays on Cultural Studies*, Durham, NC: Duke University Press, 2012.

155 Alexander Galloway, Eugene Thacker, and McKenzie Wark, *Excommunication*, Chicago: University of Chicago Press, 2013.

156 Claude Shannon and Warren Weaver, *The Mathematical Theory of Communication*, Bloomington: University of Illinois Press, 1971.

157 Jon Gertner, *The Idea Factory*, New York: Penguin, 2013.

158 Lydia Liu, *The Freudian Robot*, Chicago: University of Chicago Press, 2011.

159 Terranova, *Network Cultures*, 15.

160 Jean-François Lyotard, The Differend: Phrases in Dispute, Minneapolis: University of Minnesota Press, 1989; Jean-François Lyotard and Jean-Loup Thébaud, *Just Gaming*, Minneapolis: University of Minnesota Press, 1985; Jürgen Habermas, *Theory of Communicative Action Vol. 1*, Boston: Beacon Press, 1992.

161 Michel Serres, *The Parasite*, Minneapolis: University of Minnesota Press, 2007.

162 Gilbert Simondon, *On the Mode of Existence of Technical Objects*, Minneapolis: Univocal, 2017; Adrian MacKenzie, *Transductions: Bodies and Machines at Speed*, London: Bloomsbury, 2013.

163 Terranova, *Network Cultures*, 19.
164 Ibid., 24.
165 Karen Barad, *Meeting the Universe Halfway*, Durham, NC: Duke University Press, 2007. See also Wark, *Molecular Red*, 152ff.
166 Jean Baudrillard, *Simulations*, New York: Semiotext(e), 1983; Wark, *A Hacker Manifesto*.
167 Seb Franklin, *Control: Digitality as Cultural Logic*, Cambridge, MA: MIT Press, 2015.
168 Terranova, *Network Cultures*, 27.
169 Gilles Deleuze, *Difference and Repetition*, New York: Columbia University Press, 1995.
170 Amy Wendling, *Karl Marx on Technology and Alienation*, London: Palgrave, 2009; see Wark, *General Intellects*, chapter 1.
171 Wark, *Capital is Dead*, chapter 6.
172 Donna Haraway, *Crystals, Fabrics and Fields*, Berkeley, CA: North Atlantic Books, 2004.
173 Donna Haraway, *Modest_Witness*, New York: Routledge, 1997.
174 Terranova, *Network Cultures*, 37 (emphasis in original).
175 Henri Bergson, *Matter and Memory*, New York: Zone Books, 1990.
176 Terranova, *Network Cultures*, 51.
177 Peter Galison, *Einstein's Clocks and Poincaré's Maps*, New York: Norton, 2004.
178 Terranova, *Network Cultures*, 51.
179 McKenzie Wark, *Virtual Geography*, Bloomington: Indiana University Press, 1994.
180 Terranova, *Network Cultures*, 57, 62.
181 Ibid., 68.
182 Ibid., 69.
183 Fernandez et al., eds, *Domain Errors!*; Josephine Bosma et al., eds, *Readme!;* Kroker and Kroker, eds, *Life in the Wires*; Nigam et al., *Sarai Reader.*
184 Claire Evans, *Broad Band: The Untold Story of the Women Who Made the Internet*, New York: Portfolio, 2018.
185 Mario Tronti, *Workers and Capital*, London: Verso, 2019; Paolo Virno, *Grammar of the Multitude*, Los Angeles: Semiotext(e), 2004. See Wark, *General Intellects*, chapter 3.
186 Henry Jenkins, *Fans, Bloggers and Gamers*, New York: New York University Press, 2006.
187 Terranova, *Network Cultures*, 75.
188 Whitney Phillips, *This Is Why We Can't Have Nice Things*, Cambridge, MA: MIT Press, 2016.
189 Richard Barbrook, *The Internet Revolution*, Amsterdam: Institute for Network Cultures, 2015.

190 Terranova, *Network Cultures*, 79, 80.

191 Geert Lovink, *Uncanny Networks*, Cambridge, MA: MIT Press, 2004.

192 Wark, *Capital Is Dead*.

193 Lazzarato, *Signs and Machines*; see Wark, *General Intellects*, chapter 5.

194 Terranova, *Network Cultures*, 82, 83.

195 Ibid., 84, 84.

196 Karl Marx, "Fragment on Machines," in Mackay and Armen Avanessian, eds, *#Accelerate*; see the introduction to Wark, *General Intellects*.

197 Terranova, *Network Cultures*, 87.

198 Franco Berardi, *The Soul at Work*, Los Angeles: Semiotext(e), 2009; see Wark, *General Intellects*, chapter 6.

199 Antonio Negri, *Marx Beyond Marx*, New York: Autonomedia, 1992.

200 Bogdanov, *The Philosophy of Living Experience*.

201 Angela McRobbie, *Be Creative*, Cambridge, UK: Polity Press, 2016; see Wark, *General Intellects*, chapter 7.

202 Terranova, *Network Cultures*, 94.

203 Gilles Deleuze and Félix Guattari, *What Is Philosophy?*, New York: Columbia University Press, 1996.

204 Terranova, *Network Cultures*, 100, 101 (emphasis in the original).

205 Ibid., 102.

206 Gilles Deleuze, *Bergsonism*, New York: Zone Books, 1990.

207 Wark, *Molecular Red*, 13ff.

208 Terranova, *Network Cultures*, 103.

209 Ibid., 104, 105.

210 Ibid., 105.

211 Kate O'Riordan, *Unreal Objects*, London: Pluto Press, 2017.

212 Terranova, *Network Cultures*, 106.

213 Steven Greenblatt, *The Swerve: How the World Became Modern*, New York: Norton, 2012.

214 Terranova, *Network Cultures*, 107.

215 Galloway, *Protocol*.

216 Terranova, *Network Cultures*, 115.

217 Ibid., 116.

218 Alexander Bogdanov, *Essays in Tektology*, Seaview, CA: Intersystems Publishing, 1980.

219 Just look at the parade of reactionary sources drawn together in Latour, *Facing Gaia*.

220 Terranova, *Network Cultures*, 121.

221 Ibid., 134.

222 Jean Baudrillard, *In the Shadow of the Silent Majorities*, Los Angeles: Semiotext(e), 2007.

223 Rem Koolhaas, *Delirious New York*, New York: Monacelli Press, 1997.

224 Julio Fajardo, *Starchitects*, New York: Harper Design, 2010.

225 Jacques Rancière, *Dissensus*, London: Bloomsbury, 2010.

226 Keller Easterling, *Extrastatecraft: The Power of Infrastructure Space*, New York: Verso, 2016.

227 Armand Mattelart, *Networking the World*, Minneapolis: University of Minnesota Press, 2000.

228 Easterling, *Extrastatecraft*, 11, 13.

229 Ibid., 19.

230 Ibid., 20.

231 Ibid., 22.

232 Chuihua Judy Chung et al., eds, *Great Leap Forward*, Cologne, Germany: Taschen, 2001.

233 Manuel Castells, *Communication Power*, Oxford: Oxford University Press, 2013.

234 Easterling, *Extrastatecraft*, 45, 54.

235 Keller Easterling, "I Love DPRK," *Harvard Design Magazine*, no. 17, 2002.

236 Bogdanov, *The Philosophy of Living Experience*.

237 Easterling, *Extrastatecraft*, 72.

238 Ibid., 68.

239 Ibid., 74.

240 Ibid., 77.

241 Wark, *Gamer Theory*, chapter 3.

242 Daniel Karatzas, *Jackson Heights: A Garden in the City*, New York: Jackson Heights Beautification Group, 1990.

243 Easterling, *Extrastatecraft*, 133.

244 Keller Easterling, *Critical Spatial Practice*, Berlin: Sternberg Press, 2014.

245 Gilles Deleuze and Félix Guattari, *A Thousand Plateaus*, Minneapolis: University of Minnesota Press, 1987.

246 Easterling, *Extrastatecraft*, 148.

247 Ibid., 149.

248 Slavoj Žižek, *The Universal Exception*, London: Bloomsbury, 2014; see Wark, *General Intellects*, chapter 9.

249 Easterling, *Extrastatecraft*, 156.

250 Esther Leslie, *Synthetic Worlds*, London: Reaktion Books, 2006.

251 Jussi Parikka, *A Geology of Media*, Minneapolis: University of Minnesota Press, 2015, 137.

252 Ibid.

253 Richard Maxwell and Toby Miller, *Greening the Media*, New York: Oxford University Press, 2012; Cubitt, *Finite Media*.

254 Wark, *Gamer Theory*, chapter 9.

255 Parikka, *A Geology of Media*, 138.

256 Macarena Gómez-Barris, *The Extractive Zone: Social Ecologies and Decolonial Perspectives*, Durham, NC: Duke University Press, 2017.

257 Tim Maugham, "The Dystopian Lake Filled by the World's Tech Lust," *BBC*, April 2, 2015.

258 Reza Negarastani, *Cyclonopedia*, Melbourne: re:press, 2008; Reza Negarastani et al., *Leper Creativity: Cyclonopedia Symposium*, New York: punctum books, 2012.

259 Parikka, *A Geology of Media*, 4.

260 Ibid., x.

261 Ibid., 1.

262 Barad, *Meeting the Universe Halfway*; see Wark, *Molecular Red*, 152ff.

263 Parikka, *A Geology of Media*, 2.

264 Paul B. Preciado, *Testo Junkie*, New York: Feminist Press at City University of New York, 2013; see Wark, *General Intellects*, chapter 15.

265 Kittler, *Gramophone, Film, Typewriter*.

266 Parikka, *A Geology of Media*, 3.

267 Douglas Kahn, *Earth Sound Earth Signal,* Berkeley: University of California Press, 2013.

268 Robert Smithson, *Collected Writings*, Berkeley: University of California Press, 1996.

269 Wolfgang Ernst, *Digital Memory and the Archive*, Minneapolis: University of Minnesota Press, 2012.

270 Seigfried Zeilinski, *Deep Time of the Media*, Cambridge, MA: MIT Press, 2008.

271 Parikka, *A Geology of Media*, 13.

272 Donna Haraway, *Manifestly Haraway*, Minneapolis: University of Minnesota Press, 2016; see Wark, *General Intellects*, chapter 21.

273 Parikka, *A Geology of Media*, 14.

274 Ibid., 17.

275 Jason Moore, *Capitalism in the Web of Life*, London: Verso, 2013.

276 Parikka, *A Geology of Media*, 18.

277 Deleuze and Guattari, *A Thousand Plateaus*.

278 Bennett, *Vibrant Matter*.

279 J. D. Bernal, *Science in History*, London: Faber and Faber, 2012.

280 Gilles Deleuze and Felix Guattari, *Anti-Oedipus*, London: Penguin, 2009.

281 Parikka, *A Geology of Media*, 35.

282 Elizabeth Povinelli, *Geontologies*, Durham, NC: Duke University Press, 2017.

283 Stephen Jay Gould, *Punctuated Equilibrium*, Cambridge, MA: Harvard University Press, 2007.
284 Parikka, *A Geology of Media*, 42.
285 I have borrowed "undead labor" from my New School colleague David Bering-Porter.
286 Parikka, *A Geology of Media*, 49.
287 Cubbitt, *Finite Media*.
288 John Bellamy Foster, *Marx's Ecology: Materialism and Nature*, New York: Monthly Review Press, 2000.
289 Parikka, *A Geology of Media*, 57–8.
290 London Psychogeographics Summit, "What is Psychogeophysics?" *Mute*, August 4, 2010.
291 Roger Caillois, *The Writing of Stones*, Charlottesville: University Press of Virginia, 1985; Rosi Braidotti, *Nomadic Theory*, New York: Columbia University Press, 2012; Timothy Morton, *Hyperobjects*, Minneapolis: University of Minnesota Press, 2013; see Wark, *General Intellects*, chapter 18.
292 Parikka, *A Geology of Media*, 63.
293 Wark, *The Beach Beneath the Street*, chapter 2.
294 Parikka, *A Geology of Media*, 67, 67.
295 Margret Grebowicz, *The National Park to Come*, Stanford, CA: Stanford University Press, 2015.
296 Bernard Smith, *European Vision and the South Pacific*, New Haven, CT: Yale University Press, 1985.
297 Parikka, *A Geology of Media*, 89.
298 Ibid., 103.
299 Berardi, *The Soul at Work*; see Wark, *General Intellects*, chapter 6.
300 On soul in Platonov, see Wark, *Molecular Red*, 97ff.
301 Parikka, *A Geology of Media*, 100.
302 Moore, *Capitalism in the Web of Life*.
303 Parikka, *A Geology of Media*, 102 (emphasis in the original).
304 Ibid., 106.
305 W. J. T. Mitchell, *The Last Dinosaur Book*, Chicago, IL: University of Chicago Press, 1998.
306 Manuel De Landa, *War in the Age of Intelligent Machines*, New York: Zone Books, 1991.
307 Parikka, *A Geology of Media*, 119.
308 Paolo Virno, *When the Word Becomes Flesh*, Los Angeles: Semiotext(e), 2015.
309 Theodor Adorno, *Minima Moralia*, London: Verso, 2006; Guy Debord, *The Society of the Spectacle*, New York: Zone Books, 1994.
310 Trevor Paglen, *The Last Pictures*, Oakland: University of California

Press, 2012; Lauren Cornell, Julia Bryan-Wilson, and Omar Kholeif, *Trevor Paglen*, London: Phaidon, 2018.

311 Quentin Meillassoux, *After Finitude*, London: Bloomsbury, 2010; see Wark, *General Intellects*, chapter 19.

312 Barad, *Meeting the Universe Halfway*. See Wark, *Molecular Red*, 152ff.

313 Parikka, *A Geology of Media*, 135.

314 Georges Bataille, *Visions of Excess*, Minneapolis: University of Minnesota Press, 1985.

315 Kittler, *Gramophone, Film, Typewriter*.

316 Parikka, *A Geology of Media*, 139.

Index